GUILTY PLEASURES

Pamela Robertson

I.B.Tauris
& Co Ltd
Publishers
London
and
New York

GUILTY PLEASURES

Feminist Camp from Mae West to Madonna

Published in 1996 by I.B.Tauris & Co Ltd

45 Bloomsbury Square, London WC1A 2HY

Copyright © 1996 Duke University Press

ISBN 1 86064 087 7 (hardback)

ISBN 1 86064 088 5 (paperback)

Manufactured in the United States of America

CONTENTS

ACKNOWLEDGMENTS

I owe a lot of people thanks in connection with this book. First, my teachers. This book began as a dissertation at the University of Chicago. Corey Creekmur encouraged me to pursue this project after I made a comment about feminist camp in his seminar on film and psychoanalysis. The conceptualization of this project, its organization, and its prose benefited greatly from his careful readings of drafts and his belief in me and the project. I am deeply obliged as well to Jay Schleusener whose influence on this project and on my thinking generally, while not always apparent to him, has been immeasurable. I owe Miriam Hansen a special debt, not only for her tremendous help in shaping and guiding the dissertation, but also for her mentoring and unflagging support above and beyond the call of duty. Thanks also to earlier influences: Kevin Nolan, who introduced me to film studies, and Terry Tyler, who introduced me to Sontag's "Notes on 'Camp.'"

This book has benefited greatly from conversations with many friends and colleagues. Thanks to Shari Roberts, fellow fan of Hollywood gals, my rival and my pal, for being an insightful critic, an inspiration, a creative cocktail mixer, and a great friend. Thanks also to other friends who read and commented on drafts and supported me with infinite good humor and comradeship: Alex Doty, Terry Kapsalis, Arthur Knight, Hank Sartin, Anna McCarthy, Rick Wojcik, John Corbett, Tara McPherson, David Grubbs, David Boyd, members of the Chicago Recorded Music Reading Group, members of the Mass Culture and Gay and Lesbian Workshops at the University of Chicago, Lauren Berlant, Bill Brown, Loren Kruger, Jim Lastra, Chris Looby, Doug Bruster, Candace Mirza, Paul Young. For putting up with me, sharing pitchers at Jimmy's, being phone cronies and e-mail pals: Priscilla Barlow, David Nicholls, Sharon Rowley, Kim Miller, Ellen Nerenberg, Joe Dimuro, Larry Goodman, Ann Campbell-Goodman, Jim Chandler, Paul Hunter, Nancy Henry, Anne Balay-Wilson, Eva Fernandez, Larry Rothfield, Lynn Voskuil, Vince Bertolini, Yvette Christianse, Cathy Davidson, Kyle Robertson, Ann Robertson, the Miller family, the Roberts family, all my friends and fellow students from Chicago, all the Wellesley gals, and my colleagues at the University of Newcastle. In addition to providing other more important kinds of support, Mark Robertson, Kristine Harris, Robert Polito, and Gretchen Ford put me up during research trips and conferences. Larry MacEnerney and Joe Williams provided employment that kept me afloat and helped me with my writing.

Through workshops at the University of Chicago, I was able to meet Susan Sontag, Richard Dyer, and Ulrike Ottinger. Although our meetings were brief, being able to discuss my work with those whose work, in different ways, inspired it meant a great deal. Eve Kosofsky Sedgwick, Ramona Curry, Steve Cohan, Patricia White, Kathleen Rowe, Richard Henke, Marcos Becquer, and Jose Gatti provided me with information, papers, advice, and support. Thanks to my editor and friend Ken Wissoker for his encouragement and understanding, and to the anonymous Duke University Press readers for their very helpful critiques and suggestions for revision.

I was fortunate to receive predissertation and dissertation fellowships from the Mellon Foundation. The Research Management Committee at the University of Newcastle provided me with a grant that enabled me to finish the book. The staffs at the Manuscript Reading Room and Motion Picture Broadcasting Division of the Library of Congress and the Billy Rose Theater Collection at the New York Public Library were extremely helpful. I am also indebted to Mary Carbine and the staff at the Film Center, reference librarians and interlibrary loan staff at the University of Chicago, and to the staff of the Audio-Visual Library at the University of Newcastle.

Much of this work has been trotted out in conference papers and seminars. Thanks to respondents, participants, and organizers of conferences and seminars at: the Society for Cinema Studies, the Rutgers Gay and Lesbian Studies Conference, Chicago Humanities Institute, Chicago Film Educators Forum, the Australian National University and Humanities Research Centre, Sydney University, and the University of Newcastle. I am extremely grateful to the Society for Cinema Studies for giving me the prize for best student essay in 1991 for chapter 1 and the award for best dissertation in 1994. Thanks especially to Robert Burgoyne, Tom Gunning, Jane Gaines, Maureen Turim, and Virginia Wright Wexman. A version of chapter 1 appeared in *Cinema Journal* 32, no. 2 (Winter 1993): 57–72 and in *Campgrounds: Style and Homosexuality*, edited by David Bergman (Boston: University of Massachusetts Press, Fall 1993), 156–172. A version of chapter 3 appears in a special issue of *The Journal of Film and Video*, edited by Roberta Pearson (forthcoming).

Finally, thanks to my parents, Paul and Nancy Robertson, who have not only helped me emotionally and financially, but who have each unknowingly marked my life and work. Thanks to my father, who made me want to become an academic, and my mother, who taught me the meaning of feminist camp.

INTRODUCTION

What Makes the

Feminist Camp?

C amp, as an adjective, goes back at least to 1909. In its oldest sense, it was defined as "addicted to 'actions and gestures of exaggerated emphasis'; pleasantly ostentatious or, in manner, affected." But from 1920, in theatrical argot, camp connoted homosexual or lesbian and was in general use with that meaning by 1945.[1] In 1954, Christopher Isherwood's The World in the Evening distinguished between two forms of camp; low theatrical gay camp, an "utterly debased form," equated with "a swishy little boy with peroxided hair, dressed in a picture hat and feather boa, pretending to be Marlene Dietrich," and serious high camp, potentially gay or straight, "expressing what's basically serious to you in terms of fun and artifice and elegance."[2] Susan Sontag's famous "Notes on 'Camp'" (1964) defined camp as a failed seriousness, a love of exaggeration and artifice, the privileging of style over content, and a being alive to the double sense in which some things can be taken. While she maintained that camp taste and homosexual taste were not necessarily the same thing, Sontag claimed an affinity between the camp sensibility and homosexual aestheticism and irony.[3] Sontag's conflation of homosexuality, aestheticism, and camp, bolstered with the authority of epigraphs from Oscar Wilde, suggested a homosexual genealogy for camp originating with Wilde. Moreover, Sontag collapsed Isherwood's distinction between different forms of camp and ignored the colloquial affiliation between lesbianism and camp; and camp came to be associated almost exclusively with a gay male subculture.

Camp has been criticized for its politics—or rather, lack thereof. In "Notes on 'Camp,'" Sontag refused to assign aestheticism a politics and, therefore, asserted that camp's attention to style and artifice was, by definition, apolitical; and her claim continued to have a hold over both apologists for and critics of camp.[4] Some have argued that the point of camp resides in its frivolity, which opposes the morality and politics of satire and parody and is specifically and necessarily not a form of critique.[5] For others in the gay community, especially after the 1969 Stonewall riots (and the birth of the modern gay liberation movement),[6] camp was viewed largely as an artifact of the closet, an embarrassment fueling gay stereotypes and affirming the dominant culture's negative perception of the gay community.[7] Because of camp's partial complicity with oppressive representations, it has been seen as a sign of both oppression and the acceptance of repression.

Many critics, however, claim that camp represents a critical political practice for gay men: they equate camp with white, urban, gay male taste to explore camp's effectiveness as a form of resistance for that subculture. Richard Dyer, for instance, attributes a past-tense politics to camp when he claims that for gay men the use of camp constituted "a kind of going public or coming out before the emergence of gay liberationist politics (in which coming out was a key confrontationist tactic)."[8] This reading of camp, which links it to gay identity and cultural politics, has become dominant with the rise of gay activist politics and gay and queer studies in the academy.

While recognizing camp's appeal for "straights," most critics argue that "something happens to camp when taken over by straights—it loses its cutting edge, its identification with the gay experience, its distance from the straight sexual world view."[9] In part, this is a historical claim, positing the 1960s "outing" of camp as a betrayal of "true" gay camp. In this light, straight camp, almost an oxymoron, flattens into what Fredric Jameson has labeled postmodern "blank parody" or pastiche, the heterogeneous and random "imitation of dead styles, speech through all the masks and voices stored up in the imaginary museum of a now global culture."[10] According to Jameson, postmodern pastiche, which he equates with camp, lacks the satiric impulse of parody, and equalizes all identities, styles, and images in a depthless ahistorical nostalgia. Linda Hutcheon, in contrast, argues that postmodernism effects a denaturalizing critique through parody that is not nostalgic or de-historicizing, but critical and subversive. But Hutcheon, similar to Jameson, differentiates between high postmodern parody and the "ahistorical kitsch" of camp.

However, the postmodern equation of camp and pastiche is itself ahistorical. As a form of ironic representation and reading, camp, like Hutcheon's high parody, "is doubly coded in political terms; it both legitimates and subverts that which it parodies."[11] Whereas postmodern pastiche may privilege heterogeneity and random difference, camp is productively anachronistic and critically renders specific historical norms obsolete. What counts as excess, artifice and theatricality, for example, will differ over time. As Andrew Ross has noted, "the camp effect" occurs at the moment when cultural products (for instance, stars, fashions, genres, and stereotypes) of an earlier moment of production have lost their power to dominate cultural meanings and become available, "in the present, for redefinition according to contemporary codes of taste."[12] Camp redefines and historicizes these cultural products not just nostalgically but with a critical recognition of the temptation to nostalgia, rendering both the object and the nostalgia outmoded through an ironic, laughing distanciation. In the postmodern moment, "contemporary codes of taste" may have rendered camp's form of critique outmoded so that camp has been recoded as pastiche. But if we understand camp to have been always already mere "blank parody," we simply dehistoricize and "postmodernize" camp's parodic and critical impulse.

In addition, and prior even to the historical claim about post-1960s camp, the argument against straight camp presumes that camp's aestheticism is exclusively the province of gay men. In particular, women have been excluded from discussions of pre-1960s camp because women, lesbian and straight, are perceived to "have had even less access to the image- and culture-making processes of society than even gay men have had."[13] We tend to take for granted that many female stars are camp and that most of the stars in the gay camp pantheon are women: consider Garland, Streisand, Callas, Dietrich, Garbo, Crawford, just to name a few. We also take for granted gay men's camp appropriations of female clothing, styles, and language from women's culture: consider drag and female impersonation, or gay camp slang such as calling one another "she" or using phrases like "letting one's hair down" and "dropping hairpins," and even "coming out" (appropriated from debutante culture).[14] Most people who have written about camp assume that the exchange between gay men's and women's cultures has been wholly one-sided; in other words, that gay men appropriate a feminine aesthetic and certain female stars but that women, lesbian or heterosexual, do not similarly appropriate aspects of gay male culture. This suggests that women are camp but do not knowingly produce themselves as camp and, furthermore, do not even have access to a camp sensibility. Women, by this logic, are objects of camp and subject to it but are not camp subjects.

Assuming this one-way traffic between gay men's and women's cultures, critics emphasizing those aspects of camp most closely related to Isherwood's "low" camp have criticized camp for preferring images of female excess that are blatantly misogynistic. Most of the answers to this charge have been unsatisfactory. For instance, Mark Booth justifies the misogynist slant of camp by claiming that because gay men have been marginalized, camp commits itself to and identifies with images of the marginal and that women simply represent the primary type of the marginal in society.[15] This justification simply underlines camp's potential for affirming patriarchal oppression. Even worse is Wayne Koestenbaum's reply, in his essay on Maria Callas, to

Catherine Clement's statement that the gay male identification with female stars is "vampiristic." According to Koestenbaum, Clement recycles the myth (which he links with the "fag hag" stereotype) "that a man's projection of glamour and flamboyance onto a woman is febrile, infantile, and poisonous, and that such attentions harm the woman thus admired." He then sloughs off the criticism, stating that female stars, "as images adrift in the culture, lend themselves to acts of imaginative borrowing and refurbishing" and that these images "were not placed on the market at gay men's instigation."[16]

Like Booth, Koestenbaum's response begs the question: The question is not whether gay men put these images on the market, but rather how they deployed these images and whether that deployment partakes of misogyny. While cultural studies broadly considered and star studies, in particular, depend on the idea that texts are "adrift in the culture" and can be put to different uses by different audiences and spectators, we nonetheless need to be able to account for how texts get taken up—not simply to accept any and all appropriations as equally valid, but instead to explore how and why certain texts get taken up in certain ways by certain groups.

Koestenbaum's response sounds curiously like the familiar cliché deployed in the justification of rape. To state that female stars are "adrift in the culture" and, consequently, ripe for "refurbishing" is simply an academic form of blaming the victim: "What was she doing walking alone at night?" "Why did she wear that sexy outfit?" Not only do these remarks compound the misogyny of gay camp, but they also limit themselves to a justification of camp's misogyny for gay men only, without asking whether or how heterosexual men and women, or even lesbians, might use these images.

We can, however, reclaim camp as a political tool and rearticulate it within the theoretical framework of feminism. To counter criticisms of camp's misogyny, for instance, some critics have articulated a positive relationship between the camp spectator and images of female excess. Andrew Ross notes that camp's attention to the artifice of these images helps undermine and challenge the presumed naturalness of gender roles and to displace essentialist versions of an authentic feminine identity.[17] By this account, the very outrageousness and flamboyance of camp's preferred representations would be its most powerful tools for a critique, rather than mere affirmations of stereotypical and oppressive images of women. Thus, despite camp's seemingly exclusive affiliation with gay men and misogynist tendencies, camp offers feminists a model for critiques of gender and sex roles. Camp has an affinity with feminist discussions of gender construction, performance, and enactment; we can thereby examine forms of camp as feminist practice.

Clearly, it would be foolish to deny camp's affiliation with gay male sub-culture or to claim that women have exactly the same relation to camp as gay men do. But it seems rash to claim that women have no access to camp. If the exchange between gay men and women has been wholly one-sided, how do we account for stars like Mae West and Madonna who quite deliberately take on aspects of gay culture? Are they merely exceptions to the rule? Are there other "exceptions"? What about Texas Guinan? Bette Davis? Marlene Diet-rich? Eve Arden? Agnes Moorehead? Dolly Parton? Furthermore, if camp is exclusively the province of gay men, how do we account for the pleasure women take in camp artifacts like musicals, or Dietrich, or *Designing Women*? What are we assuming about identification if we presume that women take their stars "straight"? Do gay men automatically have a critical distance from roles and stereotypes that women blindly inhabit?

Most troubling is that women's frequent exclusion from the discourse about camp has meant not just that these questions have not been fully ad-dressed but that they have not even been asked. At the very least, would it not be important to determine why women enjoy so many of the same cul-tural texts as gay men? Asked another way: Why do gay men like so many of the same cultural texts as women? By not posing the latter question, what are we assuming about gay men? Inversion? Misogyny? By viewing the exchange between women and gay men as a two-way street we could begin to better understand gay male camp and stop taking for granted camp's reliance on feminine images and styles (as if these acts of appropriation were "natural").

We could also begin to break down some of the artificial barriers between audiences and between subcultures that theories of spectatorship and cul-tural studies have unwittingly advanced, so that we tend to talk about one audience, one subculture at a time and only in relation to the (in that case) dominant culture (one gender, race, ethnicity, class, one category, one dif-ference at a time). By thinking about subcultures in constellation, we would necessarily rethink some of our assumptions about textual address and also which subculture we discuss in relation to which kind of text. To take an example pertinent to this project, many critics acknowledge a gay male audi-ence for the musical but ignore the genre's popularity among women;[18] alter-nately, much work has been done on the female spectator of the woman's film, without considering that genre's popularity among gay men. If, how-ever, we considered gay men as spectators of the women's film (a genre chock full of eventual camp idols) or women as spectators of the musical (it seems so obvious), we would have to reconsider issues of textual address, identification, subcultures, resistance, and domination.

By looking at the links between gay men and women across cultural texts we could also begin to better understand the many close ties and friendships shared by women and gay men, which we have, as yet, almost no way to talk about—despite their very routineness, their "of-courseness." Certainly, there are stereotypes. There is the figure of the "beard," the lesbian or heterosexual woman who serves as heterosexual cover for the closeted gay man (just as men have served as "beards" for lesbians).[19] Colloquially, we also have the "fag hag," an epithet hostile to both the "fag" and the "hag." Rather than describe the love and friendship between women and gay men, the fag hag stereotype often seems to presume a failed object choice on the part of the woman, the "hag"—that is, the fag hag chooses gay men because she "can't get a man" (she is stereotypically unattractive) and/or because she desires a man who doesn't want her (she is stereotypically secretly, desperately attracted to gay men; see, for example, Robert Rodi's novel, *Fag Hag*). At the same time, it diminishes the man in the relationship, the "fag." While the term recognizes that at least some women do not share the dominant culture's disparagement of gay men, in naming the friendship this way, the term (used inside gay culture as well as being imposed from without) reinforces the initial devaluation of gay culture.[20]

We also have a new media stereotype: the gay neighbor, who provides local color to urban settings but participates little in the plot (see, for example, *Frankie and Johnny* and *The Prince of Tides*). The gay neighbor is kin to what I will call the gay enabler, the gay man whose primary function is to help the heterosexual lovers resolve their conflicts (see, for example, *Burn This, Melrose Place*, and *Mrs. Doubtfire*). While there might be some value in having at least this minimal acknowledgment of the friendships between women and gay men, these newly minted stereotypes, no less than other, overtly pejorative ones, seem a far cry from representing the routine richness of these friendships.

Part of the difficulty in talking about women's friendships with gay men can probably be blamed on the problematic formulation "some of my best friends" (given a new twist in Seinfeld's quip, "not that there's anything wrong with it"). But the fact that we don't talk about friendships between gay men and women reflects, I think, the larger academic divisions that obtain between gay and feminist theory, as well as lesbian and gay, and heterosexual and lesbian feminist, theory. Academic politics and identity politics are such that instead of seeking points of overlap between gay men and women and between lesbian and heterosexual women, we increasingly focus on differences.

In part, this is for good reason, as it represents a greater attention to the specificity of gendered and sexed experiences and seeks to counter the problem of being "spoken for" that, for instance, many lesbians feel with respect to both feminist and gay theory. But oftentimes we seem to be addressing ourselves only to the already converted—or, worse, to be self-defeating, proving the lie that only gays should be interested in gay issues or insisting on a single and singular identification (one difference at a time). Lesbians, especially, have often been forced to choose between identifying, as women, with feminist theory and politics (which tends to privilege [white] heterosexual women) and identifying, as homosexuals, with gay theory and politics (which tends to privilege [white] gay men). It thus becomes more difficult to form alliances between feminism and gay theory and politics as we focus on points of divergence.[21]

Any discussion of women's relation to camp will inevitably raise, rather than settle, questions about appropriation, co-optation, and identity politics. But as an activity and a sensibility that foregrounds cross-sex and cross-gender identifications, camp provides an opportunity to talk about the many points of intersection, as well as the real differences, between feminist and gay theory, and among lesbians, heterosexual women, and gay men. I argue that women, lesbian and heterosexual, have historically engaged in what I call feminist camp practices. This tradition of feminist camp, which runs alongside—but is not identical to—gay camp, represents oppositional modes of performance and reception. Through my analysis of feminist camp I reclaim a female form of aestheticism, related to female masquerade and rooted in burlesque, that articulates and subverts the "image- and culture-making processes" to which women have traditionally been given access.

Although I argue for the crucial role of heterosexual women as producers and consumers of camp, I hesitate to describe feminist camp as "straight" and suggest instead that camp occupies a discursive space similar to the notion of "queer" described by Alexander Doty: "[T]he terms 'queer readings,' 'queer discourses,' and 'queer positions,' . . . are attempts to account for the existence and expression of a wide range of positions within culture that are 'queer' or non-, anti-, or contra-straight."[22] In Doty's sense, "queer" refers to a variety of discourses that have grown up in opposition to or at variance with the dominant, straight, symbolic order. This sense of queerness includes gay- and lesbian-specific positions as well as non-gay and non-lesbian ones. Unlike Moe Meyer, who also describes camp as a queer discourse but clearly states that queer means exclusively gay and lesbian (and lumps all other forms of camp under the category of the "camp trace"),[23] I take camp to be a queer discourse in Doty's sense, because it enables not only

gay men, but also heterosexual and lesbian women, and perhaps heterosexual men, to express their discomfort with and alienation from the normative gender and sex roles assigned to them by straight culture. Feminist
camp, then, views the world "queerly": that is, from a non- or anti-straight,
albeit frequently non-gay, position.

This is not to say that camp or the mobile notion of queerness I am describing will always include all non- or anti-straight viewpoints. Doty points
out that not all queer texts are gay (citing *The Silence of the Lambs* as an example). Similarly, gay camp might be misogynist and feminist camp may or
may not be antihomophobic. Although both feminists and gay men engage
in discourses that are at variance with the dominant culture, those discourses
are not always identical. "Queer" then functions for me as an explanatory
term connoting a discourse or position at odds with the dominant symbolic order, the flexibility and mobility of which helps account for instances
of overlap among the interests and points-of-view of heterosexual women,
lesbians, and gay men, but which, at the same time, can account for feminist aesthetics and interpretations that are simultaneously non-gay and not
stereotypically straight.

Camp and Gender Parody

For feminists, camp's appeal resides in its potential to function as a form
of gender parody. Feminist theorists working in a variety of disciplines have
turned to gender parody as a critical tool and a promising means of initiating change in sex and gender roles. For example, at the end of her book on
the woman's film of the 1940s, Mary Ann Doane argues that women need
to map themselves in the "terrain of fantasy" in order to denaturalize representations of women. She claims that the woman's film stylizes femininity,
narrativizing and making acceptable stereotypical feminine scenarios. "What
is needed," she contends, "is a means of making these gestures and poses
fantastic, literally incredible." [24]

Doane believes that the credibility of images of the feminine can be undermined by a "double mimesis" or parodic mimicry. Parodic mimicry, Doane
claims, allows one to disengage from the roles and gestures of a seemingly
naturalized femininity: "Mimicry as a political textual strategy makes it possible for the female spectator to understand that recognition is buttressed by
misrecognition." [25] In other words, the mimicry of stereotypical images demonstrates the female spectator's recognition of herself in those images, while
it also allows the spectator to misrecognize herself, to see that her "self" does
not exist prior to the mimicry but is always already a construction.

Judith Butler similarly emphasizes the significance of parody for feminist politics. Butler accounts for the cultural construction of gender and identity as a collective activity of "gendering" and questions how gender identities might be constructed differently. She asks: "What kind of subversive repetition might call into question the regulatory practice of identity itself?" and claims that "genders can be rendered thoroughly and radically *incredible*" through a politics of gender parody.[26]

Although both Doane and Butler seek a means to render gender identities "incredible" through parody, Doane roots her notion of "double mimesis" in the concept of the "feminine masquerade," while Butler begins her discussion of feminist parody with a description of homosexual drag. Butler argues that "in imitating gender, drag implicitly reveals the imitative structure of gender itself—as well as its contingency."[27] As Esther Newton says in her book on female impersonation, "[I]f sex-role behavior can be achieved by the 'wrong' sex, it logically follows that it is in reality also achieved, not inherited, by the 'right' sex."[28]

Butler's provocative linkage in *Gender Trouble* between homosexual drag and feminist gender parody has been construed as a claim that drag subversively displaces gender norms. However, as Butler makes clear in her later work, *Bodies That Matter*, drag is subversive only "to the extent that it reflects on the imitative structure by which hegemonic gender is itself produced and disputes heterosexuality's claim on naturalness and originality."[29] To be sure, drag reveals the performative status of gender identity, but it cannot effectively dismantle gender identity. The surprise and incongruity of drag depends upon our shared recognition that the person behind the mask is really another gender. (Consider the drag performer's ritual of removing his wig and/or baring his chest at the end of the show.) While the "naturalness" of gender identities is destabilized through this practice, that destabilization might merely effect a regulatory system of identifying "unnatural" identities—for example, the stereotype of the effeminate homosexual man or the masculinized woman.

Doane has argued that in opposition to transvestism, the concept of female masquerade offers a more radical parodic potential. Joan Riviere's 1929 essay, "Womanliness as a Masquerade," has been taken up in feminist theory as a divining rod pointing to the "performative status" and "imitative structure" of the feminine.[30] Riviere's essay describes intellectual women who "wish for masculinity" and then put on a "mask of womanliness" as a defense "to avert anxiety and the retribution feared from men."[31] In other words, the woman takes on a masculine "identity" to perform in the intellectual sphere, then takes on a feminine "identity" to placate the Oedipal father whose place she has usurped. In a now famous passage, however, Riviere casually challenges the very notion of a stable feminine identity: "The reader may now ask how I define womanliness or where I draw the line between genuine womanliness and the 'masquerade.' My suggestion is not, however, that there is any such difference; whether radical or superficial, they are the same thing."[32] Stephen Heath sums up the way in which Riviere's statement points to the absence of "natural" identities: "In the masquerade the woman mimics an authentic—genuine—womanliness but then authentic womanliness is such a mimicry, is the masquerade ('they are the same thing')."[33] The masquerade mimics a constructed identity in order to conceal that there is nothing behind the mask; it simulates femininity to dissimulate the absence of a real or essential feminine identity.

Despite the theatricality of the term, masquerade can never be merely theatrical but is always also social. The trope of the masquerade deepens our sense of the activity of gendering as enactment and acting-out. Doane suggests that "a woman might flaunt her femininity, produce herself as an excess of femininity, in other words, foreground the masquerade" in order to "manufacture a lack in the form of a certain distance between oneself and one's image."[34] Doane uses the example of Stella Dallas's self-parody as an instance of "double mimesis" or self-conscious masquerade. When Stella effectively parodies herself, pretending to be an even more exaggeratedly embarrassing mother than she is in the rest of the narrative, she demonstrates her recognition of herself as a stereotype (a pose, a trope) while making the excessiveness of her role visible and strange, depriving the initial mimesis of its currency. Like Doane's notion of "double mimesis," the self-conscious masquerade discovers a discrepancy between gesture and "essence" and not simply between anatomy and costume. It makes the "natural" "unnatural"— cultural or historical.

In opposition to drag, the surprise and incongruity of same-sex female masquerade consists in the identity between she who masquerades and the role she plays—she plays at being what she is always already perceived to be. This might consist in the exaggeration of gender codes by the "right" sex, in a female masquerade of femininity or a male masquerade of masculinity, similar to lesbian "femme" role-play or the hyperbolic masculinization of gay "macho" Levi's-and-leather culture. The concept of the masquerade allows us to see that what gender parody takes as its object is not the image of the woman, but the idea—which, in camp, becomes a joke—that an essential feminine identity exists prior to the image. As Butler observes, "the parody is of the very notion of an original."[35]

Gender parody would utilize masquerade self-consciously in order to re-veal the absence behind the mask and the performative activity of gender and sexual identities. It would have to be a parody of the masquerade so that masquerade would no longer serve as a placating gesture but instead would become a gesture of defiance toward the assumption of an identity between the woman and the image of the woman. Gender parody, therefore, doesn't differ in structure from the activity of the masquerade but self-consciously theatricalizes masquerade's construction of gender identities.

In using Doane and Butler to open up my discussion of feminist camp, I do not mean to claim that they advocate camp in their discussions of "double mimesis" or gender parody, nor do I believe that camp is the only interpreta-tion available for a politics of gender parody.[36] Rather, I consider camp to be a likely candidate for helping us explore the appeal of and reason for a poli-tics of gender parody. Conversely, I want to use the notion of gender parody as a paradigm for defining a specifically feminist form of camp spectatorship.

Camp and Female Spectatorship

The often fraught and contested concept of the female spectator has been central to feminist film theory since the 1970s.[37] The concept can be traced back to 1970s semiotic and psychoanalytic theories of spectatorship, repre-sented by the work of Christian Metz and the journal *Screen*, along with the earliest feminist psychoanalytic interventions, especially as articulated by Stephen Heath and Julia Lesage and crystallized by Laura Mulvey in her famous "Visual Pleasure" essay. Feminist film theorists have grappled with Mulvey's provocative claims about the "male gaze," often in contention with her bleak assessment of the female spectatorial position. Psychoanalyti-cally informed debates initially focused on the female spectator constructed through textual address in analyses, for instance, of the female melodrama or feminine spectacle in film noir. Increasingly, feminist film theorists, influ-enced by the Frankfurt School and British Cultural Studies, have attempted to give the concept of the female spectator historical specificity and/or ethno-graphic precision in order to account for different kinds of readings and possible forms of subcultural resistance. While the debate about the nature of female spectatorship continues and models proliferate, some of the most crucial problems facing feminist film theorists today are still those prompted by Mulvey's critique: the need to (1) rescue some forms of pleasure for the female viewer; (2) conceptualize spectatorship as a process mediating be-tween the textually constructed "female spectator" and the female audience, constructed by socio-historical categories of gender, class, and race; and (3) rethink ideas of ideology, resistance, and subversion.

Miriam Hansen describes "the greater mobility required of the female spectator—a mobility that has been described in terms of transvestitism, masquerade and double identification" as "a compensatory one, responding to the patriarchal organization of classical cinematic vision and narration." She links the "structurally problematic" nature of spectatorship for women to that of "other, partly overlapping groups who are likewise, though in different ways, alienated from dominant positions of subjectivity—gays and lesbians, or racial and ethnic minorities."[38] Camp foregrounds this structural problem of female viewing. The camp spectator, in a sense, ironically enacts the female spectator's mobility through a double identification that is simultaneously critical of and complicit with the patriarchal organization of vision and narration. Camp, as a performative strategy, as well as a mode of reception, commonly foregrounds the artifice of gender and sexual roles through literal and metaphoric transvestism and masquerade. Since camp has been primarily conceived of as a gay male subcultural practice, its articulation with the concept of female spectatorship will enable us to explore the degree to which the female camp spectator shares her liminal status with another alienated group and also to explore what kind of subcultural resistances are available to women.

Although Doane locates distanciation primarily in the text, rather than reception, she underlines the masquerade's potential usefulness for understanding the spectator's activity as well as the performer's: "What might it mean to masquerade as a spectator? To assume the mask in order to see in a different way?"[39] Here, Doane begins to articulate a relationship between gender parody and a theory of spectatorship that, while not exactly about pleasure, offers a specific route to camp. In opposition to the female's presumed overidentification with or absorption in the image, camp necessarily entails assuming the mask as a spectator—to read against the grain, to create an ironic distance between oneself and one's image. Camp not only allows for the double nature of masquerade (the spectator in disguise will always see through two pairs of eyes) but also accounts for the pleasure of the masquerade (typically unacknowledged), its status as amusement and play for both the masquerading viewer and the performer.

The trope of the masquerade, then, helps describe camp's negotiation between textual address and the viewer. As Christine Gledhill explains, the concept of negotiation implies an ongoing process of give-and-take: "It suggests that a range of positions of identification may exist within any text; and that, within the social situation of their viewing, audiences may shift subject positions as they interact with the text."[40] One way to imagine the audience shifting positions is to consider subject positions as different masks, different "identities." Most theories figure the female spectator's activity as an either/or hopscotch between positions of identification; they picture the female spectator shifting unconsciously between an active masculine and a passive feminine identity, like Riviere's intellectual women or Mulvey's transvestite moviegoer.[41] Camp offers a slightly different model of negotiation to account for the overlap between passivity and activity in a viewer who sees through, simultaneously perhaps, one mask of serious femininity and another mask of laughing femininity.

Most importantly, examining camp in relation to the female spectator opens up new possibilities for describing the kinds of pleasure a female spectator might take in mass-produced objects that seem to support an oppressive patriarchal sexual regime. Too often, spectatorship studies, and (sub)cultural studies more generally, tend to reify pleasure, particularly female pleasure, as either a consciously resistant activity or a wholly passive manipulation. Judith Mayne discerns in this either/or tendency the impulse "to categorize texts and readings/responses as either conservative or radical, as celebratory of the dominant order or critical of it."[42] According to Mayne, while the first position ascribes an unqualified power to the text ("dominant"), the second ascribes that power to viewers ("resistant").

This either/or tendency is produced by the utopian desire to activate a difference between constructed and essential identities. The "dominant" model (often associated with the Frankfurt School and political modernists) argues that texts interpellate viewers into essentialist positions of subjecthood and thus believes that the ties to those texts must be broken by creating new texts that will displace essentialist identities and stereotypes. Doane and Butler, for instance, offer a concept of distanciation that echoes the Brechtian concept of estrangement, which renders the "natural" strange, and distances the viewer from his or her everyday "normal" assumptions. For them, estrangement must entail a destruction of some forms of pleasure as advocated programmatically by Mulvey.

The "dominant" model rightfully points out the problem with unexamined pleasure, its complicity with an oppressive sexual regime. Still, these models do not provide a way in which to name the pleasures taken by performers and viewers. Doane and Butler's discounting of pleasure, for example, underrates not only the communal and pleasurable aspects of performance and spectatorship but also the viewer's sense of humor and interpretive capability. Although both Doane and Butler envision the formation of gender identities as a cultural practice, neither seems to regard pleasure as an activity in which we all engage as cultural agents. Instead, like many cultural critics and political modernists from Adorno to Foucault, they view pleasure as a form of cultural domination, passively imbibed, that renders us all cultural dupes.

On the other side of the debate, however, the "resistance" model's assumption that the activity of making meaning resides solely with viewers falls into a similar determinism. American cultural studies, in particular, has been identified with the resistance model, which valorizes pleasure as redemptive. Often, as Elspeth Probyn argues, "versions of (sub)cultural analysis tend to turn out rather 'banal' descriptions of cultural resistance."[43] Meaghan Morris sums up the typical mode of argument in this "banal" "vox pop style": "People in modern mediatized societies are complex and contradictory, mass cultural texts are complex and contradictory, therefore people using them produce complex and contradictory culture."[44] In ascribing unqualified power to viewer response, this model suggests that, rather than interpellating viewers, the text produces a multiplicity of meanings from which the viewer can choose his or her point of identification. If the conservative model reifies pleasure by seeing texts as "dominant" and audiences as dupes, the viewer-oriented model similarly reifies pleasure by ignoring the force of dominant ideology in favor of a free-for-all textual and cultural ambiguity. In ascribing an unqualified power to viewers' pleasure, this model often fails to account for the ways in which pleasure can merely affirm the dominant order and preempt even the possibility of resistance as the subject goes laughing into the shopping mall.

Each of these models has its own seductive appeal. Nonetheless, neither one seems to accurately capture the deep complexities of texts and audiences, much less the contradictions of pleasure itself. Camp, however, reveals the porousness of pleasure, its locally overlapping features of passivity and activity, affirmation and critique. Rather than willfully posit what Mayne refers to as a "happy integration" of these two extreme models, I explore camp's negotiation of these two extremes in order to account for both the "complex and contradictory" nature of camp spectatorship and its deep complicity with the dominant. Through my discussion of camp as a "guilty" pleasure, I seek to challenge the basic determinism of spectator studies, especially as this determinism applies to the female spectator. With Susan Rubin Suleiman, who, like Doane and Butler, locates the potential for feminist subversion of patriarchal norms in parody, I would like to imagine women playing and laughing.[45] At the same time, I want to avoid reifying pleasure as wholly resistant. I would like to claim camp as a kind of parodic play between subject and object in which the female spectator laughs at and plays with her own image—in other words, to imagine her distancing herself from her own image by making fun of, and out of, that image—without losing sight of the real power that image has over her.

By examining the complexity and contradictions of camp's guilty pleasures, its two-sidedness, we can begin to move beyond this debate to explore what Mayne points to as "the far more difficult task of questioning what is served by the continued insistence upon this either/or, and more radically, of examining what it is in conceptions of spectators' responses and film texts that produces this ambiguity in the first place."[46] We can begin to broach these questions by complicating our sense of how dominant texts and resistant viewers interact to produce camp, and by reconceptualizing resistance and subversion to account for the way in which camp's simultaneous pleasures of alienation and absorption refuse simplistic categories of dominant-versus-resistant readings.

Camp necessarily entails a description of the relationship between the textually constructed spectator and her empirical counterparts. Although camp tends to refer to a subjective process—it "exists in the smirk of the beholder"[47]—camp is also, as Susan Sontag points out, "a quality discoverable in objects and the behavior of persons."[48] Furthermore, camp is a reading/viewing practice which, by definition, is not available to all readers; for there to be a genuinely camp spectator, there must be another hypothetical spectator who views the object "normally."

Camp further demands a reconceptualization of subcultures so as to make clear that subcultures are variable communities that are not always well-defined and easily identifiable (through, for instance, fashion) but can have differing individuated practices. Although camp has been almost wholly associated with a gay male subculture, that subculture has not necessarily always participated in camp as a group or even recognized itself as a group. While there have been public gay camp rituals (e.g., drag shows and parties, impersonation and transvestism, Judy Garland concerts), camp consists also of individual and private, even closeted, moments of consumption.[49]

Rather than retrospectively transplant a contemporary sense of camp into earlier cinematic texts, or assume anachronistically that gender parody will mean the same thing or imply the same critique at any time, it is necessary to historicize camp. I have chosen a wide range of texts to examine diverse meanings of and means of producing camp in different historical moments.

I focus on three high-camp epochs: the 1930s, the 1950s, and the 1980s through the present. Each of these periods follows on the heels of an important feminist moment: the Progressive Era and its efforts on behalf of female suffrage as well as antiprostitution movements; World War II and women's influx into the job market; and the Women's Liberation movement, respectively. Individual chapters focus on Mae West, the film *Gold Diggers of 1933*, Joan Crawford and *Johnny Guitar*, Madonna, and recycled camp in recent television, video, and film production. Given the plethora of texts available to me that are considered camp, my choice of these particular texts may seem arbitrary. In part, these texts reflect my personal taste and guilty pleasures. More importantly, however, each of these texts seems to me to be exemplary of a particular aspect of feminist camp as well as representative of how different stars, genres, styles, and media employ camp.

Camp must be understood as not only a means of negotiating subject positions, but also as a socio-historical cultural activity that negotiates between different levels of cultural practices. Rather than emphasize either performance or reception, we need to understand masquerade as both a performative strategy and a mode of reception in order to sort through the difficulty of attributing camp to texts. Camp is most often used as an adjective, referring to a quality or qualities found in an object. But camp can also be a verb (from the French *se camper* — to posture or to flaunt). Like the masquerade, the activity of producing camp can be located at both the level of performance and at the level of spectatorship — and the line between the two activities will not always be clear. A performer might produce camp as an aesthetic strategy, as my readings of Mae West and Madonna emphasize. At the same time, a spectator creates a camp effect in reading texts as camp whether those texts intentionally produce camp or not, as I suggest in my readings of *Johnny Guitar* and *Gold Diggers of 1933*. And, as the examples of recycled camp informed by camp spectatorship cited in my final chapter demonstrate, camp blurs the line between the seemingly distinct categories of production and reception. Alexander Doty, discussing the difficulty of attributing queerness to texts, writes: "The complexity and volatility of mass culture production and reception-consumption often make any attempt to attribute queerness to only (or mostly) producers, texts, or audiences seem false and limiting." [50] Similarly, attributing camp to any text requires an understanding of not only textual address but also audience, production history, and the more general historical context of a text's reception.

Unlike gay camp, typically identified as an upper-class sensibility, feminist camp tends to speak from and to a working class sensibility. [51] Therefore,

I examine textual representations of working-class women, gold diggers, and prostitutes, and I relate these images to extracinematic discourses (e.g., Progressive Era antiprostitution discourse, Friedan's analysis of the "feminine mystique") that negotiate attitudes toward women and work. Produced at moments of antifeminist backlash, the particular texts I have chosen use anachronistic images to challenge dominant ideologies about women's roles in the economic sphere and to revitalize earlier (seemingly outmoded) feminist critiques.

Since camp has been linked with gay subcultural practice, most camp objects have taken on general associations related to sex and gender roles, but I limit my discussion of camp to the practice and reception of audiovisual representations of women. These relate most closely to those aspects of gay camp culture involving drag, female impersonation, and the gay reception of female stars. By limiting my discussion in this way, I emphasize the crucial role women have played as producers and consumers of both gay and feminist camp.

I have deliberately excluded any discussion of male stars. In part, I simply want to focus on female performers as a corrective to notions that female stars are camp but do not knowingly produce themselves as camp. In addition, I believe that a discussion of male stars would detract somewhat from the model of female spectatorship I put forward. Women might take camp pleasure in the hypermasculine masquerade of Arnold Schwarzenegger or Victor Mature, and that pleasure might be described as feminist. It seems to me, however, that a description of female identification with these figures would inevitably return to a model of transvestism, until further explorations are made of heterosexual men's relation to the camp sensibility.

Similarly, I have chosen not to discuss any non-white women. It may be possible to describe certain ethnic and racial representations as camp.[52] The parodic masquerade of minstrelsy, for instance, or the over-the-top sensationalist stereotyping of 1970s Blaxploitation films might be readable as camp. But the issues raised by these practices are outside the scope of this argument. An analysis of even metaphorical racial camp requires its own historiography, one dealing, for example, with the history of African American entertainment traditions in America or with the complex history of "passing."

At the same time, however, we need to consider the relation between camp's sexual politics and race discourse. Most discussions of camp assume the adjective "white." Moe Meyer, for instance, discusses the controversy over African American drag queen Joan Jett Blak's 1991 bid for mayor of Chicago as the Queer Nation candidate as exclusively a debate in gay politics about the effectiveness of camp, without once mentioning how Blak's race could have affected the debate or mentioning what the politics of running an African American drag queen entailed for Queer Nation.[53] Alternately, in discussions of *Paris Is Burning*—a film that foregrounds the links between queerness, camp, and racial discourse—critics tend to treat the black and Hispanic use of camp to gain access to fantasies of whiteness as a special case, without fully acknowledging the degree to which the film's invocation of "realness" testifies to how inextricably race and sex are intertwined, and without considering whether or how race discourse operates in camp generally.[54]

This racial specificity becomes clear in the frequent analogies made between camp and blackness. Dennis Altman, for instance, says, "Camp is to gay what soul is to black."[55] Describing post-Stonewall attitudes toward camp, Andrew Ross refers to camp falling into disrepute "as a kind of black-face," and George Melly dubs camp "the Stepin Fetchit of the leather bars, the Auntie Tom of the denim discos."[56] We could ask why Uncle Tom and blackface have not been recuperated as camp clearly has (by queer identity politics and in academic discourse). If this question seems problematic, and it should, it points out how thin these analogies are, and it also points to the fact that the flexibility of sex and gender roles promised by theories of camp performativity does not yet extend to race. In part these analogies suggest, as David Bergman says, the fact that camp raises the issues of any minority culture—issues having to do with appropriation, representation, and difference.[57] But the consistency of the category "black" as the counterpart to camp (as opposed to other racial or ethnic categories) not only signals the degree to which camp is assumed to be white but also mirrors the way tropes of blackness operate in much white camp as an authenticating discourse that enables the performance of sex and gender roles.

Richard Dyer argues that in American culture, at least, whiteness "secures its dominance by seeming not to be anything in particular";[58] representations of normative whiteness thus foreground race and ethnicity as categories of difference. Queer and camp representations, though non-normative in terms of sex and gender, are still consistently defined through categories of racial difference and especially blackness. Mae West and Madonna, for example, both foreground their affinity with African American culture as much as gay male culture. Similarly, as Patricia Juliana Smith argues, Dusty Springfield's camp masquerade simultaneously transforms her into a black woman and a femme gay man; and Ronald Firbank's novels, according to William Lane Clark, tie their camp effect to representations of transracial desire and the employment of black jazz tropes.[59] In a different vein, Joan Crawford's status as a grotesque is reaffirmed by her blackface performance in *Torch Song*. And the Australian film *The Adventures of Priscilla, Queen of the Desert* similarly privileges its scenes with Aboriginal people—in stark contrast to its scenes with the Filipina bride—suggesting that blackness as an authenticating discourse has become part of a transnational camp aesthetic.

Authenticity may seem antithetical to camp, which is so doggedly committed to artifice. "Realness," as *Paris Is Burning* demonstrates, is a subversive category meant to dissolve difference and any notion of authenticity. We need to reconsider, though, how "realness" operates in camp—not only in terms of sex and gender identities but also as a racial fantasy for both white and non-white queers—and the degree to which camp performativity reinscribes racial difference. As more critical attention is given to race and ethnicity in mass culture, the affinity between ethnic and racial masquerade and camp will have to be explored.

I emphasize reception in my analyses of camp texts. However, without unmediated access to fans' own comments about these texts, and suspicious of strict ethnographic audience surveys, I seek primarily to recreate the conditions of reception that create different camp effects. To determine the historical conditions of reception that cause some objects to be taken as camp, I analyze archival materials related to cinematic, institutional, and fan discourses.

Each chapter reads spectatorship through a variety of lenses. Three chapters deal with individual stars: Mae West, Joan Crawford, and Madonna. In these chapters, my analysis of spectatorship relies largely on fan discourse about those stars in movie magazines, publicity materials, and, in the case of Madonna, academic articles and books. In my analyses of *Gold Diggers of 1933* and *Johnny Guitar*, I consider the structures of expectation created by genre conventions. My conclusion investigates the role of the spectator as producer, reading texts that appropriate and recontextualize "classic" camp texts. To understand how all these texts create viewing subjects, I consider textual address, and the larger discourses surrounding individual stars and films, including reviews, production and censorship materials, interviews, and biographies.

Throughout, I consider not only how feminist camp articulates the overlapping interests of women and gay men but also how it fails to do so. In my chapter on Mae West, for instance, I argue that West's appeal to women and to gay men is virtually identical. In contrast, I regard as antifeminist Crawford's transformation into a camp grotesque from the 1950s to the present and offer a feminist reading of her role in *Johnny Guitar* that depends on fans' residual identification with Crawford as a working woman's star. My analysis of Madonna questions whether the mainstreaming of camp taste obscures real difference and reduces gay politics to a discourse of style.

While I acknowledge camp's limitations as a sensibility more committed to the status quo than to effecting real change, I emphasize feminist camp's utopian aspects. By reclaiming camp as a political tool and rearticulating it within the framework of feminism, we can better understand not only female production and reception but also how women have negotiated their feelings of alienation from the normative gender and sex roles assigned to them by straight culture. If, in Richard Dyer's words, "it's being so camp as keeps us going," then perhaps, by retrieving this aspect of our cultural history, we can better understand where we have been and help move the feminist camp forward.

ONE

"The Kinda Comedy

Where They Imitate Me":

Mae West's Identification

with the Feminist Camp

Mae West in a publicity photo (author's collection).

I n 1971, when *Playboy* asked Mae West, "the indestructible queen of vamp and camp," to define camp, she responded, "Camp is the kinda comedy where they imitate me."[1] West's self-reflective definition of camp could be taken as an assertion of her own role as a producer of camp or of a style compatible with camp taste; in other words, "Camp is the kind of comedy that imitates the kind of comedy I produce." However, for a 1970s audience, West's quote would point less to her status as a producer of camp than to her role as camp object: "Camp is the kind of comedy that makes fun of Mae West."

That *Playboy*, the self-proclaimed arbiter of swinging male heterosexuality, should be celebrating camp at all could only occur after the 1960s exposure and subsequent mainstreaming of gay camp taste, marked by Susan Sontag's influential "Notes on 'Camp'" in 1964. At the same time, *Playboy*'s interest in Mae West as both an aged sex symbol and a camp icon represented the sublation of Mae West into what she referred to as "the Mae West character." From West's "comeback" in the late 1960s to her death in 1980, at age 87, she was not so much a star as a pop culture celebrity, the icon "Mae West," who was discovered by a new generation of viewers on late-night TV and in repertory theater festivals. The essence of "Mae West," a "cheerfully extravagant vulgarity,"[2] consisted of a few easily imitated traits—the hip-rolling swagger, look-em-over stares, and outrageous double entendres—and epitomized the camp sensibility for both gay and straight audiences.

A special appearance on the televised Academy Awards in 1958, when West and Rock Hudson sang a duet of "Baby It's Cold Outside," and then a 1964 appearance on the Mr. *Ed* television show had introduced West to a new TV audience. In response, in 1968, the USC cinema fraternity, Delta Kappa Alpha, presented West with an honorary award that seemed clearly intended for West the legend and personality rather than West the actress. And West played "Mae West" to perfection. When the lights came up on the banquet hall stage, a cluster of All-American football stars broke from a huddle to

reveal West, dressed in a white satin gown, platinum wig, and gobs of diamonds, reclining on a beige chaise on a white fur rug, with a gold candelabra
and a gilt-framed mirror.[3] West not only received a standing ovation from
the wildly enthusiastic crowd but reestablished herself as a major celebrity.

Following this appearance, newspapers devoted numerous columns to
West, detailing her one-liners, sexual exploits with young football players,
and beauty secrets. She was discussed regularly in gossip columns, besieged
with requests to appear on talk shows, featured in numerous film festivals,
named the "Sweetheart of Sigma Chi" by another USC fraternity and "Woman
of the Century" by UCLA; and in 1971, she made her film comeback in *Myra
Breckinridge*.[4]

Director Michael Sarne's vision of West's role in *Myra Breckinridge* underscores both camp's critical historicist impulse and its tendency toward misogyny. The narrative of *Myra Breckinridge* revolves around a transsexual fantasy,
in which Rex Reed's Myron, a gay film critic, based on Parker Tyler, under-
goes surgery to become Myra, played by Raquel Welch, whose mission is
"to destroy the last vestigial traces of manhood." Sarne litters the film with
classic film clips, presumably reflecting Myron/Myra's fantasy life, which
serve as shorthand for both a nostalgic and a gay camp sensibility. Wedged
into a hodgepodge of classical Hollywood clips roughly contemporaneous
with West's initial film career—including Shirley Temple singing "On the
Good Ship Lollipop," Marlene Dietrich singing in a masculine uniform, and
the Busby Berkeley–Carmen Miranda, number, "The Lady in the Tutti-Frutti
Hat"—West functions in a similarly iconic manner as a camp and nostalgic
touchstone, while her status as an out-of-date relic is underlined.

In *Myra Breckinridge*, the camp effect of a Shirley Temple clip may target
the presumed innocence of an earlier time, Dietrich might be recuperated
as camp for her androgynous sexuality, and the Berkeley-Miranda musical
number might reflect the outrageousness of an outmoded and camp genre.
The camp effect of West's performance in the film depends significantly
upon a shared assumption that West herself is obsolete and outmoded. As
a 1970s celebrity, West enacted and became a one-dimensional misogynist
joke. West's camp effect depended on the fact that she continued to promulgate an image of herself as a sex symbol, with a seeming disregard for her
age, pairing herself with the youthful Timothy Dalton in *Sextette* (1978) and
insisting on her own youthful appeal: "If you didn't know me, you'd think I
was twenty-six."[5]

The deliberate camp of *Myra Breckinridge* demonstrates the degree to which
West was revered in the 1970s merely as a burlesque of woman, a grotes-

querie, beloved for her ridiculous and narcissistic belief in her own sexual appeal. Despite top-billing and a star salary, West has only a bit part as the talent agent Leticia Van Allen. West's early films always featured her as the sole desirable woman among a bevy of men, but in Myra Breckinridge she competes for attention with newcomer Farrah Fawcett, as well as established sex symbol Raquel Welch. Leticia functions as an uncensored caricature of the West persona. A lascivious phallic woman, Leticia strides into her office past a row of would-be young actors and commands, "Boys, take out your resumes." She then ushers them into her garishly overdecorated office/boudoir one by one, saying, "I don't care about your credits as long as you're oversexed." To a young Texan stud who says he's six foot, seven inches, she asserts that she's only interested in the seven inches. Here, Leticia's baldly sexual jokes and aggressive sexuality represent the same kind of perversity the film associates with homosexuals and transsexuals—in scenes such as one in which Myra, wearing an American-flag bikini and cowboy hat, straps on a dildo and rapes a young actor, while screaming "ride 'em cowboy."

Neither West nor her audience seemed able to differentiate between the Mae West personae of the 1940s theatrical comeback, the 1950s Vegas rock-and-roll musclemen act, the 1970s caricatures of Myra Breckinridge and Sextette, and the initial 1930s film career, let alone her earlier vaudeville and theatrical career.[6] West's late high-camp popularity relies on, but necessarily obscures her earlier career—particularly the ten films she made between 1932 and 1943 that forged "the Mae West character." But, by examining her early film career in its historical context, we find West as a 1930s star producing a very different camp effect from that of her later career(s).

West was a deliberate anachronism already in the 1930s. Her most successful films, like her chief theatrical successes, were set in the Gay Nineties. Rather than nostalgically evoking the past, West used the 1890s setting to expose the ideological contradictions of women's roles in the 1930s. She parodically reappropriated the live-entertainment traditions of burlesque and female impersonation to create an ironic distance from the gender stereotypes supported by these traditions, thus putting into question contemporary stereotypes.

Both Traditional and Burlesque

In 1933, William Troy of the Nation described West: "Miss West's acting style is at once both traditional and burlesque. Unfortunately, there is a certain confusion possible here because one means both that Miss West's style is in the tradition of burlesque, or burleycue, and that it is a burlesque of that tradition."[7] Most accounts agree that West never appeared in burlesque. By the 1920s, burlesque was synonymous with cooch dances and stock shows centered around the display of the female body; and by the end of the 1930s, burlesque proper no longer existed except as a euphemistic misnomer for nightclub strip shows.[8] Yet Troy rightly situates West in the "tradition of burlesque," inasmuch as that tradition, from the late 1860s until the turn of the century, covered a number of forms of comic entertainment, including parodic critiques of various types of theatrical entertainment and acting styles, as well as inversions and exaggerations of sex and gender roles.

Robert C. Allen argues that burlesque was grounded in an aesthetics of transgression, inversion, and the grotesque. Allen considers burlesque a model of ordination and insubordination, rather than domination and resistance. "Ordination" attempts to regulate through the arrangement of things in ranks and orders what is high, what is low, what is us, what is them. "Insubordination," which guides burlesque, represents a transgression or inversion of existing orderings; it challenges the notion of fixed orders and the authority of other discourses. According to Allen, burlesque structured a comic inversion of the bourgeois world. Its reliance on slang challenged the right of bourgeois culture to determine the propriety of public discourse; its puns exploded the possibility of stable meanings; its gender and racial impersonations blurred fixed categories of social difference. Burlesque resisted narrative order and closure, and it especially challenged the system that made women sexual objects but not subjects.

Allen claims that Lydia Thompson and her "British Blondes" transformed America's understanding of burlesque in the 1860s and encoded it as a subversive form specifically about, and critical of, female representation and the relationship of women onstage to women in the real world. Burlesque was the most thoroughly feminized form of entertainment in the history of the American stage; women played all roles, male and female. By reorienting burlesque toward feminine spectacle, Thompsonian burlesque parodically redefined — and resexualized — the forms of theatrical feminine spectacle that had largely been relegated to "respectable" and "artistic" living pictures and ballet. The burlesque performer was distinguished from her female counterparts in girlie shows, tableaux vivants, and the ballet, by her awareness of her own "awarishness" — the directness of her address and her complicity in her own sexual objectification. According to Allen, because the sexy spectacle of burlesque consisted of male impersonation and direct female address, it "provoked desire and at the same time disturbed the ground of that desire by confusing the distinctions on which desire depended."[9] The male impersonation of female burlesque differed from both serious and comic forms of female impersonation—which relied on the audience's knowledge of a distinction between the role played and the real gender underneath—because burlesque's male impersonators represented simultaneously masculine attributes and female sexuality. Burlesque created an upside-down world in which women dominated men with their charismatic sexual power.

Early in her career, West imported the rhetorical directness and "awarish" sexuality of burlesque into small-time vaudeville. She gained notoriety as a vaudeville performer for her transgressively sexual song-and-dance style, "her enchanting, seductive, sin-promising wriggle."[10] West modeled her 1913 solo comedienne act, "The Original Brinkley Girl," in part on Eva Tanguay, known for her uninhibited antics, sexual transgressiveness, and "I Don't Care" theme song.[11] Tanguay, however, was able to achieve stardom in vaudeville only by rechanneling the transgressiveness of burlesque through the grotesque, thereby containing her threat.[12] West reactivated the spirit, if not the letter, of burlesque not simply by becoming a female grotesque but by merging burlesque with the styles of female impersonation and camp.

The Greatest Female Impersonator of All Time

West has frequently been compared to a female impersonator. Most accounts attribute the original comparison to the gay critic Parker Tyler, who called West a female impersonator in 1944, when West left Hollywood, thereby equating West's camp effect with her decline as a film star.[13] The comparison generally partakes of camp's misogyny; West seems like a female impersonator because she appears to be a grotesque, a man in drag, a joke on women, and not a woman. Some feminist critics, however, have taken on the comparison to claim West's style as an instance of deliberate and ironic female masquerade.[14] These retrospective comparisons usefully point toward a crucial element of West's persona but typically fail to acknowledge that West actually modeled herself on contemporary female impersonators, an effect recognized by contemporary audiences.

According to her biographers, the other major influence on West's solo act besides Tanguay was the female impersonator Bert Savoy, who combined two types of female impersonation—the comic dame and the sex or double entendre act—and whose signature line was "You must come over."[15] In 1934, at the height of West's stardom, George Davis of *Vanity Fair* compared West to Savoy:

Miss West, long have I loved you. Ay, long before I'm No Angel. Long
before Diamond Lil. Long, even, before your first great play, Sex. Oft did
I applaud your song-turn in the alas! now vanished two-a-day. . . . I
can pay you no greater tribute, dear lady, than to say it has healed the
wound in my heart caused by the death of the one and only Bert Savoy.
I love you, Miss West, because YOU are the greatest female impersonator of all time.[16]

Davis's extravagant tribute suggests that contemporary audiences could recognize West's affiliation with the tradition of female impersonation and that
this aspect of her persona, like her use of burlesque, was developed before
she got to Hollywood. Whether or not West copied Savoy directly, evidence
from West's play scripts suggests that in creating "the Mae West character"
West not only modeled herself on female impersonators but also explicitly
understood their style as camp.

West wrote a total of eleven plays, eight of which were produced before
she went to Hollywood. In Hollywood, she was credited with writing at
least her own dialogue if not entire screenplays. Although all of West's pre-
Hollywood scripts contain some characteristics of the West film persona,
only Diamond Lil (1928), the star vehicle that brought her to Hollywood, seems
to join these characteristics to the double entendre and aestheticism so crucial to later West characters. West's earliest scripts, The Ruby Ring (1921), The
Hussy (1922), Chick (1924), Sex (1926), and The Wicked Age (1927), all feature a
sexually aware, powerful female, but this character primarily functions as a
comic vamp and/or good-bad girl. In The Ruby Ring, a sketch West and Harry
Richman included in their eighteen-minute vaudeville act, West's character,
Gloria, proves for a bet that she can get each of five men to propose to her
in less than five minutes by using a different vamp method on each man.
For "Alonzo Mosquite of the wild and woolly west," Gloria decides to be
romantic "according to all the rules of the Amalgamated Vamp's Union." She
uses "baby vamp" stuff on an old man, "Theda Bara" for a professor, and so
on.[17] The Hussy works the same routine into a straightforward love story about
a gold digger with a heart of gold. Sex and The Wicked Age are melodramas
that depict, respectively, the self-sacrifice of a bowery prostitute unwilling
to ruin the man she loves by exposing him to her past, and the downfall
of a cold-hearted gold digger. These plays contain themes that will recur
in West's later works—love as a performative technique, men as "suckers,"
jewelry as a measure of love's value, West as friend and counselor to subordinate women, and the conflict between female sexuality and society—but
the dialogue contains almost none of the wordplay associated with West.

The characters in West's scripts who sound most like West's film persona are the gay men in The Drag (1927) and the female impersonators in The Pleasure Man (1928). West wrote both plays but did not act in either one. The Drag attempts seriously to represent the plight of homosexuals in a hypocritical society through a quasi-medical and -juridical discourse, but most of its power and verve centers around the drag ball and the dialogue of its gay characters. The play features a bevy of "queens" who express their desire and sexual identity through witty double entendres.[18] Grayson, a construction worker, plays the straight man, in a double sense, to the gay men in the play, whose lines presage those of West's own film characters. Clem, who calls all men "she" and "molls," says, "Yes, I'd love to stay and see your wonderful construction. But we have other plans." Another character, "Winnie," echoes Savoy's tag line ("You must come over") and anticipates West's famous "Come up and see me sometime" when he says, "So glad to have you meet me. Come up sometime and I'll bake you a pan of biscuits" (II,8).

West described the flamboyant and witty style of the drag queens and female impersonators as camp, which she understood to be a performative activity. In the backstage drama, The Pleasure Man, West clearly identifies the performance style of female impersonators as the activity of camping. In all her play scripts, West uses a shorthand to indicate bits for ad-libbing—for vamping, she notes "vamp bus." or just "bus." In The Pleasure Man, stage directions note the entrance of the female impersonators onstage with the shorthand, "Boys camp—enter through [central door fancy]" (I,13). Here, the verb "camp" suggests that the performers will mime some activity that will effectively announce and mark these characters as female impersonators. Later, when the lead man assaults a woman, one female dancer asks if anyone heard a scream and another dancer responds, "No, you heard them queens next door, campin'" (II,20). Throughout the play, the "campin'" of the impersonator Bird of Paradise and his "manleykins" consists of bitchy performative exchanges that express homosexual desire: "Paradise, did you ever have a platonic love affair?" "Yes, but his wife found it out" (I,24). Like the homosexual dialogue in The Drag, the dialogue attributed to the female impersonators and identified as camping anticipates West's wisecracks to a degree that most of her own theatrical roles do not.

In these play scripts, West aligns "campin'" with Wildean aestheticism, as well as verbal activity. In The Pleasure Man, references to dandies and aestheticism serve as a joking, coded language for the in-crowd of homosexuals. When a straight performer expresses concern about the peculiar proclivities of his partner who makes lamp shades, the stage manager Stanley, identified as "the Beau Brummel," says, "He's all right—nearly. There's no harm in lampshades. He's just an aesthetic type" (II,20). Descriptions of the ball gowns in *The Drag* link aestheticism with gay camp practice and emphasize the relation between gay and female aesthetics: "Wait until you see the creation I'm wearing, dearie. Virginal white, no back, with oceans of this and oceans of that, trimmed with excitement in front" (II,4). This description, which emphasizes effect over detail ("oceans of this and oceans of that"), parodies the lingo of female fashion design and, to paraphrase Wilde, asserts the primacy of style over sincerity "in matters of grave importance."

At the same time, West's play scripts acknowledge the "grave importance" of the homosexuals' social situation. While foregrounding matters of visual and verbal style, West's play scripts articulate a deep connection between the public subordination of homosexuals and women. In fact, West becomes quite moralistic when dealing with the hypocrisy of a society that condemns both gay men and women for their sexuality. When an abandoned gay man kills his lover in *The Drag*, the murderer accuses the dead man's father, "When you condemn me, you condemn him. A judge's son can be just the same as another man's son—yes, a king's son, a fool's son—Oh! I loved him—" (III,ii,6). Similarly, in *Sex*, the prostitute Margy attacks the false distinction between respectable women and prostitutes. To a society woman who goes slumming in the red-light district, she says, "Say, you've got a nerve putting yourself on a pedestal above me. The things I've done, I had to do for a living. . . . Now your [sic] down off your pedestal. You're down where you can see, it's just a matter of circumstances. The only difference between us is that you could afford to give it away" (III,i,5–6). In both cases, West collapses the distinctions between classes by revealing society's hypocrisy in dealing with the issues of gay and female sexuality.

In addition, West's gay characters identify with women's oppression in heterosexual patriarchal society. Sexual oppression motivates West's "awarish" female characters in their manipulation of men. Margy, the prostitute, says, "Why ever since I've been old enough to know Sex, I've looked at men as hunters. They're filled with Sex. In the past few years I've been a chattel to that Sex. All the bad that's in me has been put there by men. I began to hate every one of them, hated them, used them for what I could get out of them, and then laughed at them" (II,i,17). In *The Pleasure Man*, the female impersonator Bird of Paradise articulates the bond of moral identification between gay men and women in relation to patriarchal oppression. Taking a stand against the "pleasure man" who assaults a woman he impregnated and abandoned, Paradise asserts, "If you're a man, thank God I'm a female impersonator" (II,ii,24).

In a curious half-truth, Ethan Mordden describes West's personality as "the gay style exposed to the outsider." [19] Mordden recognizes the gay style in West but misunderstands, I believe, what she exposes through her use of gay style. West did not simply copy gay style but linked certain aspects of gay culture to aspects of a female sensibility. West modeled herself on a camp gay style because she believed that gay men were like women. On the one hand, she adhered to inversion models that claimed that gay men were women in men's bodies. On the other hand, she believed both gay men and women were oppressed by straight men. She impersonates gay men and female impersonators not to expose the gay style but to exaggerate, burlesque, and expose stereotypical female styles as impersonation.

We can see elements of the female impersonator in West's fetishistic costumes—like the drag queen Clem, her costumes are excessively ornamental and "trimmed with excitement." For example, in She Done Him Wrong, she wears a tight black Edith Head design with sequins on the bodice, off-the-shoulder feathers, and white satin birds accentuating the bust. She foregrounds the fetishistic character of her costumes to the point of parody, with gowns for example, that play upon female stereotypes, like the Travis Banton spider dress worn in I'm No Angel. The 1890s corseted silhouette exaggerates and constricts the woman's body, fetishizing the bust and hips in a caricature of the female form. In part, as a female female impersonator West represents an instance of deliberate and ironic female masquerade. To understand her masquerade in terms of camp, however, we must realign the concept of the masquerade with the activities of drag and cross-dressing. West's female masquerade is mediated through gay discourses on femininity and needs to be understood in the context of gay practices of drag and cross-dressing. Recognizing this, Ramona Curry describes West's female masquerade as a modified form of gender reversal or drag. While arguing for a feminist reading of West as a female female impersonator, Curry claims that West represents an instance of deliberate female masquerade through her embodiment of masculine characteristics, as a "phallic woman" and as a "female displaying a male displaying a female." [20]

West's masquerade does respond to drag, and this means it can be read as camp. But, in contradistinction to Curry, I believe that response can only be described as feminist because it parodies drag by replacing and displacing it with the hyperbolization of the feminine through the masquerade—and not because West represents masculine characteristics behind the female masquerade. Whereas Curry reads West's aggressive and defiant sexuality as "masculine," I suggest that West displaces the masculine characteristics of the drag performer to articulate a specifically feminine form of aggressivity. Female impersonators absorb and displace a female aesthetic; they mimic the dress and behavior codes of femininity. West recuperates this aesthetic as a female aesthetic. She parodically reappropriates — and hyperbolizes — the image of the woman from male female impersonators so that the object of her joke is not the woman but the idea that an essential feminine identity exists prior to the image: she reveals that feminine identity is always a masquerade or impersonation.

At least in her early career, however, West not only parodies female stereotypes and images but, at the same time, embodies and identifies with those images. To read her impersonation as wholly ironic one must ignore her status and appeal as a sex symbol and deny her affiliation with the female tradition of burlesque. For a 1930s audience, West embodied a complex and contradictory image of female sexuality that relied undeniably on gay camp but merged the effects of gay camp with female burlesque to produce a form of feminist camp available to a female as well as a gay camp audience. The epithets attached to West in the 1930s point not only to her camp qualities ("the world's best bad actress," "the greatest female impersonator of all time"), but also to her sexual allure ("the Empress of Sex," "Queen of Curves," "Siren of Sex and Sensation," "Hollywood's Number One bachelor gal"), and to the transgressive quality of her sexuality ("the bad girl friend of the world," "the first lady gangster," "the feminine Babe Ruth of the screen"). West was simultaneously sexy and a parody of sex; she was both a sex object and a sexual subject. Like her predecessors in Thompsonian burlesque, she both provoked desire and transgressed the bounds of that desire.

The Queen-B

In addition to her potential cross-sex, cross-gender identification as a female female impersonator, West also participates in complicated cross-racial identifications with blackness that are key to her transgressive image. West was generally known as a supporter of African American causes. She wrote a novel, The Constant Sinner, about an interracial love affair. According to Clarence Muse, West gave him money for an antilynching campaign. West frequently featured African American performers in her films, including Louis Armstrong, Hazel Scott, and Duke Ellington, whose band she forced Paramount to sign for Belle of the Nineties. And West garnered extremely positive receptions in the African American press. One article in the Chicago Defender, for instance, applauds her for being more attentive to the African American journalists than Hazel Scott, who is accused of acting "Hollywood" or high-hat with them.[21]

In his piece on West, John Kobal describes West as "the first white woman with a black soul" and wistfully posits the unfounded assertion that West has "a touch of color in her blood."[22] As Ramona Curry notes, as a stage performer, West adopted a style of singing characteristic of "dirty blues," similar to that of Ma Rainey and Bessie Smith and maintained this style in a somewhat modified, censored form in her films. West's performance of "dirty blues," according to Curry, associates West in the public mind with "the unbound sexual behavior that the dominant U.S. society frequently attributes to lower class African Americans."[23] Moreover, in appropriating a black female blues style, West takes on the persona of what Hazel Carby refers to as the "mythologized" blues singer and "an oral and musical woman's culture that explicitly addresses the contradictions of feminism, sexuality, and power." Carby describes women's blues of the 1920s and 30s as "a discourse that articulates a cultural and political struggle over sexual relations": "a struggle that is directed against the objectification of female sexuality within a patriarchal order but which also tries to reclaim women's bodies as the sexual and sensuous subjects of women's song."[24] Thus, West's performance of blues-inflected songs throughout her films not only aligns her with black female working-class sexuality but also enables her to address her position as a sexual subject and object in much the same way that burlesque does.

When West performs African American styles of music, she updates the burlesque tradition of minstrelsy. Performing blackness, but without blackface, West, in John Szwed's terms, "marks the detachment of culture from race and the almost full absorption of a black tradition into white culture."[25] Almost, because it is crucial that the black tradition still be marked as "other." While commodifying African American community life and culture, minstrelization requires that the commodity still signify blackness to the consumer. In West's films, this is signified and authenticated by the presence of African American performers.

The African Americans who figure most prominently in West's films play maids and include Gertrude Howard, Louise Beavers, Hattie McDaniel, and Libby Taylor, who played the role both on- and offscreen for West; their representations are stereotypical. As Donald Bogle describes them, "The domestics were always overweight, middle-aged, and made up as jolly aunt jemimas. . . . They had the usual names: Pearl, Beulah, and Jasmine. Their naive blackness generally was used as a contrast to Mae West's sophisticated whiteness."[26] West employs racist language with her maids, calling them

Eightball and Shadow, for instance, or accusing them of being slow and lazy, but the maids are also pictured as confidantes and trusted good friends, in a manner similar to movies like Jean Harlow's *Bombshell*, Claudette Colbert's *Imitation of Life*, Shirley Temple movies, and others in the '30s, a decade Bogle names "the Age of the Negro Servant."

In *I'm No Angel*, one scene shows West bantering and singing "I Found a New Way to Go to Town" with four maids. The maids serve, as Bogle says, as "foils," straight men and yes-men, "paying homage to the supreme power of their white mistress." West is clearly the boss and center of attention. The maids frame her and set off her whiteness as well as the whiteness of the room. West's glowing whiteness is carefully constructed here and throughout her career. In a recent TV documentary about West, Herbert Kenwith claims that white women in West's stage shows were required to have dark hair, to wear darker makeup and clothes than West, and even to put a gray gel on their teeth, so that West's whiteness would make her stand out as the star and center of attention.[27] West's conversation with her black maids, however, masks racial difference by focusing on gender. She talks about men, sex, and clothing and treats Libby Taylor's comment that she likes "dark men" not as a given but much like her own quip that she likes two kind of men, "domestic and foreign." West thus simultaneously foregrounds her racial difference from the maids and her gendered identification with them.

In this scene, the African American women function not only as servants and fans of West but also as, in effect, her backup singers. The figure of the black female blues singer, whose style West appropriates, was historically transplanted into the figure of the black maid, as many female blues singers, including Hattie McDaniel and Ethel Waters, moved from making race records into film careers and maid roles. In *I'm No Angel*, McDaniel and Libby Taylor not only sing along to "I Found a New Way to Go to Town" with West but also dance across the room following West's lead.

John Corbett claims that the unspoken adjectives that precede "backup singers" are always "black" and "female" and that the unspoken adjectives preceding "lead singer" are "white male."[28] Kaja Silverman argues that West's voice is coded masculine, an assertion in line with those who see West's persona as masculine.[29] Rather than a white male lead, however, West, coded simultaneously as a female impersonator and a black woman, backed up and fawned over by the maids, plays the Queen-B or Bulldagger, a figure SDiane Bogus claims is common in and peculiar to African American lesbian fiction and culture, a "female blues singer who bonds with other women," "a central figure in the community at large" whose sway over her followers relates both to her singing and her unorthodox sexuality.[30]

West's homosocial bonding with her maids might be readable as homosexual, if we consider Linda Nochlin's point that in painting "the conjunction of black and white, or dark and light female bodies, whether naked or in the guise of mistress or maidservant traditionally signified lesbianism."[31] This potential homosexuality is raised obliquely when one of the maids (whose face we never see) says, "Well, men don't mean a thing to me." But I am not suggesting that the Mae West character be read as a closet lesbian. Rather, I would emphasize that this scene demonstrates the degree to which West's affinity for African American music, in conjunction with her association with female impersonation, marks her sexuality as particularly fluid and deeply transgressive and not merely ironic.

Belle of the Gay Nineties

West's complicated star image, her ability to both parody sex and be sexy, depended not only on her transgressive identifications with marginalized figures but also on her anachronistic use of 1890s settings. From her first starring role in *She Done Him Wrong* (1933), West was identified with the 1890s. Advance publicity for *Belle of the Nineties* (1934), her fourth film, and the third with a Gay Nineties setting, featured just a silhouette drawing (towering headdress, exaggerated curves, trailing gown, parasol) identifiable simultaneously as generic '90s fashion and as West, with the caption "Coming events cast their shadows before." Publicity for *Goin' to Town* (1935), her first starring role with a contemporary setting, underscored the close identification between West and "the Mauve Decade" by insisting on the film's modernity ("down-to-the-minute modern") while detailing the absence of Gay Nineties effects ("there isn't a pearl gray derby or a handle-bar mustache to be found") and juxtaposing a photo of West in a 1935 Travis Banton design with a line drawing of a spare '90s silhouette.

In part, West evokes the fashions and entertainment forms of the '90s nostalgically, but, at the same time, she renders both the period and the nostalgia outmoded. On the one hand, West could be taken seriously as a 1930s sex symbol only by invoking an outmoded ideal of feminine beauty and recontextualizing her voluptuous figure according to those ideals. On the other hand, West recontextualizes and redefines 1890s styles according to 1930s mores. While her look was associated with the '90s, West's attitudes were recognized as decidedly modern. A *Time* magazine review of *Klondike Annie* (1936) reflects how essential this disjunction was to her star image and appeal: "As usual, the comedy depends mainly upon the incongruity between Mae West's up-to-date wisecracks and their *fin de siecle* background."[32] West's camp effect depends partly on this disjunction between social mores, and also, more pointedly, upon the intersection of and gap between outmoded 1890s live entertainment traditions and Depression-era film and music styles.

The gap between mise-en-scène and social mores serves to exaggerate West's cynicism and distance her from contemporary film stars and screen stereotypes. Contemporary fan magazines sometimes positioned West as a rival to thirties sex symbols, especially Garbo and Dietrich. One headline in *Motion Picture* reads: "Is Mae West Garbo's Greatest Rival?" Another offers a psychologist's comparative analysis of "Katharine Hepburn, Mae West—And Sex Appeal!" And an article in *Photoplay* looks for "War Clouds in the West?" by pitting West against Dietrich: "On this side, Mae West, Queen of Curves. Gossip picks her for one contender. On this side, Marlene Dietrich, Queen of Glamour, gossip's other contender." [33]

But reviewers also took West's cynicism as a welcome and critical relief from the maudlin seriousness of these screen vamps; and their perception of West's opposition to contemporary sex symbols was a crucial element of her star text. Andre Sennewald of the *New York Times*, for instance, claimed that

Advertisement for Belle of the Nineties *from Movie Classic, October 1934 (photo reproduction courtesy of the Library of Congress).*

Mae's Change of Pace...
by Ted Allen

Every big league pitcher knows the value of a change of pace. First a fast one, then a wide curve, then a high one on the inside, then another fast one right across the heart of the plate. That wins baseball games.

And Mae West, the feminine Babe Ruth of the screen, knows all about change of pace too. An expert on fast ones and wide curves, she long ago learned the value of varying her style to meet public demand.

All of which is by way of pointing out that Mae West is about to give theatre-goers a brand-new version of herself. Having set a home-run record with her characterizations of the Gay Nineties, she decided it was time to change pace. She has done it by going completely, down-to-the-minute modern in her newest Paramount Picture, "How Am I Doin'?"

Gone are the exaggerated curves and towering head-dresses of "She Done Him Wrong." In their place are the just-as-alluring 1935 model curves and the smartest of today's coiffures. The trailing gowns of the Mauve Decade have been replaced by Travis Banton's smartest creations. The sixteen-cylinder town car replaces the horse-drawn barouche. And there isn't a pearl gray derby or a handle-bar mustache to be found on either Paul Cavanaugh or Ivan Lebedeff, the "tall, dark and handsome" masculine members of the cast!

Always her own scenarist, Miss West has seen to it that the story is as modern as the characters who appear in it. But she hasn't lost sight of the basic entertainment values that have distinguished every one of her box office smashes of the past. It's a Mae West story tailored in the 1935 fashion for Mae West by Mae West and directed by Alexander Hall, the man who gave the screen "Little Miss Marker."

"How Am I Doin'?" the star asks in the title of this Paramount Picture. And the answer from an army of West fans promises to be a mighty "Okay, Mae!"

Advertisement for Goin' to Town (working title "How Am I Doin'?") from Movie Classic, May 1935 (photo reproduction courtesy of the Library of Congress).

"her cynical swagger . . . casts acid ridicule upon the sulphurous sexdramas of the Dietrichs and Garbos."[34] In an article in Photoplay, Leo McCarey, who directed West in Belle of the Nineties, asks, "I wonder how many people realize that Mae West satirizes sex? She has made our old-fashioned vampires, those mysterious, pallid, emaciated, smoky-eyed females appear as futile as they usually are in real life."[35] Similarly, Elza Schallert of Motion Picture calls West "the first and real Waterloo of the Garbo and Dietrich schools of sultry, languorous, erotic emotions" because she makes them appear "slightly foolish—as if they didn't know how to get a 'kick' out of life": "And whether the vivid and voluptuous, electric and elegant Mae is aware of it or not—and I, for one, think she is—her healthy, Amazonian, audacious presentation of the ancient appeal known as sex has made the world-weary, secretive charm of Greta and Marlene appear feeble by comparison."[36] By these accounts, West represents at once healthy sexuality and uninviting cynicism, parodic knowingness and potential obliviousness—in other words, a two-sided camp effect. But in each case, she opposes and ridicules the vamps' style of "sexdrama," making them seem "futile" and unrealistic. West pointedly parodies "sexdramas" in *Go West, Young Man* (1936), but, for the most part, West parodies contemporary types obliquely, by replacing old conventions with new ones. For the vamps' slim, "emaciated," figures she substitutes "voluptuous" curves; rather than mysterious languor, she offers "audacious" cynicism; and instead of "pallid," "sulphurous," "feeble" eroticism, she treats sex with a "healthy" practicality.

Other sex symbols were both sexy and funny, but the way in which West blended sex and humor parodied the very notion of sex symbols. Whereas a Jean Harlow could be taken as a sex symbol and comedienne who epitomized 1930s mores, the anachronism of West's humor created a camp effect that targeted contemporary types by displacing 1930s attitudes into an 1890s setting (a disjunction that, once established, carried over into even her films with a contemporary setting).

In addition to incongruous attitudes, West's camp effect depends on the gap between dominant and residual entertainment forms. Sometimes West demonstrates the incongruity between entertainment traditions by anachronistically inserting blues and jazz numbers into the Gay Nineties. In *Belle of the Nineties*, she sings "Memphis Blues," "St. Louis Woman," and "My Old Flame." In *She Done Him Wrong*, she sings the blues-influenced "I Wonder Where My Easy Rider's Gone" and "A Guy What Takes His Time," which are distinctly from the thirties; and she merges various traditions in a jazzy update of the period song "Frankie and Johnny." Her performances stand out from others in the film, like that of the Irish tenor who sings the period song "Silver Threads Among the Gold." By incorporating multiple styles, she recodes the period songs to give them a sardonic thirties flavor and tone; and she distances the viewer from the thirties songs by recontextualizing their racy cynicism.

When West performs numbers suited to the Gay Nineties setting, she parodically reworks them in a burlesque of burlesque itself. In *I'm No Angel* (1933), West's character Tira rises from a lowly circus cooch dancer to a daring lion tamer accepted by high society, paralleling West's own rise from a vaudeville specialty act to a Broadway and Hollywood star. West had gained notoriety for introducing the shimmy to Broadway audiences in 1918 after she learned the dance from black nightclub patrons in Chicago, but she dropped "the shakes," unwilling to become exclusively identified with a trend. Tira, "the girl who discovered you don't have to have feet to be a dancer," functions both as a reminder of West's past and of the "awarish" sexuality of the burlesque performer. She displays herself in a see-through, beaded gown as she sings, "I sing a passionate strain / Then I'm lowdown again / So be careful of this dame / They call me Sister Honky Tonk." The film viewer witnesses the spectacle of Tira's provocative dance, shoulders shaking and hips swiveling but also hears her sarcastically mutter "Suckers" as she exits the circus stage, thereby recognizing her control over the image and her disdain for the suckers who think they possess her and for the film viewer who identifies West with such easy objectification.

Belle of the Nineties contains West's most extensive parody of burlesque entertainment, in which she plays Ruby Carter, the "Queen of all Entertainers" and "the Greatest Sensation of our 19th century," a "St. Louis Woman" who transfers her act to New Orleans. Ruby's first number, "My American Beauty," "the most beautiful act" her emcee has ever had the "privilege to offer," consists of Ruby, in a shiny, clingy dress, posing before and "becoming" a giant butterfly, a vampire bat, a rose, and a spider, until finally, torch in hand, she personifies the Statue of Liberty—all of which, according to the song, represent different aspects of this American beauty. Ruby shifts her weight a bit from left to right, in true West style, but can't be said to perform anything—instead, she silently enacts and impersonates a series of feminine stereotypes. This number, however, functions like Doane's "double mimesis" to make these poses and the tropes they represent, incredible, literally fantastic. The act's excessive buildup and amazingly enthusiastic reception seem ridiculous in relation to what Ruby actually does, especially since the other six performances Ruby gives—including "Troubled Waters" and the numbers with Duke Ellington—demonstrate West's genuine and unique talent as a singer. "My American Beauty" anachronistically retrieves the form of 1840s girlie shows in which women posed as living statuary—which, in turn, were revived in 1890s films like Edison's American Beauties, featuring the American flag, an American beauty rose, and a woman.

In "My American Beauty," West distances the viewer from the female stereotypes the lyrics of the song seemingly support. She not only burlesques female stereotypes in becoming a virtual slide show of female tropes (vampire, spider, rose) but extends her critique to cover early voyeuristic film practice and even advertising imagery in her final incarnation as the Statue of Liberty.

Long before the statue was dedicated in 1886, numerous pictures of it appeared in newspapers and magazines, and techniques of mass reproduction made possible the manufacture and distribution of 3-D replicas of it. The statue was frequently used as an advertising image, and representations of the statue inevitably suggested certain gendered roles and situations. Favorite comic variations mimicked the pose and accessories by featuring a

West poses as an American beauty rose in "My American Beauty" in Belle of the Nineties.
Video frame enlargement (author's collection).

disgruntled matron raising her lamp to chastise errant spouses or a housewife who obtains her liberty by using a brand-name cleaning product.[37] In
addition to humorists and advertisers, feminists also recognized the statue's
symbolic potential. On the day of the statue's unveiling, suffragettes rented a
boat to circle the island and made speeches that protested the injustice of a
society that denied women true freedom while literally, in this case, putting
a woman on a pedestal.[38]

West's impersonation of the statue plays upon the statue's nineties associations with advertising imagery while also reactivating the feminist critique.
But, reflecting the turn-of-the-century split between feminists who emphasized political equality and those who focused on women's sexual freedom,
West's imitation exposes not the political injustices of society but the hidden sexuality of the image. Appropriately, George Jean Nathan dubbed West's
pose "The Statue of Libido". By impersonating the statue, West refers, on the
one hand, to the proliferation of the image in the 1890s, while, on the other,
she recodes its subversive feminist potential according to 1930s sexual mores.

In *Belle of the Nineties*, we also see the way West uses the buildup to give "the

West as "The Statue of the Libido" in "My American Beauty" in Belle of the Nineties.
Video frame enlargement (author's collection).

Mae West character" a built-in legendary status that parodies the star system. Before we see West, even before the emcee's fawning introduction, we see a billboard for "The Most Talked About Woman in the World" (a label applied to West in her *Diamond Lil* days), crowds gaping at publicity photos outside the theater, and the standing-room-only audience. In virtually all her films, the buildup for West's entrance coincides with a diegetic buildup. In *I'm No Angel*, for example, the emcee announces Tira as a "supreme marvel of feminine pulchritude," a carpet rolls out, a spotlight hits the runway entrance, trumpets play, and then Tira enters—all before we enter the enclosed tent space where she performs her cooch dance. In both *She Done Him Wrong* and *Every Day's A Holiday* (1938), the extraordinary beauty and appeal of West's character is described and anticipated in the dialogue long before West makes her entrance. Because it is West's entrance, and not just the diegetic performer's, the excessive buildup parodies the introduction and individuation of the star. As a review of *Diamond Lil* reflected, the other characters' "seeming delight in the heroine's presence brings the star system to an ironical perfection."[39]

Every Day's A Holiday makes an explicit joke about the role of the buildup to manufacture a sensation. To hide from the law, Peaches O'Day disguises herself as the temperamental French performer, Mademoiselle Fifi (interestingly, the name of a 1929 New York burlesque stripper). In a key nineties reference, Peaches and her sidekick, Nifty, plan to give Fifi more advance publicity "than P. T. Barnum ever thought of." A montage sequence shows two newspaper headlines: first "Crowds gather to get glimpse of Mademoiselle Fifi," then "Crowds fail to get glimpse of Mademoiselle Fifi." Next, we see the theater filling to standing-room-only capacity. Finally, the curtain opens to loads of chorus boys singing "Fifi," followed by chorus girls and more men, all singing "Fifi," until Fifi (West in a brunet wig) makes her glorious entrance in a carriage drawn by white horses. The buildup, we know, is a scam, a fabrication, like Fifi herself. Like the other buildups, it reflects an "awarishness" behind the self-objectification and self-consciously mirrors the prior introduction of Peaches O'Day.

In West's films, the buildup functions to make clear the self-consciousness of private as well as public performances. Just as her early plays, *The Ruby Ring* and *The Hussy*, enacted a version of sexuality as performance, in *I'm No Angel*, West makes seduction an obvious performance by using the buildup not only for her cooch dance but as an integral part of her rendezvous with Jack Clayton (Cary Grant). After arranging her costume and boudoir, she tells her maids (Libby Taylor and Hattie McDaniel) to open the door for her entrance and says, "Well, here goes my big moment." Then, while kissing Grant, she asks McDaniel, "How'm I doin'?" Earlier in the film, Tira enacts a false seduction to hook a stage-door-johnny in a blackmail scam. She sorts through a collection of records ready made for her suckers ("No One Loves Me Like That Frisco Man," ". . . Dallas Man," etc.) choosing the appropriate one, like a vaudeville star inserting "local" material. Because her sincere fondness for Clayton partakes of the same degree of theatricality, that performance, like the con, can be read as sexual huckstering and as a form of impersonation.

The link between sexuality and performance in West's films offers, then, an instance of self-conscious female masquerade. But because West situates herself in the world of nineties entertainment, the link between sexuality and performance also represents the contradictions of women's roles in the public sphere. As Kathy Peiss has pointed out, at the turn of the century, middle-class forms of leisure, including the theater and some vaudeville, witnessed the emergence of a female audience; but women's participation in popular venues (like the circuses, saloons, variety shows, and sports events depicted in West's films) was still severely limited due to the cost as well as the content that was still associated with the masculine saloon culture.[40]

Female performers associated with these forms were, moreover, culturally coded as prostitutes. Sites of working-class commercial leisure represented the intersection of feminine economic independence and social autonomy insofar as they offered women the possibility of an independent career and wages that were typically denied them in other fields. "Prostitution" meant "not so much literal sexual commerce as a whole symbolic constellation of qualities attendant upon the working-class woman's economic and social independence."[41] This system included not just the performers but also the working-class female audience for these entertainments. Peiss describes the working women who attended popular entertainments as "charity girls," women who relied on a system of "treating," trading sexual favors for male attention, gifts, and a good time.

The 1890s "Mae West character" in film is almost always a performer and sometimes a gold digger or charity girl but covertly, of course, she is a prostitute. Her role as performer functions as a code for, and is seen as of a piece with, prostitution. Lady Lou of She Done Him Wrong makes the connection explicit by referring to herself as the "finest woman who ever walked the streets." West undoubtedly downplays her characters' transgressiveness and criminality to suit Hollywood mores, but, by substituting the role of performer for that of prostitute, West displays the contradictions of working-class women's roles in society.

As Miriam Hansen notes, the "maximally inclusive" world of mass and consumer culture in the cinema gave women access to horizons of experience previously unavailable to them. She cites the 1897 filmed Corbett-Fitzsimmons fight that surprised exhibitors by drawing huge crowds of women who were for the first time able to see half-naked male bodies boxing.[42] In Belle of the Nineties, Ruby not only attends the boxing match—where she is one of only a handful of female spectators—but also determines the outcome of the fight, slipping her ex-beau a mickey in the twenty-seventh round. The scene of the boxing match at once represents female exclusion from this sphere and undermines it, by drawing the film's female audience into it, and by giving Ruby access to and control over it. "The Mae West character" may function as a kind of prostitute, a victim of the social and gender hierarchy in the public sphere, reliant on her physical attributes for luxuries; but she also undercuts that role by manipulating her place in the public sphere.

Functioning as an autonomous agent in the public entertainment sphere, West's character suggests the possibility of breaking free from prescribed roles for women in all spheres, especially in relation to sex and marriage. As

Colette described "the Mae West character", "She alone, out of an enormous and dull catalogue of heroines, does not get married at the end of the film, does not die, does not take the road to exile. . . . She alone has no parents, no children, no husband. This impudent woman is, in her style, as solitary as Chaplin used to be."[43] Although, due to pressure from the Hays office, the West character usually must get married at the end of each film, she believes in marriage "only as a last resort." The formation of the couple in West films never seems like a sellout, because her character clearly only marries after choosing from numerous men, and because the viewer doesn't necessarily believe that the "marriage" is anything more than another scam. Lady Lou of *She Done Him Wrong* articulates West's ambivalence about marriage when she says, "He'd be the kind a woman would have to marry to get rid of" (and then "marries" this same man at the end when faced with the choice between prison handcuffs and a wedding band).

This ambivalent and transgressive attitude toward marriage and women's roles was a keystone for West's star discourse. West married only once, secretly, in 1911, but separated from her husband, Frank Wallace, within a year. Later, at the height of her stardom, when Wallace made their marriage public, she denied the story as a kind of tabloid blackmail attempt, saying that hundreds of men had claimed to be her husband. She wisecracked, "Marriage is a great institution. As I've always said, no family should be without it."[44] After admitting the truth of Wallace's story, and getting a divorce, West never married again, citing her need for personal freedom and autonomy as the reason.

The Alarm Clock that Awakened
the Cleaner-Uppers

An equally important part of West's star text, and one that goes hand in hand with her sexual autonomy, is West's constant battles with the censors. During her initial theatrical career, *Sex* was listed as one of New York's "dirt shows," along with three other plays with sexual themes: *The Captive* (about lesbianism), *The Virgin Man*, and Dreiser's *An American Tragedy*.[45] West was subsequently charged with and jailed for producing an immoral play. *The Drag* was forced to close out of town after West and her manager James Timony acquiesced to claims that it would "upset the city."[46] *The Pleasure Man* went to trial for being immoral, indecent, impure, and obscene, though the jury was unable to reach a verdict, largely because the defense succeeded in making the chief witness for the prosecution appear foolish, forcing him to imitate the female impersonators in the play (and turning him into a camp object).[47]

Hollywood became interested in West after the success of her play *Diamond Lil*, but, because the play was deemed "highly censorable," Will Hays tried to keep West and her play out of Hollywood. Yet Hays's efforts only increased her allure for the studios, and Paramount brought her to Hollywood. When West arrived in Hollywood, she was initially kept idle for twelve weeks because Paramount was afraid to use her. According to Leonard J. Leff and Jerold L. Simmons, "the Mae West character" generally, and *Belle of the Nineties* in particular, was the catalyst for the formation of the Legion of Decency and the 1934 Production Code.[48] Ramona Curry disputes this claim but concedes that West played "a unique iconographic role in the public discourse about movie morality and censorship."[49]

In Hollywood, what upset the censors was not solely West's sexual explicitness. West self-censored her scripts, never appearing in costumes as revealing as other contemporary stars and never allowing her characters to consummate their relationships, believing that readiness was all. The censors were less upset about explicit dialogue (though many of her song lyrics were substantially cut), than the way she delivered her lines. In part, her employment of camp double entendres was a deliberate effort to deflect the censors, because the Production Code Administration focused on written scripts, not performance. Joseph I. Breen, the director of the Production Code Administration, stated in a memo to his staff, "Difficulty is inherent with a Mae West picture. Lines and pieces of business, which in the script seem to be thoroughly innocuous, turn out when shown on the screen to be questionable at best, when they are not definitely offensive."[50] As West put it, it was not so much what she did but how she did it, delivering seemingly "innocuous" lines in a campy style that suggested her "awarishness."

West's cynical attitude, more than her actions, proved a challenge to censors. Even after her scripts were cut and a marriage tagged on to the end, West still appeared sexually transgressive. The transgression of West's prostitutes and gold diggers could be contained within bourgeois mores, insofar as their transgression reaffirmed "normal" women's roles; but the sexual autonomy her star text represented could not be contained. West was a frequent target of theater and film censors not simply for her sexual explicitness, but also because "censors feared the independence and freedom of Mae West."[51] As Lea Jacobs argues in her book on censorship and the fallen woman film, the figure of the gold digger "associated the scenario of class rise with a representation of female sexuality which the industry's critics found especially repugnant" due to its implication of feminine aggressivity; and industry censors were particularly wary of the way comedies could justify otherwise unacceptable material.[52] West was "the alarm clock that awakened the cleaner-uppers" because "she made amorous dallying appear entirely too funny."[53] In other words, West seemed sexually transgressive because she both bur-lesqued and celebrated sex.

The fan discourse about Hollywood's efforts to censor West focused on whether or not the "real" Mae West was like the characters she portrayed. West's publicists attempted to dissociate their star from her characters, claim-ing that the woman was not the institution and offering as evidence her clean lifestyle (no smoking, drinking, or partying).[54] In response, Gladys Hall of *Motion Picture* claimed that if fans got the impression that West was not like her characters "the most glamorous and the most gaudy woman in the world today will step back into the ranks of 'just another blonde'" and that "if Mae West goes Pollyanish, she is ruined."[55] While acknowledging West's two-sided camp appeal (she is both glamorous and gaudy), Hall suggests that her image as a "first-rate sex queen" depends on her seeming transgres-sive and that this separates her from "second-rate blonde(s)". A fan letter to *Movie Classic* asserted the difference between the star and her characters: "It is my opinion that any woman who doesn't like Mae West is not using her common sense and doesn't stop to realize that Miss West is not at all the character she portrays on screen." But this same letter suggests that fans iden-tified with the star through her characters: "And, too, many women would give their right arms to be Miss West."[56] Both those who want to dissociate West from her film persona and those who insist on linking the star to her roles claim West's persona as a form of impersonation—on the one hand, her film persona is merely parodic and, on the other, her real self is always already parodic. West's "awarish" and transgressive sexuality is taken at once as a pose or joke and as a real source of power; and fans, especially female fans, could identify with both sides through camp practices.

That All-Important Female Audience

Jackie Stacey criticizes reductive models of identification assumed in psycho-analytic film theory and offers instead a model for broader cultural and social dimensions of identification in the cinema.[57] She distinguishes two basic kinds of conscious social-cinematic identification. The first consists of identificatory fantasies that involve fantasies about the relationship between the identity of the star and the identity of the spectator. These relate to the cinematic context and include relations of devotion to and worship of the star, the desire to become the star, pleasure in feminine power represented by the star, and the pleasure of escapism through the star. The second consists of identificatory practices that take place outside the cinematic context and involve the audience in some kind of self-transformation in order to become more like the star. These extracinematic identificatory practices include pretending, resembling, imitating, copying, and consumption.

The discourse on censorship indicates that West's fans partook of cinematic identificatory fantasies involving the desire to become West and pleasure in West's power and humor. These processes are not unlike the identificatory fantasies we can attribute to other star-audience relations. But West's fans also practiced forms of identification that can be aligned with camp practices. In particular, I would like to emphasize the female spectator's extracinematic practices of copying, consumption, and imitation, and her cinematic identification with West as spectacle. Without access to female fans's own comments about West, I rely on promotional materials, production statements, and fan-magazine discourse. I contend that these materials helped mediate female fans' understanding of West and made it possible for fans to subvert the image-making processes to which women have traditionally been given access—namely, an aesthetics of femininity related to fashion, consumption, spectacle, and performance.

Alexander Walker claims that West's "films never made fans out of that all important female audience." [58] His assessment, coextensive with her late camp popularity, retrospectively denies West's appeal to women in the 1930s. Reviews and articles of the time, however, assert again and again the importance of West's female audience. Fans could sympathetically identify with West as a woman not unlike themselves. Leo McCarey claimed, "Women like her as well as men. Mae understands the psychology of her own sex." [59] Elza Schallert concurred, "Any red-blooded he-man can understand Mae. . . . His lush, full-blooded sister understands her, too—and likewise becomes her pal." [60]

In her films, West's interactions with other female characters are mediated by class and race. While racial difference might limit West's appeal to non-white female fans, her barely concealed status as a prostitute enables her to have a livelier camaraderie with lower-class women of all races than with upper-class women. Upper-class white women are often portrayed as failed rivals and enemies. But West's character frequently functions as counselor to subordinate women, like the fallen Sally in She Done Him Wrong whom she counsels on men ("Men's all alike . . . it's their game. I happen to be smart enough to play it their way.") and whose shame she ameliorates with the worldly wisdom that "when women go wrong, men go right after 'em." Similarly, in Belle of the Nineties, when her maid Libby asks, "What kind of husband do you think I should get?" West advises her, "Why don't you take a single man, and leave the husbands alone?" In *Klondike Annie*, West helps her Chinese maid, Fah Wong, played by Soo Yong, escape to her lover and even speaks Chinese with her.

West's friendships with these women suggest the possibility of West having an "authentic" self beneath or behind the discourses of camp and masquerade. Across her films, West's maids (whether African American, Chinese, or French) are consistently pictured as knowing the real West better than anybody else. West, in effect, lets her hair down with them, and tells them her true feelings. In *I'm No Angel*, West never tells Cary Grant that she loves him. Instead, he finds out from Getrude Howard's Beulah, who testifies in a breach of promise suit that West's character Tira said "she never knew she could love a man like she loves him."

At the same time that West appeals to women as a friend, fan discourse emphasized West's difference from her female fans, especially with respect to body type. This served, in part, to offset West's potential status as a rival. As Madame Sylvia of *Photoplay* put it, women didn't resent her "because she was so far removed in physical type from the modern woman of today, that they figured she wouldn't be serious competition."[61] But women also presumably desired West's curves and wanted to be more like her. An article in *Motion Picture* noted the "influence of Mae West" in creating a "new deal in feminine film figures."[62] The article proclaimed the new curvaceous styles to be "'IT' with the bones covered": "There's a revolution on against the once-popular 'washboard silhouette.' The girls are craving that 'upholstered' look again. They're convinced they won't break any scales if they add a few pounds in the right places—and might break a few box-office records (as Mae West has)." *Vogue* magazine featured a photo of West in her corset with West's claims that the corset gave evidence of "a return to normal," "a ladies way of saying that the depression is over" and a recognition that women need heft, confidence, vitality, and stamina.[63] For Colette, West's plumpness was of a piece with her independence, so that when West appeared to have lost some weight in *I'm No Angel*, Colette mourned it as "a violation of principle."[64] West popularized plump female figures to such a large degree that the Central Association of Obstetricians and Gynecologists congratulated her and called her style "a boon to motherhood";[65] while Madame Sylvia, on a less congratulatory note, accused women of using West as an "elegant alibi" for letting themselves get too fat.

In her autobiography, West claimed that she wrote the play *Diamond Lil* in order to attract a female audience: "In my new play, I would give a little thought to bringing in the women. I got to thinking I should do a period

play of the Gay Nineties. I had always admired the fabulous fashions just before the turn of the century, when Lillian Russell and Lillie Langtry were
around. . . . It was the style that really attracted me to the colorful background of the Nineties."[66] Her choice of an 1890s mise-en-scène was a determined effort to win female audiences who, she felt, would be attracted
to the fashions and glamour of the period. When West brought Lil to Hollywood in the enormously successful *She Done Him Wrong*, Edith Head's Lady Lou
outfits started a fashion craze toward a return to the frills, plumes, ruffles,
and proportions of the Victorian era.[67] In addition to this extracinematic
identificatory process of copying and consumption, female spectators could
also identify with the cinematic spectacle of the costumes, enjoying them in
themselves, apart from their narrative context.

Similarly, fans could identify with the spectacle of West herself. Noting
that reviewers and spectators sat through *She Done Him Wrong* two or more
times, while others waited to get in for a first viewing, Jay Brian Chapman
claimed that its appeal resided in the spectacle of personality: "This tendency
to hold seats means just one thing to seasoned showmen and critics. Experience has taught them that when an audience likes a picture because of its
story, it does not remain to see the show a second time, which tends to spoil
the plot's effect. It is when the star's personality is the attraction that seat-
holding becomes a nuisance."[68] The plots of West's films could not account
for her extraordinary popularity. Because West's character changed very little
from film to film, her personality functioned as an attraction. It is "the Mae
West character" that appeals, and it operates as an extranarrative attraction,
justifying the melodramatic plots that serve as a mere pretense for the star's
wisecracking personality and hip-rolling swagger.

Female fans, attracted to this spectacle of personality, engaged in the extracinematic camp practice of playfully imitating West. Stacey differentiates
between copying, which reflects a desire to look like the star, and imitating, which involves a partial taking-on of the star's identity, by replicating
her behavior and activities. Female spectators identified with and imitated
West's cynical attitude and her mannerisms. West described herself as "the
woman's ego": "When women'd be leaving the theater at intermission, you'd
see them sort of walking like the Mae West character, you know, giving
an attitude—and the talk, too."[69] According to one fan magazine, when the
Mayfair nobility gave parties, they gave Mae West parties, and "everyone
from Mayfair duchesses to kindergarten tots" (including Shirley Temple, in
her earliest films) imitated her cynical style, repeated her wisecracks, and
replicated her gestures.[70] Imitating West gave women imaginary access to her
autonomy, transgression, and humor. Like West's female female imperson-

ation, their imitations created a "double mimesis" that was at once a form of identification with West and with her masquerade.

Going West

I began with *Myra Breckinridge*, which encapsulates and contributes to West's late camp appeal. I conclude with *Go West, Young Man*, which brings together various elements of West's 1930s star text and the identificatory relationship between West and her female fans.

In *Go West, Young Man*, West plays film star Mavis Arden. The film begins with a fast tracking shot into a movie theater, past crowds of patrons and a picture of Arden in the lobby, in a buildup similar to the opening of *Belle of the Nineties*. Then, the camera tracks down the aisle until we see Arden on the screen. We enter the film within the film, titled *The Drifting Lady*, a clever play on West's one-liner "I used to be Snow White, but I drifted." The film seems to be a parody of a Garbo film. It takes place in an exotic locale, with Spanish sailors and army officers. Arden's character speaks in a formal diction and appears to be more of a femme fatale than West's characters. A shot of the film's audience shows a couple clinging to each other, weeping. The girl sobs, "Isn't she wonderful?" The boy replies, "Uh-huh." We return to the film within the film to watch Arden's character melodramatically dismiss her lover: "But when you're gone, remember me kindly sometimes for just a brief moment when April comes around again with its blue skies and sudden showers—remember that April woman who drifted into your life as casually as a summer cloud drifts over a green field and then—drifts on again. Now go, Phillip, go." This melodramatic speech, though perfectly in keeping with the tone of *The Drifting Lady*, parodies West's distance from contemporary vamps. For the viewer familiar with West's previous films, this imitation of the vamp stereotype would exaggerate the disjunction between her typically cynical and practical persona and the sacrificial, maudlin persona here.

After the film, Mavis Arden makes a personal appearance, in which she repeats her "April showers" speech. She describes herself as a simple country girl, completely unlike the "fascinatin' sirens" she portrays, similar to the way in which West's publicity insisted on the discrepancy between the real Mae West and her roles. But she stumbles over a few words in her speech and mispronounces "Italian villa" as "Eyetalian," demonstrating that the "real" Arden, like the "real" West, is a public relations construction.

As the film progresses, the "real" Arden proves to be a real prima donna, mercilessly bossing her servants around. In 1934, fan magazines accused West of going "high hat," letting success spoil her so that she imagined herself to be a great actress, "out-Garboing Garbo."[71] Her publicists countered with articles proclaiming her a simple, modest girl, even featuring an early photo of West planting corn in a patriotic wartime gesture! *Go West, Young Man* jokingly transplants the discourse about the "real" West onto Arden, whose "high hat" attitude is juxtaposed with her definition of herself as a "simple country girl" against her image as a "fascinatin' siren." When Mavis Arden's limousine breaks down, she gets trapped in a simple country boardinghouse with some of her male and female fans. The men ogle her body, but it is the women who truly "go West" in their appreciation for Mavis. The young girl Gladys (Isabel Jewell), who saw *The Drifting Lady* with her boyfriend the night before, works as a maid at the boardinghouse. She is an ardent Arden fan, who sees every one of her films and pays close attention to fan-magazine discourse about Arden. She worships Arden and views her as a glamorous idol. She excitedly reports to Aunt Kate, her coworker, that Arden won first place in the "IT" contest last month, according to the fan magazines. She also engages in identificatory practices: after watching Arden for a bit, she does an impersonation of her, walking with one hand behind her head, the other on her hip, while she swivels her hips. Her imitation reflects her desire to be like Arden, enticing, beautiful, and talented. She also imitates Dietrich singing "Falling in Love Again" in her effort to convince Arden's publicity manager to give her a screen test. But the old maid, Aunt Kate (Elizabeth Patterson), also imitates Arden in a private, playful moment, just after Arden's exit from the boardinghouse. Previously, Kate expressed her disapproval of Arden on moral grounds: "In my time, women with hair like that didn't come out in the daytime." Her subsequent imitation reflects a humorous identification with Arden, a fantasy that stems from admiration but recodes that admiration into a joke.

The camp effect of *Myra Breckinridge* channels and diffuses West's transgression through her construction as a grotesque figure, which disqualifies her as an object of erotic desire and distances her from a female audience. In contrast, *Go West, Young Man* represents the way in which West's early camp effect allowed her to parody herself while still functioning as both an object and subject of desire with whom female spectators could identify. In the 1970s, West represented camp to female spectators only as a misogynist joke, the "kinda comedy that makes fun of me." In the 1930s, "the kinda comedy where they imitate me" was a practice of camp identification between the female spectator and West. Through cinematic and extracinematic identificatory fantasies and practices, West's female fans "went West," gaining access to a form of camp that enabled them to distance themselves from sex and gender stereotypes and to view women's everyday roles as female impersonation.

T W O

What Trixie and God

Know: Feminist Camp in

Gold Diggers of 1933

Ginger Rogers as Fay Fortune performs "We're in the Money"
in Gold Diggers of 1933. Video frame enlargement
(author's collection).

A|t the opening of the backstage musical *Gold Diggers of 1933*, choreo-graphed by Busby Berkeley, we see a dress rehearsal for "We're in the Money," in which, Fay Fortune (Ginger Rogers) leads a troupe of chorus girls bedecked in fetishistic coin-costumes that explic-itly link female sexuality and performance to economics—a large coin at the crotch and smaller coins decorating the midriff top. Further aestheticizing the number, Fay cheerfully sings a chorus in pig latin ("E'reway inay ethay oneymay") and Berkeley edits the image of the chorus line singing so that Fay appears at both the far left and far right ends of the line. The chorus sings, "We're in the money / We're in the money / We've got a lot of what it takes / to get along. . . . We never see a headline / 'Bout a breadline today. . . . We're in the money." Underscoring the song's irony and the visual links among female performance, sexuality, and economics, the sheriff interrupts this number, stripping the girls of their costumes ("*Corpus delecti*—seize the body!"), closing the show, and initiating a Depression-era plot about the lack of work on Broadway.

Following this apt overture, the backstage plot of *Gold Diggers of 1933*, di-rected by Mervyn LeRoy, primarily concerns the professional, economic, and romantic careers of three showgirls: Carol King (Joan Blondell), Trixie Lorraine (Aline MacMahon), and Polly Parker (Ruby Keeler). The first part of the film deals with the necessity for and mechanics of putting on a show. After the sheriff closes Barney Hopkins's (Ned Sparks) show due to unpaid debts, we discover that all the theaters in New York are closed due to the Depression. In the next scene, after an undisclosed period has passed, we find Trixie, Carol, and Polly sleeping three in a bed in a cramped apart-ment, stealing milk from neighbors, dodging the landlady, and reminiscing about better times. They learn from their friend Fay Fortune that Barney is putting on a new show. Gathering all their girlfriends together, they discuss the show with Barney. Barney doesn't have a backer, so Polly's boyfriend, an apparently poor composer named Brad Roberts (Dick Powell) loans Barney

$15,000. The source of Brad's contribution remains unclear until he is forced to step into the juvenile's role opposite Polly on opening night, and newspaper reviewers disclose that "Brad Roberts" is really Robert Treat Bradford, a wealthy Bostonian.

With the show already a major success and the girls established in a new glamorous art deco apartment, the second half of the film deals with the efforts of Brad's family to stop his marriage to Polly. Brad's brother, J. Lawrence Bradford (Warren William), and the family lawyer, Faneuil H. Peabody (Guy Kibbee), mistakenly identify Carol as Polly and attempt to pay her off if she will leave Brad alone. Lawrence tells Carol that a marriage to a showgirl would disgrace the family: "Showgirls are—are—reputed to be—parasites, chiselers, gold diggers!" Hearing this, Trixie convinces Carol not to clear up the confusion but to exact revenge, mimicking the false stereotype of gold-digging showgirls to take the two men for a ride. At film's end, Polly and Brad are married, and Carol and Trixie are engaged to Lawrence and Faneuil, respectively.

This chapter focuses on *Gold Diggers of 1933* to suggest that feminist camp is a sensibility that is particularly attuned to historically determined attitudes toward women and work and that the comic gold digger is to feminist camp what the dandy is to gay camp—its original personification, its defining voice. *Gold Diggers of 1933* plays upon many of the same concerns that Mae West's films do—female performance, economics, gold digging, and prostitution—and was contemporaneous with West's initial appearance in Hollywood. West offers one model for feminist camp—a model of unique female performance and agency, linked to burlesque and female masquerade, that generates camp fan activity on the part of female and gay male spectators alike. *Gold Diggers of 1933* offers another model that helps to broaden our notion of feminist camp away from the personality of the star and toward more communal strategies and pleasures. In its combination of a knowing address to women at the narrative level with feminine spectacle in the numbers, the film harkens back to Thompsonian burlesque even more explicitly than West does. It, therefore, enables us to connect feminist camp to the tradition of female burlesque through the figure of the showgirl and the chorus line, as opposed to the star. In addition, by aligning the figure of the showgirl with the stereotype of the gold digger—and linking both to prostitution—the film provides a historical context for viewing feminist camp as a working women's strategy. This film suggests that the conjunction between West's "awarish" female masquerade and her role as performer and prostitute are not accidental but fundamental to feminist camp. My goal in this chapter is twofold: first, to consider the musical's camp effect from a feminist perspective; and second, to investigate the links between the figure of the gold digger, the showgirl, and feminist camp.

Camp and the Musical

Camp, according to Sontag, represents the "victory of style over content, aesthetics over morality, irony over tragedy." It is a sensibility committed to the unnatural, to artifice and exaggeration; it converts the serious into the frivolous. Sontag acknowledges that camp's deflationary attitude mocks the critic, and, in taking it seriously, she risks producing an inferior piece of camp herself.[1] In academic film criticism, the Hollywood musical has posed a similar critical challenge, seeming to resist serious analysis. More than any other major film genre, the musical seems singularly dedicated to the trivial and to style over content. Jane Feuer notes, "Musicals seem particularly resistant to analysis; peel away the tinsel and you find the real tinsel underneath."[2] Like camp, the musical is artificial and unnatural, highly aestheticized and stylized. Whereas camp archly promotes the frivolous, the musical, as Gerald Mast observes, "paradoxically proclaims its own worthlessness and the importance of its worthlessness."[3] To analyze the musical can seem, therefore, almost automatically to overanalyze it.

Most critics describe the musical's "real tinsel" as an ideology of self-reflexivity. Insofar as the musical purports to be about anything, at its most basic, the musical is about entertainment. Although entertainment is not, strictly speaking, a camp category, the basic concept of entertainment promoted by the musical relates closely to a camp sensibility. Most musicals assert the primacy of entertainment over "art" (swing over classical, tap over ballet, folk music over opera). Alternately, some musicals, particularly in the 1950s (consider The Band Wagon or An American in Paris), deflate and democratize "art," absorbing ballet, for example, by granting it entertainment value, as opposed to highbrow legitimacy. Like the musical, camp converts the serious into the frivolous and bridges the gap between high culture and low, without being merely pluralistic. The ballet, pulp fiction, decorative art, B movies, Aubrey Beardsley, and Maria Callas are all equally precious metals in the melting pot of camp. The populist principles of the song "That's Entertainment," which serves as a kind of credo for the musical's ideology of entertainment, are easily assimilable to a camp sensibility. By ironically dubbing Hamlet as "where a ghost and a prince meet, and everyone ends up mincemeat," and Oedipus Rex, as "where a chap kills his father and causes a lot of bother," "That's Entertainment" suggests that what is basically serious to us should be appreciated in terms of fun and artifice and elegance. If musicals, both entertaining and camp, are about entertainment, they are potentially as much about camp. For the most part, however, critics have treated the camp effect of the musical as little more than an embarrassment, an unfortunate side effect produced by combining musical numbers with narrative and not a primary symptom to be investigated. Some critics, though, have begun to explore the musical's affinity with camp.

Mast, for instance, implicitly acknowledges the close tie between musicals and camp when he notes the importance of the gay male contribution to the musical (from composers, actors, designers, etc.) and speculates why musical theater and film seem "so congenial to gay people and so receptive to the gay sensibility": "Perhaps there is something in two cultural clichés that make musicals and gay people especially suited to one another: musicals represent an extravagant and excessive frippery and gay people possess some special sensibility that finds a creative outlet in extravagance, excess, and frippery."[4] The "special sensibility" Mast notices has the qualities of camp, though he does not name it as such. By this account, rather than simply bearing a superficial similarity to camp, the musical genre expresses a camp sensibility and those committed to camp often express themselves in and through the musical.

Mast suggests the potential value of studying the musical's camp effect: "Like musicals themselves, gay people can translate their alternative vision of human and social relationships into forms that both disguise it as societal critique and allow its implications to be clearly read."[5] Taken as camp, we can perhaps better see the musical's alternative vision, and camp may be a privileged position from which to view the musical. Mast, though, stops short of describing the musical's social critique *as* a camp strategy or of asking what difference it makes to understand the musical's "alternative vision" *through* camp.

More explicitly, in the postscript to the second edition of her book on the musical, Feuer suggests that the "gay sensibility" "permeates the genre" of the musical and she clearly links this sensibility to camp: "This sensibility finds expression in the aesthetic of camp which in turn provides a link between a subcultural 'structure of feeling' and certain ways of reading musicals."[6]

Despite the close correspondence between camp and the musical (it "permeates the genre"), when critics discuss the musical's camp effect, they generally align the musical's camp effect exclusively with gay male subcultural practices. Feuer and Mast both focus their analyses of camp in the musical on gay men's authorship and reading practices. Feuer's analysis stems from a discussion of Judy Garland's star text, and Feuer, following Dyer, mentions that Garland's own sensibility might be considered "queer" and "camp"; but this reading of Garland, is, according to Feuer, "authorized" only by conceptualizing "musicals as gay male texts created by and addressed to gay men."[7] Thus, while acknowledging the musical's camp effect as a mode of both production and reception, Feuer effectively denies female agency in the production of camp; and Feuer, like Mast, does not mention women at all in her discussion of camp as a reading practice, except obliquely as part of the "dominant" heterosexual and "family" audience that are the "of course" point of address for MGM musicals.

In Feuer's account, then, both the female performer and spectator are denied access to the camp effect of the musical. With respect to spectatorship, Feuer suggests that after recognizing alternate subcultural readings of musicals (she includes youth audiences as well as gay men) "we can no longer feel confident in speaking of an 'ideal' or 'model' audience for the musical or even of a 'dominant' or 'mass audience' of the genre."[8] By linking camp reception to gay men only, the logic of Feuer's argument suggests that the female spectator must either be blind to the camp that "permeates" the musical or perform an active gesture of disavowal, to identify herself with a now marginal "dominant" reading.

At the same time that analyses of the musical as camp ignore female production and reception, analyses of the musical from a feminist perspective do not generally address the question of camp. Instead, feminist critics have primarily considered the ways in which the male gaze operates in the musical, with a particular concentration on female spectacle in musical numbers. These analyses typically adhere to a Mulveyan model of female spectatorship and describe female pleasure in the musical as masochistic.

If, however, camp "permeates" the musical, we need to consider how the musical's "queer sensibility" affects notions of a male gaze, since that concept depends upon heterosexist structures of looking. If, furthermore, as I have suggested, women do have access to a camp sensibility and that sensibility is rooted in burlesque, then it seems that both the musical's female performers and spectators may be able to access the musical's "alternative vision" through camp. In Janet Staiger's contribution to "Garland studies," she examines the public perception of Garland in mainstream press accounts from the 1950s and 1960s. While she locates in mainstream press accounts many of the same issues and terms that gay male critics have cited as important for Garland's appeal to gay men, Staiger doesn't "read" Garland's camp effect as available to the so-called dominant audience. Instead, she uses this material to historically locate gay male readings. I would suggest that if representations of Garland in magazines like *Vogue*, *Life*, *Photoplay*, and *Newsweek* closely resemble readings of her star text by gay men, then the "alternative" reading of Garland may be dominant and women may have liked Garland for many of the same reasons as gay men.[9] I am not suggesting that all musicals can be read as feminist camp. In fact, the camp effect of many musicals, like other forms of camp, may be misogynist. Instead, I suggest that feminist analyses need to take camp into account when considering female musical performance and reception, and that, in certain instances, we can read the musical as feminist camp.

Busby Berkeley's Camp Aesthetic

Although the camp sensibility can be productively traced throughout the genre of the Hollywood musical, the musicals Berkeley worked on are the most stylized and extravagant in the canon. Further, because Berkeley's numbers equate entertainment so outrageously with feminine spectacle, his choreographic style has provoked other feminist analyses. Berkeley contributed four numbers to *Gold Diggers of 1933* besides "We're in the Money." The other three numbers, "Pettin' in the Park," "Shadow Waltz," and "Forgotten Man" (to which I will return below), represent Barney's second successful show. In brief, "Pettin' in the Park" and "Shadow Waltz," both featuring Dick Powell and Ruby Keeler, are songs of love and romance visually expressed through trademark Berkeley feminine spectacle. "Forgotten Man," a call to remember the poverty-stricken "forgotten men" of the First World War, features Joan Blondell as a prostitute and substitutes a bevy of not-so-beautiful men (the Bonus Marchers) for feminine spectacle.

Throughout his career, Berkeley's signature style adheres to the philosophy of the title song of *Dames* (1934): "What do you go for? Go see the show for? / Tell the truth—you go to see those beautiful dames." The chief structuring elements of the Berkeley aesthetic are so identifiable that Berkeley has earned a place in the slang lexicon: "busby berkeley: A very elaborate musical number; any bevy of beautiful girls; a spectacular."[10] The typical Berkeley number showcases scores of beautiful white women who form intricate, fairly abstract patterns, who do not necessarily dance but walk and smile, and/or are mechanically transported; it kaleidoscopes female forms in ever changing cinematic designs.

Berkeley was assigned most often to a film as the choreographer/director of dance sequences, while another director was assigned to the narrative sequences. In many Berkeley films, the numbers seem like separable, isolated units, bearing little obvious relation to the rest of the film. In and of themselves, Berkeley's numbers produce a camp effect that renders the live Ziegfeld tradition outmoded. After an establishing shot that places the number on a live stage, Berkeley abandons all pretense to theatrical verisimilitude and instead offers a "stage" spectacle available only to a film audience.

Consider, for example, the second number of Gold Diggers of 1933, "Pettin' in the Park." The first chorus begins with a medium shot of Ruby Keeler and Dick Powell on a park bench singing to each other. Close-ups of the couple follow. Then, as they rise to leave the bench, the camera tracks to a close-up of a box of animal crackers on the bench. A drawing of two chimps on the box dissolves into an image of live-action chimps in a zoo cage.

In the second chorus, panning the park zoo, we see numerous couples each "pettin' " in the park and a "baby" (midget Billy Barty) in a carriage. A cut removes us to another area of the park where a policewoman (Aline MacMahon) shows Ruby Keeler the entrance to a roller-skating service "For Little Girls Who Need an Escort." First, loads of women in matching costumes skate out of the entrance. Then, a large number of policemen on skates join Ruby Keeler to escort her home. The baby/midget intervenes, shooting a spitball at the police, and a chase ensues. Snow begins to fall, and the camera cuts to a row of girls with huge "snowballs."

The third chorus begins with a pan left in close shots of the girls' faces, then the camera cuts to an overhead shot as the girls form abstract, quasi-organic patterns with the lines of their bodies and the spherical snowballs. Cutting from the overhead shot to a medium shot, we see the baby/midget exit the circle of women. He rolls a snowball to the camera. A match cut shows a rubber beach ball rolling back from the camera to the baby/midget, who is suddenly dressed in summer play clothes. He runs back into the park, now filled with couples lounging on the grass. The camera tracks forward showing numerous panty shots of the women in revealing costumes and poses. It begins to rain and the women run for cover behind a sheer backlit screen. As we see their presumably nude silhouettes in the background, the baby/midget, dressed in a rain hat and slicker, looks for a way to raise the curtain as Dick Powell, similarly attired, watches. When the baby/midget raises the curtain, the women appear in metallic swimsuits. Ruby Keeler joins Dick Powell on a bench where he discovers to his chagrin that the swimsuit is really made of tin. The baby/midget supplies a can opener and the curtain falls.

This typical Berkeley number exemplifies the way in which Berkeley used the camera and editing to divorce objects and images from clear referents in time and space. In most backstage musicals, a filmed version of a live stage show might use close-ups, tracks, and pans to assure the film spectator of the "best seat in the house" and to bridge the distance between spectator and spectacle created by the proscenium arch. At the same time, shots of the theatrical audience would be used to establish continuity between theater seats and movie-theater seats and to create an identification between the internal audience and the film audience.[11] Berkeley's extraordinarily fluid camera movements, dissolves, and match cuts dismiss the fiction of theatrical space and live performance altogether. Yet the numbers still open and close with establishing shots of the theater audience, who presumably provide a relay for our look. However, after watching a Berkeley number, a dizzying enough experience for a film spectator, the follow-up shot of a theater audience politely and appreciatively clapping comes like a jolt, reminding us of how far removed we are from them. It is impossible to imagine what show they have seen. Without the benefit of extremely rapid set changes, a theater with rotating overhead seats, and an audience willing to take miraculous leaps of faith, the notion that a Berkeley number could ever be a live performance falls apart.

For Berkeley, aesthetic effect was more important than adherence to backstage convention. When Zanuck first saw Berkeley in the rafters of a Goldwyn soundstage, he said, "You can't take an audience up there." "I know," Berkeley replied, "but I'd like to. It's awfully pretty from up here."[12] In emphasizing cinematic technique, rather than live performance, Berkeley's numbers remove the show from the fictional theater space and jettison it to the film studio's back lot, optical lab, and editing room. In addition to displacing the theatrical spectator, Berkeley effaces the myth of live entertainment, denying both the labor and the appeal of song and dance. Instead, he offers a purely cinematic vision of entertainment in which the camera itself dances and the spectator identifies with its movements, rather than with characters who sing and dance.

The camp effect of Berkeley's numbers depends not on the viewer appreciating the beautiful effects of artifice and style but on the viewer perceiving the dissonance between the purported object represented—a live musical number—and the mode of representation, which gleefully abandons verisimilitude. Rather than being moved by the aesthetic or utopian effect of song and dance, the film spectator's experience is one of sheer astonishment—at the product qua produced, at the fact that Berkeley transforms live action into such amazing and impossible abstractions.

Berkeley's camp effect consists in part in this assertion of the primacy of extravagant style over the demands of plot, of the pleasure principle over reality, cinematic effect over backstage convention. To abstract the camp effect of the numbers from their narrative motivation, however, endlessly reproduces the camp effect. Such a reading obscures the representational aspects of the spectacle (the numbers rely, after all, on the spectacle of female bodies) and reasserts the primacy of style over content without examining what work this camp style does in the narrative. Although Berkeley operated with some degree of independence from the directors of the narrative sequences, the numbers he choreographed were still conceived as part of specific films and were exhibited to audiences as parts of a whole.

Narrative versus Number in Berkeley Musicals

Berkeley's three 1933 films—*42nd Street* (dir. Bacon), *Footlight Parade* (dir. Bacon), *Gold Diggers of 1933* (dir. LeRoy)—are the first and probably the best in Berkeley's Warner Brothers period; and they are the three most obviously conceived as a unit.[13] These films take the Depression as their subject matter and depict the success of the show as an economic necessity for the hundreds of performers and technicians involved. The stylistic disparity between Berkeley's numbers and the rest of the diegesis in these films exaggerates the apparent frivolity and meaninglessness of Berkeley's numbers.

The backstage musical notably has two diegetic levels, apparent in the contrast between the backstage plot and the show-within-the-show. These separate diegetic levels are created in order to be overcome and united; the success of the romantic plot and the success of the show are made mutually dependent; the world offstage and the world onstage are synthesized in the end through the union of the romantic couple. Berkeley musicals, however, resist this synthesis. As Jane Feuer observes, "Busby Berkeley musicals rope off the show as a separate universe, a world of cinematic excess and voyeuristic pleasure in sharp contrast to the low-budget verisimilitude of the backstage sequences. . . . The Berkeley number epitomizes the show as secondary diegesis."[14] The backstage pattern limits the extreme stylization of the Berkeley number to the secondary diegesis of the show, but the degree to which the excess and camp of the secondary diegesis are ultimately contained by and synthesized with the primary diegesis is unclear.

According to Arthur Hove, the narrative sequences root Berkeley's numbers in reality and offset the camp effect: "Berkeley's numbers provide an augmentation that certainly makes [*Gold Diggers of 1933*] more appealing. Without the story, however, the musical numbers would be meaningless fragments, a visual tutti-frutti with no reason for being other than to show off the director's imagination and skill."[15] Rather than seeing a close interaction between narrative and musical sequences, Hove posits a content/style split between story and numbers. According to Hove, the Depression is not the primary focus of the show-within-the-film: "Pettin' in the Park" and "Shadow Waltz" are "puff pieces that have no bite whatsoever" and "Forgotten Man" is an incongruous footnote. Hove views the numbers and their "tutti-frutti" excess as contained by the narrative, the emphasis of which is on romance.[16] Mast, by contrast, foregrounds the manner in which stylistic excess undermines narrative concerns. Mast asserts that the "paradoxical effect today of many Berkeley numbers" consists of "laughter at the monstrous audacity of his not seeing anything about a social situation except an opportunity for decorative design; wonder at his energetic execution of that design and absolute commitment to its visual execution."[17] Mast and Hove view the disjunction between narrative and number from different angles, but both highlight the threat Berkeley's numbers pose to narrative coherence. Reflecting the sense that Berkeley's numbers fail to fit easily into narrative sequences, Sontag places Berkeley in the category of "unintentional" camp, as an example of something that aims to be dead serious but fails. For Mast and Hove, the seeming naïveté of Berkeley's 1930s numbers consists in the irony and incongruity of inserting the excessive kaleidoscopic spectacle of female bodies into progressive narratives of the Depression.

Disregarding the camp effect of Berkeley's numbers, Mark Roth has analyzed Berkeley's Warner Brothers numbers as not incongruent but complementary to the primary diegesis. 42nd Street, Footlight Parade, and Gold Diggers of 1933 were made at the most Democratic, pro-Roosevelt studio in the same year that FDR and the New Deal were inaugurated. Roth parallels the strong directors of the show-within-the-film featured in 42nd Street and Footlight Parade (Warner Baxter and James Cagney, respectively) and the new strong leadership in the country. He argues that Berkeley's numbers in these films, in downplaying the role of individual stars in favor of blocks of figures moving in tandem, symbolize the spirit of cooperation and community characteristic of the early stages of Roosevelt's presidency. Connoting the New Deal spirit, these films transform the ideal of individual success into an ideal of success through collective effort under the leadership of a strong male director. Roth thus offers a Great Man theory that posits a New Deal symbolism in all three of Berkeley's 1933 films, but he largely ignores the role feminine spectacle plays in Berkeley's aesthetic, and he cannot account for the relationship between the primary and secondary level of diegesis in Gold Diggers of 1933. "*Gold Diggers of 1933* is a good film," Roth concedes, "but is weakened by the lack of a strong male lead (such as Baxter or Cagney)."[18] Roth discounts the role of the actual leads in *Gold Diggers of 1933* to make his point, yet the strong female presence in *Gold Diggers of 1933* offers a potentially more complex view of the Depression than either *42nd Street* or *Footlight Parade*, one related not so much to New Deal solutions but to the economic problems facing working women in the Depression.

Richard Dyer, in line with Hove and Mast, notes a shift in *Gold Diggers of 1933* between the narrative "realist" aesthetic—which reinforces the film's "realistic" emphasis on the Depression, poverty, the quest for capital, gold digging, and prostitution—and the "non-real," nonrepresentational numbers. The numbers express a utopian sensibility, offering abundant spectacle in place of poverty and energy in place of Depression-induced dispiritedness. Dyer argues that the spectacular mode of presentation undercuts the palliative effect of the numbers by denying it the validity of "realism." Instead of ultimately undermining the narrative, however, the nonrepresentational level "reprises the lessons of the narrative—above all, that women's only capital is their bodies as objects."[19] For Dyer, neither the narrative nor the numbers, though rooted in the Depression, are specifically about 1930s New Deal economics but are more generally about women's role in the sexual economy.

Dyer's analysis incorporates many of the conclusions drawn by Lucy Fischer's discussion of the "optical politics" of *Dames* (1934) and Paula Rabinowitz's investigation of commodity fetishism in *Gold Diggers of 1933*.[20] Fischer interprets Berkeley's "plastic abstractions" as "the essence of image itself—a vision of female stereotypes in their purest, most distillable form." Noting that "stereotype" denotes on one level "having no individuality," Fischer asserts that the Berkeley showgirl loses her individuality because each girl's physical appearance is so similar (Berkeley described his "girls" as matched pearls on a string) and because their identities are consumed in the creation of an overall abstract design. The women, passive and objectified, function as fetishized objects, while the men take the role of voyeur.

Rabinowitz plays on both the Freudian and Marxist meanings of fetish in her discussion of *Gold Diggers of 1933*. Berkeley's abstractions of the female form signify both the Freudian fetish, the substitution of an object for the phallus, and the Marxist model of commodity fetishism, a process of reification and alienation engendered by capitalist relations. Their individuality abstracted into an assembly line–like production, the women in the Berkeley musical function as both fetishized image and fetishized commodity. "We're in the Money," which visually links female sexuality and money, establishes the dual commodification of women and money. With the film's conflation of female performance, gold digging, and prostitution, *Gold Diggers of 1933* asserts that a woman's only resource is her body—which can be used legitimately, on stage or film, or illegitimately, as a sellable commodity. Rabinowitz argues that by refuting the cinematic conventions of the narrative (Dyer's "realist" aesthetic) the musical structure overpowers the narrative structure. The numbers represent an alienated use of female imagery as fetish that effectively controls and neutralizes the strength of the female protagonists in the plot.

Departing somewhat from these critical models, Patricia Mellencamp emphasizes the role of the female protagonists in *Gold Diggers of 1933* and characterizes the disjunction between narrative and number not as a content/style split, but as a representation of an apportionment of female and male spectatorial address:

> With the crucial qualification that Berkeley's spectacles are addressed to the male spectator, literally coded as voyeur or fetishist, LeRoy's narrative demonstrates the pleasure of female friendship—the solidarity between Trixie, Carol, and Polly—and is propelled by fast-talking, inventive women (who are transformed into identical, anonymous, Freudian symbols in the spectacles that stop the advance of the story) who are infinitely more interesting, idiosyncratic, and clever than the wimpy men.[21]

With its emphasis on female leads in the primary diegesis and its reliance on feminine spectacle in the secondary diegesis, *Gold Diggers of 1933* belies theories that presume an organizing male spectatorial address in all classical Hollywood films. Instead, according to Mellencamp, it "suggests an address and appeal to women—who are let in on the joke" at the primary level of the diegesis while it still conforms to a Mulveyian model (the spectator as masculine voyeur and fetishist) in the spectacles that temporarily halt narrative progress.

Although Mellencamp raises interesting questions about textual address, she eventually abandons the promise of a dual feminine/masculine address and warns that the pleasure this film offers to the female spectator is compromised by the musical numbers, which use women as commodities, and by the final unions of the romantic couples, which separate the women from each other and contain them in a patriarchal institution. Ultimately, like Dyer and Rabinowitz, Mellencamp claims that the film's sexual economy reasserts masculine authority: "Knowledge, which the women have about men, is not power; money is."[22] The female spectator's pleasure is thus coded in hind-

sight as masochistic, a quality Mellencamp aligns with masculine sadism and
fetishism.[23] This claim confirms a Mulveyian view of the female spectator's
position. While the male spectator comfortably assumes the role of voyeur
and sadist, the female spectator shifts from an empowered, knowledgeable
spectator position to a masochistic transvestite identification with the masculine point of view. Her knowledge, and the appeal to her knowingness,
are undermined and turned against her.

I would suggest, however, that the tension between narrative and number
that Mellencamp describes might work in the opposite direction: in other
words, that the textual address to women at the narrative level may undermine the film's spectacles and its ending. According to Mellencamp, the
female spectator identifies with the gold diggers who know "about men."
But the gold diggers also know about money, about power, and about the relation between sexuality and economics—the same knowledge and relationships represented by the fetishistic coin-costumes in "We're in the Money."
If the female spectator is "let in on the joke," and the joke is on the men
in the film, why must we assume that she stops laughing when confronted
with feminine spectacle or the resolution of a romance plot? The knowledge
that the female spectator gains about men, money, power, and economics in
the primary diegesis provides her with a means to read the spectacles from a
feminist camp perspective, one which enables her to recognize herself in the
fetishized images but from which she is able to knowingly distance herself.

Mellencamp, Fischer, and Rabinowitz predicate their assessment of Berkeley's sexual politics on the assumption that Berkeley's numbers are unequivo-
cally addressed to a masculine spectator and that they wholeheartedly support the patriarchal ideology that they, undoubtedly, portray. They attribute
fetishism solely to men—even when, as Fischer argues, a Berkeley number
like "The Girl at the Ironing Board" in *Dames* ascribes this classically male
fantasy to the behavior of a female protagonist. (Here, Joan Blondell, playing
a laundress, attaches herself fetishistically to men's underwear as a substitute
for the "normal" sexual object.) This assumption also ignores female spectators whose same-sex desire might locate a lesbian erotic in the numbers. A
number like the title song of *Dames* (which features images of women two by
two in bed, exercising in sexy pajamas, and bathing together before turning
into black-and-white abstractions) seems equally available to be read as lesbian imagery as well as in terms of the girl-girl eroticism favored in straight
male pornography.[24] Even if we assume a masculine address, we need to
understand these and other potentially oppositional ways in which female
spectators might be able to negotiate their experience of these texts.

At face value, Dyer too represents the numbers in fairly dogmatic terms, as "lessons" taught to gullible (female) spectators. But Dyer acknowledges that contradictions inhere in the numbers themselves—contradictions between the materialist abundance of the spectacle and its association with the immaterial (magic, the imaginary) and between the creative energy of the dances and their mindless automatism. These contradictions are intrinsic to Berkeley's elevation of a mode of cinematic entertainment over "realistic" live entertainment. To return to Mast's description of the musical's "alternative vision," which both disguises social critique and allows its implications to be read, these tensions may reflect a dual view of the palliative effect of numbers, one which simultaneously proffers relief while mocking its own offer, recognizing the absurdity of substituting feminine spectacle for material aid. In representing a two-sided view of entertainment's ameliorative possibilities, the numbers in Gold Diggers of 1933 also offer a two-sided view of women, which both supports and critiques the notion that women's only capital is their bodies. This two-sided view inheres both in the camp spectacle of the numbers and in the activity of the gold diggers, who jokingly and knowingly manipulate their commodity status and further promulgate their commodification.

These contradictions at the representational level in both the narrative and numbers of Gold Diggers of 1933 furnish the female spectator with sufficient material to enable her to read the film through a double vision: not as a transvestite who identifies with male voyeurs but as a camp spectator who simultaneously identifies with and laughs at her image. While the Berkeley numbers in Gold Diggers of 1933 are certainly part of the film's camp effect, to discern what makes the film feminist camp—as distinct from other, even campier Berkeley films—requires that we situate the camp effect of the musical numbers in the film in their narrative context and analyze how the camp masquerade of the gold diggers in the narrative recodes the camp effect of the numbers—an effect that taken out of context could be read as antifeminist—from a feminist perspective. At the same time, I suggest that we can read "spectacular elements" in the narrative itself, elements that work against closure and lend the film to a feminist camp reading.

Narrative Spectacle and Feminine Vision

Fischer's claim that the women are rendered passive objects by the active and voyeuristic male gaze depends on the presence of a diegetic male figure of identification. According to Fischer, this diegetic male functions as bearer of the look and organizer of the vision, and he stands in for Berkeley. In Dames's "I Only Have Eyes for You," for instance, Dick Powell's fantasmatic imagination "produces" hundres of Ruby Keelers. Similarly, in *Footlight Parade*, James Cagney plays a Berkeley-like figure who produces gimmicky and spectacular live musical prologues to cinema attractions. In the film's most outrageous moment, his bizarre gaze lights on a group of black children playing by an open fire hydrant and "sees" a Berkeley spectacle: "Say, that's what that wood nymph needs—a large waterfall splashing on beautiful white bodies." The policeman standing nearby confirms the patriarchal authority of this extraordinary—and racist—vision when he tells Cagney, "I've got ideas, too, Mr. Kent." *42nd Street* aligns the male gaze so closely with the director (Warner Baxter) that he seemingly exudes the spectacle from his own body—his spent body virtually expires once the show ends.

In *Gold Diggers of 1933*, however, as Mark Roth suggests, it is difficult to pinpoint a diegetic male character—among those Mellencamp characterizes as the "wimpy men"—who functions as the bearer of the look. Brad provides the cash and writes the songs for the show and, as in Powell's other films with Ruby Keeler, he sings the opening chorus of two numbers with Keeler. "Pettin' in the Park" and "Shadow Waltz" potentially do represent his fantasy. "Pettin' in the Park," as I mentioned earlier, ends with Powell opening Keeler's metallic chastity suit; and in "Shadow Waltz," he intones "Let me dream a song that / I can bring to you" and "dreams" a song rife with Freudian symbols in which women play neon violins and form a highly sexualized violin-and-bow shaped pattern. Nevertheless, the narrative minimizes the degree to which a spectator could be said to identify with Brad or attribute authority to him. In *Dames*, Powell directs and produces the show, as Cagney and Baxter do in *Footlight Parade* and *42nd Street*. Powell's Brad, though, is hardly in charge. He obtains the money from inherited, not earned wealth. When he expresses his desire to marry Polly, he loses control over that money to his brother, over whom the women take charge. Even within the numbers, the only one of the three leads whom he manipulates is Polly, who plays the ingenue in relation to the other two women as well as filling that role in the show-within-the-film. Carol does not appear in either "Pettin' in the Park" or "Shadow Waltz" and Trixie only appears in "Pettin' in the Park," where, dressed in a policeman's uniform, she represents a counter authority figure.

As director of the show, Barney presents the next logical choice of a male figure for voyeuristic or sadistic identification. Barney's "vision," however, extends primarily to the "Forgotten Man" number:

> That's just what this show's about—the Depression—men marching—
> marching in the rain—marching—marching—doughnuts and crullers

—jobs—jobs—marching—marching—marching in the rain—and in
the background will be Carol—spirit of the Depression—a blue song—
no, not a blue song—but a wailing—a wailing—and this woman—this
gorgeous woman—singing this number that tears your heart out—the
big parade—the big parade of tears.

Barney envisions not a female spectacle but "men marching." The "gorgeous
woman" will be "in the background" and not passive or mute but "wailing" and tearing "your heart out." His vision reverses the structure of most
Berkeley numbers: it delegates men to the role of mass spectacle and grants
a woman both voice and empowered vision; the forgotten men will be produced and thus remembered by Carol's "wailing" song.

Moreover, unlike the directors played by Cagney and Baxter, Barney dis-
appears for the better part of the film. For a backstage musical, Gold Diggers
of 1933 devotes very little screen time to rehearsals. Aside from the dress
rehearsal for "We're in the Money," we get only one brief glimpse of a rehearsal—for "Pettin' in the Park." This scene establishes Brad's superiority to
the juvenile lead; Barney figures only in the background. And, while Footlight
Parade, 42nd Street, and Dames each concludes with the show's opening night,
focusing all narrative energy on producing the show, Gold Diggers of 1933 uses
opening night to propel the second half of the narrative, the gold-digging
scheme, in which Carol and Trixie function as our main points of identification, the principal organizers of our vision.

The show produced through the collaboration of Barney and Brad frames
and complements the narrative but does not determine it. Rather than taking
place backstage, the primary plot of Gold Diggers of 1933 unfolds offstage in
the everyday world of the showgirls. This plot effects a synthesis with the
secondary level of the diegesis, not by making the show serve narrative demands, but by incorporating thematic and symbolic concerns of the show
into the narrative in a production staged by the women protagonists themselves. Apparently bored by Barney's vision of "men marching" and by Brad's
drippy songs, Trixie asks Barney if this show will have any comedy, her
speciality. He responds, "Plenty. . . . The gay side, the hard-boiled side, the
cynical and funny side of the Depression. . . . Be the best thing you ever
did, Trixie." Aside from "Forgotten Man," which could be called cynical, the
numbers we see bear little relation to Barney's promise of showing the many
sides of the Depression. In the show-within-the-show that we see, Trixie's
only role is a silent bit as a policewoman in "Pettin' in the Park." Trixie does,
however, perform her comic specialty in the film. She produces this comic,

Trixie (Aline MacMahon), Carol (Joan Blondell) and Polly (Ruby Keeler) in Gold Diggers of 1933. *Video frame enlargement (author's collection).*

multifaceted show "backstage," as it were, in producing the show of gold-digging show girls for Lawrence and Faneuil.

In acting out the stereotype of the gold digger, Trixie and Carol (and Polly, to a degree) make a spectacle of themselves. This spectacle, unlike the musical numbers, features active and controlling women who manipulate passive men. In pretending to be gold diggers, the women play upon the trope of female commodification and undermine the viewer's belief in that trope by suggesting that it is only an act. At the same time, the show they produce, like the show Barney produces, has the Depression as its primary subject matter, and the narrative acknowledges the limitations women face in the economic sphere, limitations that make their act a necessity. We need, therefore, to understand the particular historical circumstances that gave rise to the stereotype of the gold digger and how that stereotype reflects and represses economic and social conditions related specifically to the Depression.

The Stereotype of the Gold Digger

The gold digger first entered the American lexicon with the production of Avery Hopwood's play *The Gold Diggers* in 1919. Warners had filmed two versions of the play before 1933: a silent version in 1923 and a talking version, *Gold Diggers of Broadway*, in 1929. Encouraged by the success of the latter, Warners revived the play yet again in *Gold Diggers of 1933*.[25] In a different arena, the literary prototype of the gold digger, Lorelei Lee, was born in 1925 with the publication of Anita Loos's *Gentlemen Prefer Blondes: The Illuminating Diary of a Professional Lady*. The stereotype of the gold digger was thus produced and popularized on the heels of the Progressive Era, a time of extraordinary reform ferment and activism targeting a variety of social ills, notably prostitution.

During the first two decades of the twentieth century, Progressive Era reform set in motion the most intensive antiprostitution campaign ever waged in America. Antiprostitution movements addressed social and psychological anxieties related to the changes that were corrupting and invading American society—particularly commercialization, urbanization, and industrialization.[26] The prostitute symbolized the failure of women to gain access to the material benefits of industrial society due to low wages and a sexual double standard in the workplace. Antiprostitution reform movements linked prostitution to the second-class status of women and, therefore, created a forum for addressing women's economic and political inequality. Ultimately, however, the focus on prostitution deflected these broader concerns, as reformers focused more on eradicating prostitution rather than the unequal conditions that fostered prostitution.

In the 1920s, as the image of the "new woman" and the flapper entered the public imagination, antiprostitution reform discourse moved away from policies embracing economic, social, and political issues. Instead, the discussion narrowed and shifted almost exclusively to the character of the prostitute—her inherited traits, criminal tendencies, and psychological disorders—so as to define her sexuality and social position as deviant.[27] Reformers divided prostitutes into two very different stereotypes: the innocent victim, on one hand, and the sinister polluter, on the other. The stereotype of the innocent victim responded to behaviorist theories of the Progressive Era. The innocent victim was pictured as an all-American girl—young, rural, and white—whose innocence, ignorance, and poverty had been manipulated by urban male pimps or white-slave traders; potentially, if not actually, a lady, she was coerced or tricked into vice by external forces.[28] The sinister polluter, by contrast, was typically portrayed as a naturally depraved lower-class non-white or immigrant who craved excitement and material goods. She was pictured as a polluter both literally, spreading venereal disease, and figuratively, as a corrupter of morals.[29] While targeting the failure of industrial society to meet women's changing needs, antiprostitution movements contradictorily blamed women's new position in industrialized America for altering the essential nature of "good" women and for rewarding "bad" women.

The stereotype of the gold digger was established just as the stereotype of the prostitute underwent this transformation. If the prostitute represented the new woman's leaning toward deviant sexuality and criminal tendencies, the newly minted stereotype of the gold digger represented her greed and amorality. Dictionaries define the gold digger as "a girl or woman who attaches herself to a man merely for gain"; "a young woman who accepts a man's attention for the sake of his gifts"; "a woman who uses her charms and favors to get money, presents, etc. from wealthy men."[30]

When antiprostitution discourse abandoned Progressive Era arguments about women's rights and the effects of commercialization, industrialization, and urbanization, the behaviorist explanation formerly allocated to the innocent victim was, in a sense, transferred to the gold digger. But instead of being seen as motivated by low wages, the gold digger's actions were attributed to an excessive desire for material goods and leisure suited to the giddy prosperity of the 1920s. The stereotype of the gold digger serves to empty Progressive Era antiprostitution discourse of its content. The concept of gold digging still raises questions related to the effects of commercialization, industrialization, and urbanization on sex roles and sexual behavior. But, because the gold digger's actions are attributed to greed and not need, her image is divorced from the broader issue of women's inequality that had previously grounded feminist concern over the cultural emphasis on material acquisition and commercialized leisure. As I discuss in the next chapter, melodramatic treatments of the fallen-women theme in the 1930s and 1940s virtually equate the gold digger, the prostitute, and the kept woman. Generally, though, the gold digger serves as a comic and cynical counterpart to the prostitute.

Not coincidentally, the comic gold digger generally appears on the cultural scene in times of perceived prosperity. Born in the Roaring Twenties, she was revitalized in the 1950s in films like Howard Hawks's *Gentlemen Prefer Blondes* and Jean Negulesco's *How to Marry a Millionaire* (both starring Marilyn Monroe), and she reappeared in the Reagan era as the quintessential "material girl," Madonna. In times of prosperity, the figure of the gold digger parodically mimics the culture's emphasis on consumption and deflects feminist issues related to women's work and equal rights by suggesting that women desire to achieve the material benefits of industrial society but not to labor in the workforce for them. In the comic variant, the figure of the gold digger aestheticizes and makes a joke of prostitution; she parodically appropriates the behavior of the prostitute for camp effect.

The comic gold digger would seem to be an outmoded stereotype in the 1930s insofar as her excessive greed can no longer be imagined or justified in a time of real economic worry.[31] *Gold Diggers of 1933*, however, inserts the comic gold digger into a narrative of the Depression. During the Depression, a new round of federal and state laws forced thousands of women out of the workforce and new federal wage codes institutionalized lower pay rates for women. The film responds to these changes, linking gold digging not to the greedy acquisitiveness of prosperous times but to the economic concerns of women trying to survive in the Depression. It revitalizes Progressive Era critiques of unfair labor practices and women's low wages. To achieve this end, *Gold Diggers of 1933* anachronistically inserts various tropes of Progressive Era antiprostitution discourse into the diegesis.

Gold Digging and the Masquerade

In enacting the stereotype of the comic gold digger the film plays upon the outdated stereotypes of the sinister polluter and innocent victim. Lawrence and Faneuil invoke the image of the sinister polluter in characterizing the gold-digging showgirl as a "parasite." Lawrence believes he can outmaneuver the women, getting Carol (whom he mistakes for Polly) to transfer her affections to him, thereby proving that she is a gold digger. But he confesses that he is "afraid"—"Polly" (Carol) "fascinates" him and presents a danger to which he may "succumb." Trixie and Carol play on this image to parody the stereotype of the gold digger, exaggerating the gold digger's traits for comic effect, hyperbolizing the gold digger's masquerade, theatricalizing it to create an ironic distance from it. They exaggerate their desire for material goods—Trixie, for instance, catches sight of Faneuil's lighter and exclaims "GOLD!"—and force the men to buy them hats, corsages, furs, and a slew of other goods. They mimic the stereotype of the "bad" woman. In order to discuss how much money "Polly" (Carol) will take to leave Brad alone, they go to a speakeasy, where they drink lots of champagne and Trixie fondles Faneuil's knee. At a nightclub, Carol snuggles provocatively with Lawrence on the dance floor: "You think it's vulgar, don't you, dancing this way?" In the final act of their masquerade, the women act out a scenario of actual prostitution: when Lawrence passes out drunk in the girls' apartment, Trixie convinces him that he slept with Carol and demands $10,000 payment for services rendered.

While Trixie and Carol mimic the behavior of the sinister polluter, Polly plays upon the trope of the innocent victim, revealing the element of masquerade in her seemingly genuine status as the ingenue of the trio. Lawrence links acting as a profession to prostitution when he states that Polly is unlike the "cheap" and "vulgar" women of the theater and that she is the woman his brother should be interested in: "How did a girl like you—? What are you doing in the theater?" Polly tells Lawrence that she is an orphan, whose father was an official in the government and whose mother was an invalid: "I had to find something to do—earn money—and all I could find was—[shrugs]. You see?" Trixie, Carol, and Brad watch and listen to Polly's discussion with Lawrence from a balcony above, providing an audience for this staged spectacle. In comic asides, Trixie deciphers the codes of Polly's masquerade: "Her father was a letter carrier!"; "Her mother could have licked John L. Sullivan." Polly has previously been delegated to the role of ingenue in relation to the other two women in the film, as well as in the musical numbers of the show. Here, in parodying her status as ingenue, she suggests that all stereotypes, even her goody-two-shoes persona, are masquerade, performance.

Instead of viewing women as fitting into one of two categories, wholly good or wholly bad, Gold Diggers of 1933 represents a range of types and gradations between these two poles. It is not the case that the film denies that gold diggers exist—Fay Fortune is, after all, a "true" gold digger. Rather, it blurs the distinction between gold diggers and other women, between authenticity and masquerade. By contrast, the final shooting script reinforces these distinctions. According to the final script, Trixie cannot continue with the hustle and confesses her genuine love for Faneuil, just as Carol confesses hers for Lawrence and Polly truly loves Brad. In the film's final cut, however, Trixie's motivation in marrying Faneuil is left ambiguous. She may truly love him or she may just decide to fully enact the role of the gold digger and take Faneuil for his wealth. In another vein, even as Carol admits to being in love with Lawrence, she plays the sinister polluter to his corruptable heart. She describes herself as "cheap and vulgar." "Everytime you say cheap and vulgar," Lawrence proclaims, "I'm going to kiss you." The film depicts a range of heterosexual relationships—young, innocent love (Polly and Brad), mature, sexual, sophisticated love (Carol and Lawrence), and older, asexual, cynical love (Trixie and Faneuil)—each of which is brought about through the masquerade and none of which is without an element of masquerade, no matter how genuine the love that informs it. In theatricalizing the masquerade's construction of gender identities, the women protagonists force the recognition of these heterosexual relations as culturally constructed.

Gold Diggers of 1933, therefore, deepens and confirms the psychoanalytic view that genuine womanliness and the masquerade are "the same thing," points on a continuum. However, the film also reveals the class bias inherent to the notion of masquerade by associating the masquerade with working-women's survival strategies. Riviere models her original conception of female masquerade on her observation of certain intellectual women who have gained a measure of power in the intellectual sphere and then have put on a "mask of womanliness" to placate men who resent their power. Although Riviere claims that all women participate in the masquerade, she conceives of the masquerade as primarily a gesture of disavowal, denying and abrogating "masculine" power and knowledge. In a patriarchal and oppressive society, however, most women do not have such privileged access to masculine power. Feminists have primarily used Riviere's notion of the masquerade to support theories related to the constructedness of gender identities; we need, however, to reconsider what relation, if any, the everyday masquerade has to female empowerment.

If, as I claim, female masquerade is a camp strategy, it also partakes of the pathos of camp and reflects the fact that camp is a product of oppression. As Richard Dyer argues, gay men developed an eye and ear for surfaces because they had to be skilled at disguise to adapt to society's conventions: "We couldn't afford to stand out in any way, for it might give the game away about our gayness." [32] Gold Diggers of 1933 reverses the order of Riviere's examples and suggests that women can use masquerade not only to disavow masculine power but also to gain strategic access to power and privilege typically denied them as women. This masquerade merges the thin theatricality of performance with the deeper drama of the lived. Here, the person who has real needs and desires consciously takes on a persona to realize those needs and desires. Her masquerade entails a camp recognition of herself as a stereotype and her manipulation of that stereotype for her own ends. She not only camps, creating an artificial masquerade, but perceives herself as camp, as enacting the serious joke that is her life. The women protagonists in the film theatricalize the masquerade, both to create an ironic distance from oppressive stereotypes (exacting revenge on Lawrence and Faneuil), and to use those stereotypes to their advantage (becoming effective and successful gold diggers who, in fact, use feminine charms to marry three rich men).

The masquerade in Gold Diggers of 1933 represents a working-class women's strategy of survival and not simply a placating gesture to patriarchal authority. The film evokes the threat of prostitution at both levels of the diegesis to make clear that the choice for working women in the Depression is not a choice between masculine power and feminine disavowal but between unsuccessful and successful masquerade, between prostitution and gold digging.

An Aesthetics of Prostitution

Unlike most backstage musicals that make the success of the show and the success of the romance mutually dependent, Gold Diggers of 1933 establishes the success of the show before introducing the question of romance. The success of the show enables the women to seek romance, but first they must avoid becoming prostitutes. For the show to be a success, Brad must take the juvenile's lead. Still trying to conceal his true identity, Brad resists. Trixie convinces him to think of the consequences for the female performers:

> Listen. I don't care if you have to go to jail after this performance. . . . Do you know what this means—if the show doesn't go on? It means that all those girls, all those poor kids who gave up jobs, and who'll never get other jobs in these times, all those kids who've been living on nothing, starving themselves these five weeks we've been rehearsing, hoping for this show to go on, and be a success—They're depending on you! . . . God knows what will happen to those girls—They'll have to do things I wouldn't want on my conscience.

In asking Brad to think of the community before himself, Trixie's speech could be taken as simply representing the New Deal spirit. But she appeals to Brad's conscience not by enunciating New Deal ideals but by enlisting Progressive Era–tinged arguments about the effects of low wages on female behavior. If the show does not go on, the women will not have access to jobs and will have to do "God knows what" simply in order to survive. What Trixie and God know, and what Brad realizes, is that these women will turn to prostitution, because the Depression severely restricts their options for other means of survival.

In linking the concept of entertainment to prostitution, the film acknowledges, as Dyer and others claim, that women's capital is their bodies. However, rather than simply affirming this, the film's invocation of Progressive Era discourses on prostitution in its diegesis enables us to view the feminine spectacle of the musical numbers through a lens that both affirms and undermines the trope of female commodification. Countering the sense that Berkeley's numbers in *Gold Diggers of 1933* offer a "non-real" aesthetic effect different in kind from the "realistic" narrative, I would argue that Berkeley's numbers refer symbolically to the issues that inform the narrative, not reprising "lessons" but exposing the contradictions in the narrative's use of Progressive Era antiprostitution discourse. The spectacle of mass-produced, abstract female bodies in Berkeley's numbers creates an aesthetic of prostitution that the film eventually unmasks, leading not to an affirmation of female commodification but to a critique of the conditions that cause women to commodify themselves.

As Mellencamp notes, "the Berkeley sequences are spectacles of the glories of capitalist technique and hence are visual demonstrations of the narrative."[33] She supports this contention mentioning Siegfried Kracauer's 1931 essay, "The Mass Ornament," which provocatively links the mass ornament to the capitalist production process. The mass ornament Kracauer describes closely mirrors a Berkeley spectacle. He refers to spectacular pageants, modeled on the "Tiller Girls,"[34] popular in Berlin and throughout the world, in live performances and newsreels; these pageants consist of "thousands of . . . sexless bodies in bathing suits" who form intricate patterns. In a sentence that could come straight from Fischer's analysis of Berkeley, Kracauer writes, "These products of American 'distraction factories' are no longer individual girls but indissoluble female units whose movements are mathematical demonstrations."[35] For Kracauer, the interest of the mass ornament consists in its "reality level"; it makes visible the capitalist production process. First, the ornament is an end in itself; the constellations of women, like the commodity, have no meaning outside themselves. Second, the ornament is conceived according to rationalist principles—each woman performs a partial function without knowing the entirety, the organization hovering above, like an assembly line. Despite its "reality level," however, Sabine Hake observes that, for Kracauer, the feminized mass ornament, like the female movie audience, is denied its revolutionary potential and placed instead in the category of kitsch.[36]

How then to reserve the revolutionary potential of diversion in the mass ornament and how to claim that potential for women? "The problem," as Peter Wollen remarks, commenting on Kracauer in his essay on Fordism and the cinema, "is that of reintegrating reason not only with truth, but also with the body. . . . What form of bodily movement would correspond to a process of production which displayed a different, transformed rationality— and, of course, a transformed gender division and sexuality?"[37]

A detour through Walter Benjamin's scattered comments on prostitution in his fragmentary essay, "Central Park," on Baudelaire, leads to one possible answer. Benjamin links both the figure of the nineteenth-century prostitute and the showgirl to the onset of industrialization: "One of the *arcana* which has fallen to prostitution only with the development of the metropolis, is the development of the masses. . . . In the form which prostitution took in the great cities woman appears not merely as a commodity but as a mass-produced article. This is indicated in the artificial disguise of the individual expression in favor of a professional one, such as is brought about by the application of make-up."[38] Like the twentieth-century chorus girl, the prostitute loses her individuality in becoming a commodified object. Her makeup, which serves as a marker of her profession, turns her into commodity, sign, and type all at once. Benjamin's analysis resembles the Progressive Era arguments about the effects of industrialization on women, but rather than seeking to curb the effects of massification on women, he implicitly values the prostitute precisely because she displaces the myth of natural femininity.[39]

In her analysis of his comments on prostitution, Christine Buci-Glucksman links Benjamin's comments on prostitution to his utopian vision of mechanical reproduction in the "Work of Art" essay: "Women become mass-produced, widely available commodities with the "massification" of industrial labor and society, simultaneously losing their "natural" qualities (a feminine essence, a nature determined by child bearing) and their poetic aura (beauty as the sublimating idealization that surrounds Dante's Beatrice)."[40] According to Buci-Glucksman, Benjamin's equation of the figure of the prostitute with the masses describes a form of modernity that rests on a lack, on the destruction of feminine aura. This loss and destruction serve as critical forces.[41] Similar to the way in which Benjamin imagines that mechanical reproducibility will destroy the aura of a work of art, freeing the viewer from hierarchic contemplative culture, he envisions (as Baudelaire did before him) the prostitute freed from the aura of "natural" femininity, of the family, of idealized beauty, and of the illusions of love.

Returning to Berkeley's spectacles, we see that the "reality level" in Berkeley's numbers consists in disclosing the joint articulation of massification and prostitution: Berkeley's unique visual style may possess the revolutionary feminist potential seemingly absent from the mass ornament in Kracauer's reading. The plastic abstractions in Berkeley numbers reduce women, on the one hand, to commodified objects, creating an aesthetics of prostitution; but, on the other hand, rather than fetishize the image of the woman, the very abstractness of Berkeley's images creates an ironic distance from the image of woman, destroying the aura of the fetish. In turning women into mass-produced images, linked to the technology of film as well as other technologies (neon, electricity), Berkeley displaces the eroticism of the image from the woman to technology.

At the same time, the order in which the numbers of *Gold Diggers of 1933* are presented ultimately humanizes and individuates the prostitute, exposing the way in which modern industrialization invests the image of the woman with the aura of the commodity. Susan Buck-Morss notes: "The gesture of mimicking the commodity world could be redeemed as well. If adults— assembly-line workers, goose-stepping soldiers, "girls" in the chorus line— have been regimented and transformed into machines, one has only to reverse the image to recover the child's dream of utopia, where things are humanized rather than humans reified."[42] *Gold Diggers of 1933* reverses the image not only in the narrative that humanizes and individuates female stereotypes but also in the numbers. According to the shooting script, the three couples get engaged or married, then Brad and Polly perform "Shadow Waltz" and the film concludes with a reprise of "We're in the Money" sung by Brad and Carol. In the final version of the film, however, "Shadow Waltz" precedes the resolution of the romance plot and the film ends with "Forgotten Man," not "We're in the Money." At the narrative level, the specter of prostitution is raised in order to be avoided through the success of the show and the success of the romance plot. The secondary diegesis, however, reverses the order of the narrative, moving from comic and metaphoric images of prostitution in the first three numbers to a concrete image in the last.

In "Forgotten Man," Carol plays a prostitute both commodified and cognizant. The number provides a history of the forgotten men of the First World War. It begins with images of men marching as soldiers in the rain, then as wounded soldiers returning from the war, then in breadlines. Carol sings,

> Remember my forgotten man / You put a rifle in his hand / You sent him far away / You shouted "Hip Hooray" / But look at him today— / Remember my forgotten man / You had him cultivate the land / He walked behind a plow / The sweat fell from his brow / But look at him right now— / And once he used to love me / I was happy then— / He used to take care of me / Won't you bring him back again?— / Cause ever since the world began / A woman's got to have a man / Forgetting him, you see, means / You're forgetting me / Like my forgotten man.

Instead of identical and glamorous women, the number features portraits of highly individuated women—a thin, sad woman, an old woman, an African American woman—reminiscent of portraits by Dorothea Lange and Walker

Evans of poor rural women in the Depression. In addition, an African American woman (Etta Moten) sings a solo version of the verse, lending the song the presumed "authenticity" of African American blues culture. These images remind us of the women who have been "forgotten" in the rest of the diegesis. In part, the lyrics reinforce the ideals of romance — "and once he used to love me / I was happy then." But the song also serves to remind the viewer that romance is a conditional illusion. In using the figure of the pros-titute to summon the forgotten man and creating a causal link between her massification and that of alienated soldiers and workers, the song forcefully reminds us of the conditions lurking behind the romance plot: "Forgetting him, you see, means / You're forgetting me." Ending here, inside the number rather than in the primary diegesis, undercuts the palliative effect of the ro-mance plot. It robs the film of its illusions; the alternative vision contained in the camp effect of the gold-digging plot and the aesthetics of prostitution in the numbers is no longer disguised. Instead of reprising the lesson that women's only capital is their bodies, "Forgotten Man" insists that the social implications of female commodification — in industrial society and through mass-produced images — be clearly read and remembered.

Without acknowledging the text's camp qualities at both the primary and secondary level of the diegesis, describing Berkeley's style as an aesthetics of prostitution would merely reiterate the claims of earlier feminist critics. By analyzing this aesthetics of prostitution as a camp aesthetic and by placing the numbers in the context of the plot's camp masquerade, we can see the aesthetics of prostitution as a form of feminist camp. The film addresses women at the narrative level, creating an identification between the female spectator and the gold diggers, who acknowledge and overcome oppression through the discourses of masquerade and camp. The female spectator, then, without changing subject position, views the camp effect of Berkeley's num-bers — the astonishment one experiences at the sight of a Berkeley spectacle, the perception of dissonance between the number's purported object, and its mode of representation — through a lens that perceives a dissonance in both the numbers and the stereotypes they represent. She, like the gold dig-ger, recognizes the stereotype of woman as image and commodity as merely a stereotype (a false image), and as partial truth, as both a camp joke and as her lot. She also knows that the stereotype is socially constructed (artificial, unreal) and motivated by alterable economic conditions — and she is aston-ished.

Gold Diggers of 1933 thus demonstrates how a specifically feminist form of camp can operate in the musical and how acknowledging the musical's camp effect as dominant, rather than subcultural, might enrich feminist interpretations of the musical. This reading of *Gold Diggers of 1933* as feminist camp depends upon acknowledging the film's textual address to female spectators at the narrative level. Despite its attention to textual address, however, this reading is not ahistorical. By taking seriously the film's linking of gold diggers, showgirls, and the present threat of prostitution, we can better understand how 1930s audiences might have read the film and how the feminine spectacle in the numbers may have been read.

If, as I am suggesting, the figure of the gold digger is central to feminist camp, then prostitution is the hidden threat behind feminist camp. West enacts the shift from prostitution to feminist camp in her shift from theater—where she wrote roles for drags and female impersonators but played prostitutes—to film—where she combines the camp style of the drags and impersonators with the role of prostitute. In the next two chapters, the star texts of Joan Crawford and Madonna will, in different ways, also play on the tropes of prostitution and gold digging and create feminist camp effects that speak to a working-class women's sensibility. These tropes, however, will register differently as attitudes toward women and work change in the 1950s and 1980s; and, as conditions of reading and reception change, the form and meaning of feminist camp will also change.

THREE

Camping under Western

Stars: Joan Crawford

in Johnny Guitar

Joan Crawford in a publicity still for Johnny Guitar
(author's collection).

So while some were born camp and some achieved campness, some had campness thrust upon them. . . . Around the time of *Torch Song* and *Johnny Guitar*, it became impossible for any sane person to see Crawford as anything but camp and that was the moment her star began to fall. —Evelyn Satz, "Camping It Up"

What the hell is a cult except a gang of rebels without a cause! *I have fans.* There's a big difference. —Joan Crawford, on Bette Davis's "cult" following [1]

C amp classics like *Whatever Happened to Baby Jane?* (1962) and *Berserk* (1967) imprinted the image of Joan Crawford as a neurotic female grotesque—all flashing eyes, padded shoulders, and maniacally clenched teeth. This cruel camp image was transmogrified after Crawford's death into a real-life comedy of horrors by daughter Christina Crawford's best-selling expose and the biopic of the same title, *Mommie Dearest* (1981). But Crawford's status as camp queen developed relatively late in her career; it was not firmly established until the third decade of what was one of the longest and most durable careers in Hollywood, encompassing over eighty films between 1925 and 1970. Unlike Mae West, who if not born camp certainly achieved it, Crawford seems to have "had campness thrust upon [her]." Before Crawford had a cultish camp following, she had fans, and particularly working-class female fans, for whom she was a fantasy figure of identification who was anything but camp.

Richard Dyer has argued that we need to examine star images as a "structured polysemy, that is, the finite multiplicity of meanings and affects they embody" that are structured so that some meanings and affects are foregrounded and others obscured for ideological effect. Rather than a simplistic relation between a given star text and a single ideology, Dyer claims that stars exist "within and between ideologies" so that they may either manage and resolve contradictions, expose contradictions, "or embody an alternative or oppositional ideological position (itself usually contradictory) to dominant ideology." [2] Robert C. Allen and Douglas Gomery have demonstrated convincingly that Crawford's "polysemy" embodies a contradiction between, on the one hand, notions of success (professional and romantic) and how it might be achieved, and, on the other, expectations about women and their appropriate roles in society.[3] However, because Crawford's career spans five decades in which notions of success and expectations about women's roles changed dramatically, the meanings and effects of this polysemic structure change across different historical periods. The kinds of success women want and the social expectations addressed to women shift throughout Crawford's career, shifts that are played out in her films; further, the cultural (and market) value of the contradiction between ideals of success and norms of femininity is itself more or less conflicted at different points in time. Crawford's film persona sometimes exposes the contradiction, sometimes resolves it, and sometimes becomes the stuff of camp.

This chapter examines the 1950s as a turning point in Crawford's career, when her status as a "straight" star who appeals primarily to women and her status as a camp object briefly overlap. Focusing on her role in Nicholas Ray's Johnny Guitar (1954), I historicize Crawford's evolution into a camp object and claim that her initial camp effect simultaneously resolves and exposes the contradictions of her star image.

My primary purpose is to examine how and why Crawford became a camp object in the 1950s and whether, in fact, there is a "big difference" between her pre- and post-camp persona. For this purpose, Johnny Guitar will be considered in the larger context of Crawford's career. I suggest that the central contradiction of her star text, revolving around notions of professional female success, becomes recoded as camp because Crawford represents the problem of an aging female star in Hollywood, insofar as she is no longer seen as sexually desirable, and because she embodies an ideal of American femininity rendered outmoded by 1950s standards. I argue that precisely those elements of Crawford's star text that appealed most strongly to her female audience in the 1920s and 1930s are "maligned" in the 1940s, and especially the 1950s, as part of a backlash against a genre, the fallen woman's film, and a type of woman, associated with class rise and hard professionalism, which Crawford represented. At the same time, I reevaluate Johnny Guitar, a text that has received considerable attention in auteur and genre studies and, more recently, as a reflection of McCarthyism, but which has not been examined as a star vehicle. I analyze Johnny Guitar as a crossing of a female star vehicle and a stereotypically masculine genre, the Western, which creates a camp effect dependent not only on Crawford's role but also on 1950s' sexual politics.

More Like a Man

The first time we see Joan Crawford as Vienna in *Johnny Guitar*, she is wear-ing black jeans and a fitted black shirt, buttoned at the throat and laced up with a string tie. Her hair is short and severe. Shot from below, the framing emphasizes her power. From a balcony above Vienna's gambling house and saloon, she barks orders to the men who work for her before disappearing into her boudoir at the top of the stairs. In case we did not notice, Sam, one of the dealers, explains, "I've never seen a woman who was more like a man. She thinks like one, acts like one, and sometimes makes me feel I'm not." Vienna's masculine costume underlines not only her empowerment but also her threat as a castrating female. As if there is only a limited amount of phallic power to go around, her added masculinity diminishes that of "real" men. When Sam says she makes him feel he's "not," he suggests not only that he is not a man (because Vienna is too much man), but also that his very existence has been challenged, his identity eradicated along with his man-hood. The film emphatically foregrounds and endorses this fear by having Sam seemingly make his point in a direct address to the viewer, his comment then relocated in the diegesis by a cut.

Vienna is not the first castrating bitch in Crawford's career. She is, though, the first undeniably butch variation on the theme. Vienna can be seen as fol-lowing a trajectory of Crawford's film career that began with her "comeback" in *Mildred Pierce* (1945). In this regard, Vienna, like Mildred, represents the cas-trating woman who usurps masculine power and must be punished or re-turned to femininity, thus reflecting a backlash against professional women coincident with the return of American GIs after the war and the need to reassert masculine authority in the workplace after the unprecedented war-time employment of women.[4] But the sexual politics of *Johnny Guitar* express deeper concerns about women's roles and gender boundaries. By 1954, the attitude toward the working women Crawford represents has taken a much crueler turn. Vienna is not merely masculinized but quite butch. Whereas Mildred was able to maintain a "straight" friendship with other women (Eve Arden's Ida), the plot of *Johnny Guitar* turns upon the eroticized antagonism between Vienna and Emma (Mercedes McCambridge). *Mildred Pierce* breathed new life into Crawford's flagging career, and she won her first and only Academy Award. *Johnny Guitar* coincided with a downturn in her status as a Hollywood star. And, as Evelyn Satz argues, while Crawford may have be-come camp in the 1940s, this was still a "minority taste"; her success in the 1940s came from people who took her perfectly seriously. By the time of *Johnny Guitar*, however, "it became impossible for any sane person to see Crawford as anything but camp."

Crawford's camp persona—nascent in *Johnny Guitar*, full-blown in her late high-camp films—combines features of a certain kind of artificiality with a hard professionalism. By artificiality, I mean, in part, the evident construct-edness of her physical image—padded shoulders, thickly drawn eyebrows, the slash of a mouth formed with dark red lipstick, and the perfect, be-cause strictly regimented, body. At the same time, artificiality also relates to hard professionalism in the perceived difference between this hard sur-face and the bitter, lonely woman "beneath" the surface. Crawford's camp persona encodes professionalism as masculinization, physically—the broad shoulders and severe face—and characterologically—domineering and cas-trating, competitive with men, jealous of other women, and determinedly self-reliant.

These structuring elements of Crawford's camp effect have their roots in corresponding features of her early star text. At the high-point of her popu-larity, the trope of artificiality had a different value, and Crawford was por-trayed positively as a self-made and regenerating star; instead of hard pro-fessionalism, her star text represented female independence and class rise, which created an identification between her and working-class women.

The Dramatic Rise and Fall of a Self-Made Star

I'm no queen. I started as a hoofer in a chorus line and by hard work and good breaks became a woman, learning and growing.—Joan Crawford [5]

"Joan Crawford" was literally manufactured by her fans. A 1925 contest in *Movie Weekly* offered $1000 to the person who could come up with a new name for Lucille Le Sueur, "an auburn-haired, blue-eyed beauty" selected from hundreds of girls as the one who best personified "the ideal young American girl of today." [6] When the winning name, Joan Arden, was discov-ered to be the name of another contract player at MGM, studio executives chose the second-place name, Joan Crawford. Crawford reciprocated and cultivated strong bonds with her female fans. She answered all fan letters personally, never refused an interview, and frequently asserted that her fans had made her what she was. She gave jobs as secretaries to some devoted fans and knew many by name. Each month, she wrote a letter for the Joan Crawford Club news.

In the 1920s, the "ideal young American girl" was embodied by the image of the carefree flapper. Crawford got a name for herself in Hollywood as the "hey-hey" and "hotcha" girl, the young starlet who played hard, danced all night, and won countless trophies in Charleston contests. F. Scott Fitzgerald described the actress at the time: "Joan Crawford is doubtless the best example of the flapper, the girl you see in smart nightclubs, gowned to the apex of sophistication, toying iced glasses with a remote, faintly bitter expression, dancing deliciously, laughing a great deal, with wide, hurt eyes — a young thing with a talent for living."[7] Her breakthrough roles in *Sally, Irene and Mary* (1925) and *Our Dancing Daughters* (1928) merged this offscreen image with her film persona. She played variations on the flapper theme in movies such as the *Hollywood Revue of 1929*, playing "herself," *Our Modern Maidens* (1929) and *Our Blushing Brides* (1930), continuing the saga of the dancing daughters, and films whose titles capture the reckless and modern spirit Crawford personified: *Untamed* (1929), *Dance, Fools, Dance* (1931), *Laughing Sinners* (1931), and *This Modern Age* (1931).

Crawford's image as carefree "hey-hey" girl was tempered by fan-magazine discourse, which emphasized the obstacles she had overcome to achieve her success. A typical article, "The Story of a Dancing Girl," recounts details of Crawford's almost Dickensian childhood — suffering physical abuse while working as a maid to earn her tuition in a private school, snubbed by sorority girls who looked down on her domestic work, molested by a stepfather, and overcoming a crippling accident to become a dancer.

According to Allen and Gomery, in their case study of Crawford's tenure at Metro-Goldwyn-Mayer (1925–43), the chief structuring element of Joan Crawford's star text is the idea of a "self-made" star. Fan magazines consistently detailed how Crawford "deliberately manufactured a personality."[8] Because Crawford had overcome severe obstacles to gain success, her self-creation seemed less artificial than triumphant, an American success story. A three-part series in *Photoplay*, "Joan Crawford: The Dramatic Rise of a Self-Made Star," compared Crawford to "the self-made men of pioneer days" and suggested that her self-creation, taken as typically American, was a point of identification. Reflecting on a series of photographs depicting Crawford's change from pudgy starlet to sophisticated star, the article directly addresses and assures her: "If you'd always been just what you are today, you couldn't possibly be so closely identified with us, with all that's American in us, with all that's human in us."[9] If Crawford was artificial, manufactured, this meant that other women could also manufacture a better self: "If Lucille Le Sueur could acquire Joan Crawford's glamour in a few short years, there is hope for you and You and YOU!"[10]

Examining the influence of Crawford's Adrian gowns on female fashion consumption in the 1930s, Charlotte Herzog and Jane Gaines emphasize
that Crawford's image as a self-made star "was repeated in a way calculated
to appeal to fans with similar economic struggles."[11] Dubbed "Cinderella,"
"Horatia Alger," "Queen of the Working Girls," and "A Shopgirl's Dream,"
Joan Crawford came to embody notions of female success and class rise with
which American women were meant to identify. Working-class women were
encouraged to believe that, through "hard work and good breaks," they could
achieve the same kind of success Crawford had. One magazine urged, "Every
ambitious girl who is struggling for success against odds should read this
story of Joan Crawford's brave fight!"[12] Another told women who doubted
the efficacy of will power to "consider the amazing case of Joan Crawford
and admit that any lack of success in your own life is due to plain laziness
and a refusal to grab the breaks."[13]

By the 1930s, Allen and Gomery argue that as Crawford became Mrs.
Douglas Fairbanks Jr. (1929–33) and then Mrs. Franchot Tone (1935–39), she
represented not just a self-made but a regenerating star.[14] Married to these
modern Pygmalions, who introduced her to Hollywood high society and
the New York intelligentsia, respectively, Crawford changed to suit each new
role. She transformed her reckless flapper image into that of "a woman,
learning and growing." Fan magazines noted the change through a simultaneous invocation and erasure of her past, constantly depicting her evolution
from chunky "hotcha" girl to glamorous star, while calling her "the girl
without a past" whose every new phase was a stranger to the previous one.[15]

Similarly, Crawford's film persona changed in the 1930s from that of the
reckless flapper to a more mature, independent woman. Her starring roles in
the 1930s, her most successful decade in films, played upon her image as a
self-made woman who overcame tough obstacles to succeed. Crawford's ve-
hicles were a subset of what Lea Jacobs has termed "the fallen woman film."[16]
In these films, the heroine commits a sexual transgression (adultery or pre-
marital sex) to become either a victim of society (prostitute, outcast, dead)
or a success (gold digger, "kept" woman). Crawford played a prostitute in
Rain (1932) and Strange Cargo (1940). Most often, however, she played working
women—shopgirls, factory workers, dancers, stenographers—determined
to rise from the working class to a better life. But while she starts out associated with legitimate work, the scenario of class rise was associated with
her sexuality, not her work; or, rather, her sexuality was what she worked
at in order to succeed as a gold digger or kept woman. More than simply
a figure of upward mobility, Crawford represents a figure of female desire,

an unapologetic figure, neither sentimental nor exotic, who desires—and gets—material wealth and true love by using her sexuality.

Sometimes Crawford portrays the comic gold digger, like the shopgirl Crystal in *The Women* (1939), who wants easy success and gets it by taking away another woman's husband, only to lose him and her newfound wealth at the end. More often, however, her characters "fall" because the films represent legitimate work as a dead end for women. In *Grand Hotel* (1932), for example, she plays a stenographer who matter-of-factly supplements her income through prostitution, ultimately finding a kind and wealthy mate who will take care of her. In *Possessed* (1931), Crawford's character is a small-town girl working in a paper-box factory who wants a finer life. She decides to leave her unsuccessful boyfriend (Wallace Ford) to move to New York "to be done right by," using her sexuality as her ticket to success. She tells her boyfriend, "All I've got is my looks and my youth and whatever it is about me that the fellas like, that you like. You think I'm gonna trade that in on a chance that'll never come?" In New York, she becomes the mistress of a high-society lawyer (Clark Gable), after she tells him straight out that she is after him for his money. Instead of being punished, she gets the man and his wealth. Thus, while Crawford embodied American ideals of hard work and self-determination, her films contradictorily depict the limitations that prevent women from succeeding through hard work alone. The films mask this conflict over the meaning of and means to female success, however, by suggesting that being a gold digger or kept woman will actually lead to increased wealth and true love.

Crawford's star text was also manipulated to gloss over the contradictions between female success and social expectations about women's roles, especially with respect to marriage. While her films downplayed the sexual transgressiveness of her characters to turn her into a symbol of female success in work and love, extratextual materials concerning Crawford's "private" life negotiated a different conflict between female professional success and romantic love. Crawford's first three marriages failed because she was more successful than her mates, but publicity materials depicted Crawford as a success in both business and love. On the one hand, as Allen and Gomery point out, each new marriage was treated as a new opportunity for Crawford to recreate herself. Articles on her married life mask the tension between ambition and marriage by asserting that, for Crawford, the latter aids in the realization of the former—each husband teaches her new things that help her become more successful.[17] On the other hand, much of her publicity material suggested that Crawford was a success in love because, despite her three divorces, she managed always to find a new husband or boyfriend. In interviews, she frequently gave advice about men to young women. Fan magazines asked "Can You Pass Joan Crawford's Love Test?" and explained "How Joan Crawford Keeps Her Men Friends Interested." [18]

Publicity materials focused on her real-life rags-to-riches story, rather than the sexually transgressive characters she portrayed, and turned her into a symbol of professional success. Crawford was wildly popular with women in the 1930s—movie magazines sold out if they featured her on the cover [19]— and her popularity was considered as correlating with her identification with working women. On a second honeymoon in London with Douglas Fairbanks Jr. in 1932, MGM arranged for Crawford to talk to three thousand working-class women, fans of "the American star with whom they identified most." [20] *Movie Classic* proclaimed her "a cult, a tradition, a symbol of what millions of women would like to be." [21] In 1936, *Life* magazine named Crawford First Queen of the Movies: "It is an axiom in Hollywood that movie favorites are usually created by women. Joan Crawford's public is predominantly female, predominantly lowbrow. A former shopgirl herself, she has risen to stardom as the Shopgirl's Dream." [22] Since 1932, Crawford had appeared among the top ten stars in *Motion Picture Herald*'s poll of movie theater owners who were asked to name the stars who made the most money for them. In 1936, she was number seven, the top female dramatic star, preceded by only four men (Clark Gable, Robert Taylor, Joe E. Brown, Dick Powell), a child (Shirley Temple) and a musical team (Fred Astaire and Ginger Rogers).

In the late 1930s, however, Crawford's star fell. In 1937, she was dropped from the list of the top ten moneymaking stars; and in 1938, an influential article by Harry Brandt, the owner of a small chain of movie theaters, named her "Box Office Poison," along with Mae West, Katharine Hepburn, Marlene Dietrich, Greta Garbo, Fred Astaire and Edward Arnold. In 1942, after a string of mediocre films, she was released from her contract at MGM.

Crawford's demise parallels that of other "independent" women—not coincidentally, all the women named as "box-office poison" represent a mixture of independence and sexual transgressiveness, and each has become a camp idol. Her fall also signals the end of the fallen woman genre, a cycle which Jacobs brackets from 1928 to 1942. The fallen woman film can be seen as a genre whose parameters were defined by the Depression. These films reflect, on the one hand, the financial difficulties of middle- and lower-class women who faced economic hardship. On the other hand, those films, like Crawford's, in which the heroine succeeds in gaining material wealth while ironically exposing the failure of women to achieve upward mobility through wage labor and professional work, still address the fantasies and wishes of women denied material goods in the Depression. The fallen woman's film was also affected by the increased enforcement of the 1934 Hays Code, which limited depictions of sexual transgression, and, as Jacobs emphasizes, by re-form movements concerned with the potential influence of these films on female spectators.[23] In addition, as MGM turned to its younger stars (Judy Garland, Lana Turner, Esther Williams), Crawford's slow death at the studio suggests that Crawford, almost forty, was perceived as an old and, therefore, undesirable star.

It is tempting to locate Crawford's evolution into a camp object at the mo-ment of her "comeback" in *Mildred Pierce* (1945). As Richard Dyer has demon-strated, the comeback can itself be a crucial element in a star's camp persona. In the case of Judy Garland, for example, Dyer argues that the comeback was a "decisive motif," played and replayed in each of Garland's post-1950 performances. This motif signified equally suffering and survival, a tears-beneath-the-greasepaint, show-must-go-on ethic. According to Dyer, the emotional intensity of Garland's constant comeback carried connotations of theatricality and irony, vulnerability and strength, passion and irony — quali-ties that for gay male fans paralleled in some way the experience of being gay in a homophobic society.[24] In Crawford's case, by contrast, her come-back can be taken as yet another instance of self-transformation. Whereas Garland constantly amazed us with her ability to keep going despite her well-documented suffering, Crawford's comeback repeated and further en-sconced the image of her as a trouper, able to surmount all obstacles. At the same time, Crawford's comeback underlined the longevity of her career, and, with the recognition signaled by an Academy Award, legitimated her work as an actress. She seemingly manages, then, another aspect of the contradic-tion between notions of success and expectations about women's roles — in this instance, between notions of professional success in Hollywood and ex-pectations about the desirability of older female stars.

Paradoxically, however, while Crawford's comeback asserts the star's durable professional power and attractiveness, her film roles expose the problem of rendering an older woman both desirable and desiring. In the 1940s, Crawford's films increasingly unmask the concealed relation between sexuality and work in her earlier films, thereby transforming the Crawford character from a figure of desire to a figure of dissatisfaction. As I noted above, *Mildred Pierce* exposes the contradiction in Crawford's star text between female success and expectations about women's roles, because Mildred's suc-cess conflicts with the postwar ideology that demands that women give up

their careers. Whereas Crawford's fallen woman films suggested an easy resolution between ambition and romantic love, downplaying the sexual transgressiveness that linked the two, her later films make ambition transgressive
and punish that transgression by denying the possibility of reconciling it
with romantic love.

After *Mildred Pierce*, Crawford plays upper-class women. Rather than a triumphant scenario of class rise, her films depict the dissatisfaction women
face when they have reached the top. In part, the "new" Crawford of the
1940s reflects a backlash against the professional type she represented in the
1930s and serves to refigure the appropriate object of desire for women as
domestic and maternal satisfaction, rather than professional or material success. Yet, the rootless dissatisfaction of this figure suggests a cause to her
troubles that will not be solved by simply leaving the professional sphere.
Stephen Harvey aptly describes the "new Crawford" as a "lacquered woman
of a certain age whose aura of assurance fails to mask her deep-rooted
discontent and loneliness." [25] The problems her characters face range from
alcoholism (*Humoresque* [1946]) to murderous schizophrenia (*Possessed* [1947])
to compulsiveness (*Harriet Craig* [1950]). As Mary Ann Doane observes, the
woman's film of the 1940s assumes a "compatibility between the idea of
female fantasy and that of persecution. . . . an almost obsessive association of
the female protagonist with some norm of mental stability or health, result-
ing in the recurrent investigation of psychical mechanisms frequently linked
with the "feminine condition"—masochism, hysteria, neurosis, paranoia." [26]
Unlike Crawford's 1930s roles, these characters are not victims of society
but of their own neuroses. Rather than figures of desire, these characters, in
Doane's term, desire to desire; they inhabit a mode of desire that is displayed
to the viewer as lack or as an excess of dissatisfaction.

Crawford's film roles in the 1940s clearly set the stage for her transformation into a camp object. Her physical appearance becomes increasingly
severe, and her film roles capture the artificiality and hard professionalism
that structure her camp image. Still, at this moment in her career, Crawford is not yet fully readable as a camp object. For one thing, the extracinematic elements of her star persona—her "private" self as constructed in
fan magazines, publicity materials, et cetera—did not yet support this image.
Although interviews describe Crawford as lonely, she compares her loneliness to that of women waiting for sweethearts to return from the war and
to the men who miss their sweethearts. [27] Fan discourse and publicity materials of the time focus primarily on Crawford's role as the "bachelor mother"
of her adopted children and, similarly, on her maternal role as supporter of
numerous children's charities, thereby sidetracking the issue of her sexual

desirability. Read from a contemporary viewpoint, Crawford's descriptions in these articles of the discipline she inflicts on her children are nothing but camp. At the time, however, they offered a counterpoint to the neurotic loneliness of her film roles by asserting that the private woman found the "answer to the feeling of incompleteness" in motherhood.[28] Moreover, the "new Crawford" of the 1940s woman's films suits contemporary codes of taste, whereas for an object to become camp, it must seem anachronistic and out of place. The rootless dissatisfaction she embodies is still fully conceivable in postwar America, and, crucially, she supports the dominant ideology's view of the appropriate role for women.

In the next decade, though, Crawford becomes a camp object, as the figure of nameless dissatisfaction she represents comes to conflict with the dominant ideology, which Betty Friedan famously termed the 1950s "feminine mystique." According to Friedan, the mystique was an image of women promoted in women's magazines, public and private educational systems, and institutions of psychoanalysis and psychotherapy, which dictated that women should be content with the role of housewife and mother. It defined the ideal American woman as a dependent and happy homemaker and sex object, kept childlike by a permanently arrested development. Supporting the dominant ideology's emphasis on female passivity was the 1950s discourse on female sexuality. The widely discussed 1953 Kinsey report on female sexuality contributed to a growing emphasis on female sexual satisfaction, but psychoanalysis was still the most decisive discourse on female sexuality at the time, and psychoanalysts typically proclaimed that women could only achieve pleasure by being passive and receptive to the active male sex drive.[29]

Of course, as numerous historians and cultural critics have shown, the "feminine mystique" offers a one-dimensional portrait of the realities of women's lives in the 1950s. Rather than retreating to the home, for instance, the reality of women's lives in the 1950s proved that, despite the mystique, women were a major force in the workplace, greater even than during the war. Yet it is precisely the one-dimensionality of the model that gives the mystique its force as a defining 1950s antifeminist discourse, a discourse that clashed with crucial aspects of Crawford's star text. Susan Faludi observes, "It was precisely women's unrelenting influx into the job market, not a retreat to the home, that provoked and sustained the antifeminist furor . . . [and] heightened cultural fantasies of the compliant homebody and playmate."[30] For women who continued to enter the workforce, the dominant ideology about women's appropriate roles influenced the way they (and, of course, men) thought about their professional lives and ambitions. Friedan claims that many women felt dissatisfaction ("a strange stirring . . . a yearning")

with society's expectations about the role of women but that the culture refused to legitimate these feelings. Women who wanted more were told that
their "problem" in the past had been that they had tried to rival men in
business and intellectual endeavors and that they could and should find satisfaction in the domestic sphere.

Both aspects of the Crawford persona, the figure of desire and the figure of
dissatisfaction, were, therefore, rendered outmoded by contemporary taste.
The feminine mystique dictated that the object of female desire and the basis
for female satisfaction should be maternal and domestic. Crawford, too old
to fulfill the new feminine ideal, represented not only an outmoded type,
linked to urban and professional life, but also an undesirable reminder of
the ambitions and desires of women in the past. Her dissatisfaction, instead
of suggesting a real lack in female lives, seemed to represent an excess of
desire for inappropriate objects. Hence, Crawford becomes recoded as, and
presumably contained by, camp; her persona becomes that of an excessive
grotesque unsuited to the dominant ideology.

Two events in 1953, the year prior to the release of *Johnny Guitar*, suggest
how Crawford's star image became fully recoded as camp in the 1950s. In
the first, Crawford publicly attacks Marilyn Monroe, consequently marking
herself as a bitter aging star. The second, the release of *Torch Song*, serves as
metacommentary on Crawford's star text to remake her image from that of a
hardworking, self-made star into that of a pathetic and lonely shrew whose
career is her only fulfillment.

Halfway through the 1953 *Photoplay* awards dinner at the Beverly Hills
Hotel, twenty-seven-year-old Marilyn Monroe made a grand entrance. The
recipient of the award for "Fastest-Rising Star of 1952" wore a very low-
cut, gold-lame pleated gown with paper-thin lining, which had been hand-
stitched to her nude body. As she made her way slowly through the crowd
(unable to move any faster in the tight dress), the host for the evening, Jerry
Lewis, stood on a chair to get a better look, and the whole room exploded
with whistles and wolf calls. Days later, in an AP article, Joan Crawford responded. Her message to Marilyn Monroe: "Stop believing your own publicity." Crawford claimed that Monroe's pictures were not doing any business
because people didn't want to see sex flaunted. To her, Monroe's appearance
was a "burlesque show," unsuited to the event. "The public likes provocative
feminine personalities," Crawford explained, "but it also likes to know that
underneath it all the actresses are ladies." Privately, Crawford lamented, "I
had to work damn hard before I got that much attention. Today an artificial
chin, a nose job, and a bottle of peroxide's more important than talent and
class." The story was a sensation and there were follow-up items in the gossip

columns for days. Hollywood took sides. Louella Parsons, Walter Winchell, Betty Grable, and others defended Monroe. Although some people agreed that Marilyn's outfit had been in bad taste, most insisted that Crawford was jealous of Monroe's fast-rising career, youth, and beauty, as Crawford grew older and her career waned.[31]

That same year, Crawford returned to MGM to appear in Charles Walters's *Torch Song*, the most frighteningly self-referential of Crawford's films (on a par with Gloria Swanson's role in *Sunset Boulevard*). *Torch Song* merges Crawford's on-screen image with her offscreen persona by playing on aspects of her career and private life well known to her fans. She plays Jenny Stewart, a song-and-dance star, like the dancing ladies of Crawford's initial decade in films. Glamour photos of Crawford from the twenties and thirties decorate her dressing room and apartment, despite the fact that Stewart's career is only seven years old. Most tellingly, the film plays upon Crawford's famous attachment to her fans. Stewart, like Crawford, knows a coterie of female fans by name and writes personal autographs for them. Greeting them at the stage door, she tells them where she is going and when she will be back to rehearsal. She is described as being "in love" with her audience, and she states that they are more important than anything or anyone else in her life.

Torch Song yokes these aspects of Crawford's offscreen image to her recent screen image. Stewart exemplifies hard professionalism and artificiality. She works hard and is dedicated to the show, but she is domineering and brutal to her cast and crew, especially to the blind pianist who loves her. An inside joke underlines her bitchiness — the pianist's seeing-eye dog, a female, is named "Duchess," Gable's nickname for Crawford in *The Dancing Lady*. Stewart, "a handmade child of destiny," is utterly powerful and successful; her sometimes beau says she can "take a swatch of life, twist it into the shape you want and then shove it down the throats of the weaklings." But, underneath it all, she is, of course, lonely and bitter. Rehearsing lines for the play, alone in her meticulous high-tech bedroom, Jenny breaks down:

> "[Rehearsing] "I'm not afraid of being alone. . . . I'm tough, George,
>   that's why I'll never be lonely."
> [Jenny] Look who's talking . . .
> [Rehearsing] "I'll nev . . .". . . [sob]

Jealous of all other women, she gives a party at which she is the only female, an aging woman desperately trying to assert her sex appeal and desirability. Her strong attachment to her fans reads as a poor substitute for real love and admiration.

Torch Song was Crawford's first color film, and technicolor exaggerated the artificiality of her physical appearance. Stewart has acid-orange hair, which contrasts sharply with Crawford's thick dark eyebrows and deep red mouth. Her looks are further undermined by references to her vanity (constantly checking her figure, comparing her legs to a cardboard cutout of herself) and vulgarity. The blind man repeats to her that he heard "that you had a sensational figure, but you threw it about like a burlesque queen." Later, his prediction of her downfall matches nicely the image already before us: he says she will be "a cheap, vulgar has-been. And there'll be the bottle. . . . You'll dye . . . that Gypsy Madonna hair . . . all colors of the rainbow." In the film's most outlandish scene, Stewart performs a blackface number, "Two-Faced Woman," in full-body makeup. At the end, she tears off her wig in a fury, so that her orange hair tops the dark skin as her eyes and teeth flash wildly.

By the time of *Johnny Guitar*, then, Crawford's image was almost wholly transformed into that of a domineering shrew, jealous of women and competitive with men. Publicity for *Johnny Guitar* reinforced this image and provided a subtext for the film's antagonism between Vienna and Emma. Aside from the Monroe incident, Crawford had always been treated well by the press. But during the filming of *Johnny Guitar* the press viciously attacked her, claiming that her behavior on the set was unprofessional and erratic and that she was bullying her costar, Mercedes McCambridge. Newspapers in Phoenix and Los Angeles, as well as *Confidential* magazine, reported feuding on the set. Crawford reportedly announced, "I wouldn't trust her [McCambridge] as far as I could throw a battleship." Sterling Hayden jumped into the fray saying he would never work with Crawford again due to her treatment of McCambridge; and he added, "There is one thing about Crawford you must admire: her ability to create a myth, a legend about herself." His wife declared, "Joan Crawford hates all women, except those who can help her." [32] If Crawford had created a myth about herself as a woman's star, by the time of *Johnny Guitar*'s release, that myth was effectively destroyed.

There Was Never a Man like My Johnny,
like the One They Call Johnny Guitar

We can only understand the camp effect of *Johnny Guitar* by examining the interrelationship between star vehicle and genre. Usually when we talk about the relation between star vehicle and genre, we assume a comfortable fit—a John Wayne western, a Chaplin comedy, a Gene Kelly musical. But in a case where star vehicle and genre seem incongruent, as in a Joan Crawford Western, an analysis of the dissonance created by the juxtaposition of star and genre can be extremely productive. Analyzing the uncomfortable fit between star vehicle and genre will not create coherence in *Johnny Guitar* but will help to explain why it is incoherent and what the appeal, feminist and antifeminist, of that incoherence might be.

Most academic criticism of *Johnny Guitar* downplays not only Crawford's starring role but also, significantly, the centrality and the kinky eroticism of the relationship between the film's chief protagonists, Vienna (Crawford) and Emma (McCambridge). The film's narrative emerges out of the relationship between these two women; they announce in their first encounter what the options for the film's denouement will be: "I'm going to kill you," Emma tells Vienna, who responds, "I know, if I don't kill you first." At the end, as the male characters—including the eponymic hero, Johnny Guitar (Hayden)—drop out of the action to let Vienna and Emma shoot it out, McIvers (Ward Bond) excuses the members of Emma's posse from further duty, saying, "It's their fight. Has been all along." Yet "their fight" has, in academic criticism, been primarily treated as a secondary characteristic of the film.

For critics committed to the auteur theory, for instance, the female plot has played second fiddle to the genius of the auteur, director Nicholas Ray. Ray himself, asked what he thought were the major innovations of *Johnny Guitar*, pointed to the film's aestheticism, as the first color film to use color to its full potential, as well as its being "the first Hollywood Western where women were both the major protagonists and antagonists": "It contains quite a few psychological innovations. Men can be seen as cowards and stupid. Women can be seen as leaders."[33] Auteurist readings of *Johnny Guitar* acknowledge the film's aestheticism. François Truffaut claimed, for instance, that the film's qualities "cannot possibly be seen by anyone who has never ventured a look through a camera eyepiece."[34] With respect to narrative, however, auteurist critics privilege the character of Johnny Guitar over the female characters, placing his story within the larger context of Ray's rebels without causes, and equating him with such figures as Dixon Steele of *In a Lonely Place* (1950), Bowie of *They Live by Night* (1948) and Jim of *Rebel Without a Cause* (1955).

For the auteurists, Johnny's famous "I'm a stranger here myself" crystallizes Ray's central preoccupation; accordingly, the film is interpreted as the story of a man's struggle and alienation. Truffaut, for example, asserts that all of Ray's films "tell the same story": "The story of a violent man who wants to stop being violent, and his relationship with a woman who has more moral strength than himself."[35] Jacques Rivette similarly generalizes about Ray's output: "Everything always proceeds from a simple situation where two or three people encounter some elementary and fundamental concepts of life.

And the real struggle takes place in only one of them, against the interior demon of violence, or of a more secret sin, which seems linked to man and his solitude." Making clear that "man" here is not the generic for "human," Rivette, like Truffaut, emphasizes the supporting role of the woman: "It may happen sometimes that a woman saves him; it even seems that she alone can have the power to do so; we are a long way from misogyny." [36] Not surprisingly, in auteurist readings, the most striking feature of Johnny Guitar is "the inaction of its hero"; [37] the actions of its heroines are almost entirely suppressed in a critical framework that does not seem to be very far from misogyny at all.

Auteur theory definitionally downplays genre to posit a unique directorial authorship that marks each film in the director's canon, transcending generic constraints; in other words, auteurists link Johnny Guitar to Ray's other films rather than to other Westerns. In contrast, genre theorists generally treat the film as an extreme instance of late, self-reflective Westerns, as a self-conscious critique and hybridization of the genre. Discussing Johnny Guitar, genre theorists usually qualify the generic category, "Western," with "noir," "psychoanalytic," or "intellectual." While genre theorists acknowledge the "strong whiff of erotic perversity" [38] when women take the center stage, analyses of Johnny Guitar as a self-conscious Western do not make it clear how the film comments on the Western as form or how this self-reflexivity relates to the women's roles. Insofar as the film represents a hybrid genre of the Western with some other category, the latter is conceived in exclusively masculine terms—whether the tough guy genre film noir, the "science" of psychoanalysis, or intellectualism, usually considered the "masculine" counterpart to "feminine" feelings. Having a female protagonist may parodically undermine the masculinity of the genre, but genre theory, with its emphasis on formal codes, and without a recognition of the influence of the woman's film, cannot account for the full impact and potential self-reflexivity of a female star's role. Consequently, the predominant female presence in Johnny Guitar is treated as little more than another aberration in the realm of generic expectation.

Leo Charney's essay on Johnny Guitar argues that the film needs to be understood not solely in terms of its production, as an auteurist work or a failed Western, but also in its broader sociopolitical context. He mobilizes the trope of containment to describe 1950s policies in foreign and domestic affairs—encompassing the Cold War and McCarthyist containment of Soviet communism at home and abroad, as well as more subtle forms of containment with respect to sex and gender roles. In American films of the fifties, "containment describes both the film's formal mechanism and its larger social context." According to Charney, "Everything conspires against restraint: territory expands, time recurs, genre bends, sex roles fluctuate, and, above all, socio-political realities mix allegorically into the fictional tapestry"; and, therefore, *Johnny Guitar* manifests the "dialogue between containment and excess."[39]

As Charney explains, the film's depiction of mob mentality through its representation of the posse allegorizes McCarthyism to explore blacklisting's roots. In the film's most clear-cut reference to McCarthyist tactics, Emma and McIvers force Turkey, a member of the Dancing Kid's gang, to "name names" in a bank holdup. "The truth, son, that's all we want," McIvers implores. Then Emma tells him which truth to tell, "Just tell us she was one of ya, Turkey, and you'll go *free!*" The film's "canny casting" further allegorizes McCarthyism, particularly Hollywood blacklisting. Sterling Hayden, "named names" and then spent the rest of his career recanting his own informing. As Johnny, a man who has renounced his past and his former name (Johnny Logan), his "first chance" to redeem himself comes when he rescues Vienna from the lynch mob. Ward Bond's portrayal of McIvers, the wealthy landowner who sets his own laws and, along with Emma, leads the posse, self-reflexively refers to his role as "a founding member of the Motion Picture Alliance for the Preservation of Ideals, which took it upon itself to 'clear' the names of industry figures."[40]

In addition to these explicit references to McCarthyist witch-hunts, Charney claims that the women's roles in *Johnny Guitar* also manifest the tropes of excess and containment. First, as an unwanted intruder into Emma and McIvers's territory, Vienna evokes a spatial and ideological threat; and Vienna's fluctuations between "masculine" and "feminine" costumes and behavior represent threats to the stability and containment of gender roles. In addition, Emma's over-the-top hysteria and neurotic vengeance represent an excess that, in the terms of trickle-down fifties Freudianism, stems from too much containment—she represents the stereotype of the repressed spinster, externalizing and projecting her drives onto others whom she seeks to destroy. Charney usefully analyzes these aspects of *Johnny Guitar*, and I will return to the issues of gender bending and to Emma's characterization as neurotic. However, Charney's analysis enacts its own strategy of containment, insisting that the film ultimately succeeds in keeping "both women and excess in their place."

Charney claims that the film's narrative and enunciatory strategies grant the spotlight to the plot of Johnny Guitar. First, the film's title frames the narrative; then, the film opens with a shot of Johnny alone, followed by a series of Johnny's privileged point-of-view shots of the stagecoach holdup and of Vienna's saloon; and finally, the film returns to this initial frame. Vienna ends up in Johnny's arms as the nondiegetic song "Johnny Guitar" reminds us whose story this is: "The film's clear closure . . . tips the balance of the film's gender tensions, structurally subordinating the female plot to the reaffirmed masculinity of Johnny Guitar."[41] By this account, the film's excess is contained, virtually boxed in, by the narrative frame. Johnny's privileged position at the opening and close of the film masculinizes the plot, effectively eradicating the tensions produced by the feminine plot and narrative excess inside the film.

Although Charney suggests deeply complicated and contradictory aspects of the depiction of women in the film, his explanation of the relation between the film's context and the role of women is ultimately too limited to account for these complexities. Charney curtails his assessment of the film's gender bending with a description of "postwar sex roles . . . a period in which expectations of American women hung between their replacement of male workers during the war and their reversal to 'homemaking' afterwards."[42] The film's gender bending certainly needs to be understood in relation to the ideology of domestic satisfaction. In addition, however, the film's gender bending needs to be contextualized within Crawford's career. The "canny casting" of the film not only utilizes references to Hollywood blacklisting but also, and even more importantly, to Crawford's star text, which embodies exactly this contradiction between female success and expectations about women's roles.

We need to examine how Crawford's star text contributes to the film, and, by analyzing her role in the film, to determine what, if anything, is the residual power and attraction of the outmoded figure of dissatisfaction she represents. The film's gender reversal, Vienna's gender fluctuations, and Emma's hysteria all reflect a concern with female sexuality, and, in coded terms, with lesbianism, which was explicitly linked to communism in McCarthyist politics, a subtext we cannot ignore if we are to assess the film's gender politics.

Charney's analysis of Johnny Guitar provides a crucial understanding of the film's ideological strategies; but we need to reverse the direction of Charney's argument to note not only how certain strategies aim to contain excess, but also how certain marks of excess undermine the film's narrative strategies of containment. The excess that has no name in Charney's argument, and in most academic criticism of Johnny Guitar, is camp. To assert that the film's excess is contained by narrative and enunciatory strategies is to deny the film's camp appeal. Consistent with Sontag's "good because it's awful" criterion for camp objects, *Johnny Guitar* is camp because it is a fundamentally incoherent text, both a failed Western and an awkward star vehicle, which reflects a set of early-1950s ambivalences about female sexuality. Camp operates in the film both as a strategy of containment and as a mark of excess. Just as the film can be read as both an enactment and a critique of McCarthyism, it can be read as both an enactment and a critique of the suppression of women and excess.

When we claim that a text is available for a camp reading, we assume that there is an equally available, "normal," reading and that the camp interpretation goes against the grain of the text's presumed objective. In the case of *Johnny Guitar*, however, the "normal" reading is absent, recognizable only in the film's "failure"—as genre film or as star vehicle. By examining how the film "fails" and thereby creates its camp effect, we can see how it seeks to contain women; and by acknowledging the text's camp qualities, we can potentially read the excess and the contradictions of the female roles in the film at the expense of the containment and the presumed resolution of the contradictions.

That Curious Composite Animal

Taken as a star vehicle, *Johnny Guitar* certainly relies upon thematic and stylistic features that are keyed to the presence of Joan Crawford. Vienna captures residual qualities of Crawford's early career. Once a showgirl in a saloon, Vienna, much like Mildred Pierce, has effected a rapid rise in status, becoming the owner of a gambling house; and she is on the verge of even greater wealth with the imminent arrival of the railroad to town. Her rise in material wealth coincides with a perceived class rise. Emma complains that the men of the town act "like she's some fine lady." As in the fallen woman films, her ascent entails a "fall," in this case liaisons with a number of men, each of whom has presumably provided a portion of her wealth. And Vienna, like her 1930s precursors, remains unashamed of her transgressions. "I'm not ashamed of how I got what I have," she says. "The important thing is I've got it." She dismantles the double standard that would punish her for her transgressions: "A man can lie, steal, and even kill. All a woman has to do is slip—once—and she's a tramp." However, Vienna also contains emergent aspects of Crawford's camp persona—which in this film are encoded as masculinizing tendencies, inappropriate for a woman. On the one hand, characteristics of Crawford's early star text are incorporated in order to be rendered outmoded, as Crawford herself has been in becoming camp. On the other hand, fans familiar with Crawford's early star image may sympathetically identify with the conflict between female success and expectations about appropriate female behavior in the film, recognizing and resisting an effort to contain female independence in the camp excess of her masculinization. *Johnny Guitar* thus acknowledges the residual power and attraction of the Crawford persona while attempting to undermine it.

Although the importance of Crawford's star image should not be overlooked, the camp effect of Crawford's role in *Johnny Guitar* differs somewhat from that of her other camp films, and this difference has to do with genre. Crawford made a few Westerns in her career (*The Law of the Range* [1928], *Montana Moon* [1930]) before she made the transition to the woman's films of the 1930s. But *Johnny Guitar* is her first and only Western after she is linked with the woman's film. It departs from the model of her other camp films, all of which can still be loosely categorized as woman's films, although they combine features of the horror film and/or the backstage drama. This film negotiates features of the star vehicle and woman's film with those of the Western to create its camp effect. The intervention of Crawford's star text into the masculine genre of the Western helps dismantle the film's phallic economy. In addition, the anachronistic insertion of the decidedly urban and twentieth-century type Crawford represents into a rural nineteenth-century setting exaggerates the anachronism of this figure in 1950s suburban America.

Charney observes that newspaper and magazine reviewers were unanimous in their distaste for *Johnny Guitar*, locating the film's failure in the realm of genre expectation and using genre as a vehicle of containment for the film's excess. What is striking about the reviews, however, is how excessive the language of these reviews are and the large degree to which they are *about* excess. Although they sometimes suggest that the film fails as a Western, more often they suggest that the film parodies the Western by hyperbolically inverting its codes. Unlike the academic auteurist- and genre-oriented strategies of containment that assert the primacy of the masculine plot over the feminine excess, contemporary reviewers acknowledged that the film's narrative and enunciatory emphasis on Johnny Guitar does not ultimately work. Most reviews refer obliquely, but quite clearly, to the film's unintentional camp effect, describing a successful camp object by detailing the effects of what they consider to be an awful Western. *Catholic World*, for example, finds *Johnny Guitar* "unintentionally hilarious," and Virginia Graham calls it "a parody of itself," which "gives a perverted pleasure" to "this poor unsuspecting film."[43]

Reviewers emphasized the importance of Crawford's star text, the female plot, melodramatic acting styles, and Freudianism as important aspects of its genre bending. Many reviews attribute the film's parodic effect to its feminization of the genre. The New Yorker, for instance, labels it "the maddest western you are likely to encounter this year," because "it has not only male but female gunfighters . . . [and] derives its title from the name of a pal of Miss Crawford's, who functions as her defender—a supererogatory post if ever there was one."[44] Moira Walsh's review in America calls Johnny Guitar "a king-size, adult Western designed as a vehicle for Joan Crawford": "Perhaps to buttress further the picture's backhanded tribute to feminine initiative, her chief adversary is also female, a uniquely psychopathic newspaperwoman (overplayed to the point of burlesque by Mercedes McCambridge). . . . Most of them are twice as large as life and three times as ridiculous, and the unfortunate males . . . are given short shrift by the script."[45] In both these reviews, the feminization of the genre undermines the role of men, who are contained, rendered useless, by the excessive power of the women. In particular, they question the titular hero's role. Rather than seeing Johnny as the center of the film, they rightfully emphasize "feminine initiative." The "king-size" characters are Vienna and Emma, not the "unfortunate" and "supererogatory" Johnny.

In expressing their disdain for the intrusion of psychoanalysis into the genre, some critics underline the blurring of gender boundaries and sexual identities in the film. Variety writes, "Had the makers played it straight it would have been much better entertainment for the masses."[46] Rather than playing it "straight," the makers "become so involved with character nuances and neuroses, all wrapped up in dialog [sic], that Johnny Guitar never has enough chance to rear up in the saddle and ride at an acceptable outdoor pace."[47] Time emphasizes the film's hybrid quality as a "crossbreeding of the Western with a psychoanalytic case history" and suggests that this mixed breed is something like a third sex: "Johnny Guitar is one of those curious composite animals, like the tiglon, the hippolope and the peccadillo, that most people would rather talk about than see."[48] Time makes clear that the "curious composite animal" is not merely a crossbred genre but a confusion of sex and gender roles. The review refers to the camp and potentially gay effect of Crawford's confrontation with the posse: "[D]ressed to the nines in a Paris gown," playing the grand piano, she seems like "a cowtown Liberace."

The excessive language and attempts at categorization in these reviews reflect a nervousness that can be interpreted as an effort to contain excess through a form of mocking. Psychoanalysis represents an unwanted intrusion into the Western, presumably a wholly external ("outdoor") genre,

which should not be contaminated by signs of interiority or the uncon-
scious. However, rather than a nervousness about genre, these critics are pre-
occupied with the boundaries of sex and gender roles. The camp effect they
delineate and attempt to contain, which they tag "psychoanalysis," depends
upon the masculinization and potential lesbianism of the female characters,
who are coded as such by their embodiment of a mixture of psychoanalytic
stereotypes, including the castrating/phallic woman and the neurotic spinster.

The stereotypes of the castrating woman and the neurotic spinster symbolized the two extreme poles of women's failures to live up to the ideal
female image promulgated in the 1950s. As Friedan argues, the feminine mystique derived its power, in large part, from a misinterpretation of Freudian
thought. Under the ideology of the mystique, a literal interpretation of
Freud's notion of penis envy was used to explain away female ambition, and,
therefore, to promulgate a negative image of the castrating woman. In addition, functionalism, influenced by Margaret Mead's interpretation of Freud,
emphasized women's reproductive role as the essential determining factor in
sexual difference and female identity—hence, the stereotype of the neurotic
spinster, resistant to her "natural" role.[49]

Between the end of World War II and the early 1960s, "the historical
conjuncture of social problems, the difficulty of gender roles, and the institutions of American psychoanalysis and psychiatry became an obsession
of the media."[50] A number of films during this period (e.g., Crawford's *Possessed* [1947]) took women and psychotherapy as their explicit subject matter.
Although *Johnny Guitar* does not take psychoanalysis or psychotherapy as its
overt subject matter, critics of the film do not seem far from the mark when
they complain about the intrusion of psychoanalysis into the film. The film
invokes psychoanalysis in its use of stereotypes familiar to the American
public from the popularization of psychoanalysis, and particularly Freudianism, in films, television, and even comic books of the time.

In part, the discourse of psychoanalysis functions as an additional strategy
of containment in the film. In *Johnny Guitar*, the invocation of psychoanalysis
is felt most strongly in the characterizations of the two women, Vienna and
Emma, singularly and in relation to each other. As I noted above, Vienna can
be characterized as a stereotypical castrating or phallic woman. Emma, too,
can be read as castrating—her wealth enables her to dictate actions to the
men of the town. If Vienna's problem is that she is simultaneously too masculine and too sexually transgressive, Emma's is that she is not woman (i.e.,
not sexual) enough. Vienna analyzes the roots of Emma's hostility toward

her: "She's in love with the Kid. He makes her feel like a woman and that frightens her." As Charney claims, Emma's neurotic desire for vengeance is that of the repressed spinster. These stereotypes function in the film to contain, label, and punish the female characters. But, as contemporary reviews suggest, the "neuroses" of these female characters point not simply to a reversal of sex roles but also to a blurring of gender and sex boundaries.

What if You're Cruel, You Can Be Kind, I Know

If, as I have argued, the "normal" reading of *Johnny Guitar*'s "failure" is always already available to a camp reading, it is because the film pushes its strategies of containment too hard, blurring the very boundaries it aims to delineate by exaggerating psychoanalytic stereotypes to the point of parody. By forcing the dominant ideology about female sexuality, the film distorts that ideology such that it creates dissonance, reflecting an ambivalence about female sexuality. Whether intentionally or not, the heavy-handed effort to signify the masculinization of Emma and Vienna ultimately fails to contain them and instead makes them markers of camp excess, who represent not simply the stereotypes of the neurotic spinster and castrating female but also the psychotic and mannish lesbian, respectively. In particular, McCambridge's melodramatic acting style and Crawford's costumes are both coded in such a way as to open a space for a feminist camp reading of the film, most apparent to lesbians, but potentially registering more broadly for all female spectators. This subverts the film's strategies of containment and weakens the terms of the film's phallic economy.

If Emma seems "uniquely psychopathic," it is due to McCambridge's melodramatic performance. When one witnesses the devilishly psychotic traits she brings to Emma, it is no surprise that McCambridge was asked to dub in the devil's voice in *The Exorcist*. Whether speaking with a halting, almost automatic inflection, fondling her pistol, skipping giddily after torching her rival's saloon, or galloping off to a lynching with her mourning veil flying away behind her, McCambridge's Emma is a woman possessed. But what desire possesses her? Presumably, her repressed desire for the Dancing Kid. But she directs all her manic energy and enmity toward a former dancing lady, Crawford's Vienna.

In Roy Chanslor's novel *Johnny Guitar*, Emma Small is the "sharp-nosed wife" of Leonard Small.[51] Unhappy in her marriage, Emma decides to leave Small; but before she does, Turkey, a member of the Dancing Kid's gang, kills him. Guilt-ridden, she transfers her guilt onto Vienna and Johnny Guitar and initiates her quest for vengeance. In the film, Emma is a spinster and her antagonism toward Vienna is presumably motivated by her repressed attraction toward the Dancing Kid. In making Emma a spinster, the film-makers turn her quest for vengeance into the chief sign of imbalance in a jealous and repressed woman. At the same time, her status as an unmarried woman in a family-centered town makes her available to be read both as an unmarriageable (because repressed) woman and as a closet lesbian.

While Emma can be considered the embodiment of the lonely spinster, the sensationalist characterization of Emma's twisted and psychotic mind also reflects stereotypical 1950s images of sick or evil lesbians, who lived in shame and self-hatred. These images were circulated in "cautionary" pulp novels, mass-circulation magazines, and government literature that converged in the fifties as part of a concerted public effort to control and contain lesbianism. The 1953 Kinsey report claimed a high incidence of lesbian activity (28 percent of American women were said to have "homosexual tendencies"), while the persecution of lesbians became part of the McCarthyist witch-hunts. Most notably, lesbians were routed out of military and government jobs. The Republican floor leader, asked why the Senate wanted to dismiss lesbians from government jobs, explained, "You can't hardly separate homosexuals from subversives." [52] This provides a subtext for understanding the relation between gender and McCarthyism in the film, as well as a more complicated sense of the film's dialogue between excess and containment.

I do not mean to suggest that Emma is "really" a lesbian but rather suggest that lesbians might have been able to decode her representation as a negative yet subversive image of lesbianism. The film historically has had a lesbian following. For instance, the lesbian feminist video Dry Kisses Only samples and redoes the "If I don't kill you" exchange between Vienna and Emma to become "If I don't kiss you first" (dir. Jane Cottis and Kaucyila Brooke, 1990). I am suggesting that this reading was available at the time of the film's release. On the surface, 1950s images of lesbians, most exaggerated in the pulp novels, tended to confirm social prejudices against lesbians. But lesbians read the pulp novels avidly. Hungry for images of women loving women, lesbians were able to read between the lines, putting up with propaganda for the sake of eroticism. [53]

After Vienna accuses Emma of being in love with the Dancing Kid, the Kid grabs Emma for a spin around the dance floor. Michael Wilmington describes Emma's reaction as "tense, flailing backward, hand cupped to mouth" and calls it "a mime of repression so fragile and awkward it hurts." [54] One can infer from this scene that Emma, embarrassed and frightened by her pleasure in the Kid's attention, repels precisely what she desires. At the same time, it is possible to read her gestures as genuine horror at being in the arms of a man. Furthermore, dialogue conflates the Kid and Vienna as objects of Emma's attraction-repulsion. For instance, Vienna says, "You want the Kid and you're so ashamed of it you want him dead. And you want me dead, too. Then maybe you can sleep nights." If desire keeps Emma awake at night, her desire extends to Vienna as well as the Kid. Emma herself claims of Vienna and the Kid, "They both cast the same shadow." As Wilmington notes, Emma's remark "carries the same poisonous undertones as Iago's prurient metaphor, 'the beast with two backs.' " [55] But, in Emma's case, the repository of her imagination may be less an image of two persons coupling than of a couple of people, both of whom she wants and wants dead.

Crawford's costumes in *Johnny Guitar* similarly tip the scales of gender bending to suggest a lesbian subtext. As Gaines and Herzog argue, referring to the "clothes-horse" phase of Crawford's career at MGM, "both the sheer number of costumes and the look of expense were important to Crawford's promotion." Clothing reflected changes in Crawford's career, and women were encouraged to copy her style as part of their identification with her.[56] Even describing her as a camp grotesque, Philip Core calls her a "couture dummy." [57] Indicating that Crawford's fans in the 1950s would still be interested in her costumes, *Newsweek* summed up its review of *Johnny Guitar* with the comment that "Joan Crawford shapes up well in her Levi's." [58]

Rebecca Bell-Metereau argues that Vienna combines in her costuming features of the Western's tomboyish cowgirls and ultrafeminine prostitutes.[59] But, whereas the cowgirl gets tamed by putting on a dress to have sex appeal, Crawford alternates between masculine and feminine attire with ease. Charney observes, "More purely androgynous than Emma, Vienna can adopt femininity as easily as masculinity, depending on need." [60] In part, Vienna's alternations reflect strictly codified sex roles. She wears extremely masculine costumes when she wields her "masculine" power—in the saloon, as she lays down the law for both her men and the townspeople, and when she confronts and kills Emma at the end. In contrast, when she lets Johnny seduce her, she wears a sexy red negligee, and on "the morning after" she wears a tailored but feminine dress. However, she wears her most frilly and feminine outfit, a white gown with puffed sleeves (much like her famous Adrian *Letty Lynton* dress), to greet the lynch mob and bravely face her imminent death. And, at the end, when she and Johnny kiss under a waterfall, she wears Turkey's jeans and shirt. For a lesbian audience, Crawford's alternation between "masculine" and "feminine" costumes in *Johnny Guitar* may have reflected less a masculine/feminine dichotomy than one between butch and femme.

Crawford's masculine costumes, in concert with the erotic antagonism between Vienna and Emma, could be read as the habiliments of what Esther Newton refers to as "the mythic mannish lesbian," the cross-gendered/cross-dressed figure who became the public symbol of the lesbian.[61] More accurately, she represents the "butch" lesbian, an anachronistic term for the film's nineteenth-century setting, but one which I use because it belongs to the 1950s—a figure defined as lesbian because her behavior and/or dress manifest elements designated as masculine. Not coincidentally, the McCarthyist persecution of lesbians was concurrent with the formation of lesbian subcultures, including urban working-class lesbian bars where lesbians could act out butch-femme roles.[62]

The film's dialogue, riddled with double entendre, advances a reading of the film in terms of butch-femme role-play. When the townspeople first accuse Vienna of being part of the Dancing Kid's gang, a showdown occurs with Vienna on the stairs, blocking entrance to her bedroom: "All you can buy up these stairs is a bullet in the head." Emma intones, "That's big talk for a little gun." This sexual innuendo could be seen as simultaneously imparting a phallus to Vienna and robbing her of it, by pointing out that it is only a phallic symbol, a little gun, thus emphasizing Vienna's inappropriate masculinization. At the same time, the remark could be taken as making an oblique reference to the clitoris, understood in Freudian terms as a "small penis," more suggestive of butch femininity than masculinization. Later, the marshal urges Vienna to choose whether to side with the law or the Kid, telling her, "You can't stay on the fence no longer." For a viewer already attuned to the lesbian subtext, the fences Vienna straddles would be not merely those between the law and the Kid but also those between masculine and feminine, between butch and femme, and between heterosexuality and homosexuality.

Some have argued that butch-femme roles are modeled on heterosexual sex roles. And butch style has been taken as a negative stereotype of the lesbian as a man trapped in a woman's body. Because, however, Vienna alternates between "butch" and "femme," she seems to play with gender and sex roles, never fully inhabiting either a masculine or feminine persona. I want to retain the term "butch," rather than "masculinized" or "tomboyish," to counter the sense that Vienna's appropriation of masculine accoutrements reflects a desire to be a man or a failure to be a woman. The anachronistic reading of butch style into a nineteenth-century frontier setting helps distance us from the film's equally anachronistic imposition of the 1950s stereotype of the castrating woman as nemesis to the happy housewife. Because Vienna is, after all, despite innuendo, marked as a heterosexual, her gender bending, unlike Emma's, can be read as a parodic form of masquerade.

Sue-Ellen Case claims that the butch-femme couple consciously play out the masquerade in "a discourse of camp":

> The butch is the lesbian woman who proudly displays the possession of the penis, while the femme takes on the compensatory masquerade of womanliness. The femme, however, foregrounds her masquerade by playing to a butch, another woman in a role; likewise, the butch exhibits her penis to a woman who is playing the role of compensatory castration. This raises the question of "penis, penis, who's got the penis," because there is no referent in sight; rather, the fictions of penis and castration become ironized and "camped up." Unlike Riviere's patient, these women play on the phallic economy rather than to it.[63]

Since Vienna occupies butch and femme images in alternation, even when engaged in homoerotic play with Emma, her costumes foreground the masquerade. Her costumes represent social identities rather than sexual identities. Most noticeably, when Vienna confronts the lynch mob in her frilly gown, she plays the role of the "fine lady" that the townspeople imagine her to be in order to diffuse their anger: "I'm sitting here in my own house, minding my own business, playing my own piano." Vienna's costumes resist the codification of the antifeminist psychoanalytic stereotypes that the film seemingly promotes; her masquerade plays on lesbian stereotypes to disengage the viewer from the dominant ideology's insistence on rigid sex and gender boundaries.

My point in underlining the lesbian and butch-femme aesthetic in *Johnny Guitar* is not solely to acknowledge a lesbian reading of the film. Instead, I suggest that a lesbian reading of the film helps deconstruct the tropes of containment in the film and serves as an analytic tool as well as a source of potential pleasure for female and feminist spectators. Although butch-femme role-play is unique to gay subcultures, Case suggests that the butch-femme aesthetic provides the strong subject position that feminism requires—a feminist subject who is more knowing and active than the female subject—a position that affirms the overlapping interests of straight and lesbian women.

While a lesbian audience may have had privileged access to this reading, I believe that the ambivalences about female sexuality created here could have translated to all women, especially to those who felt uncomfortable or out of place in the culture of the mystique (and who didn't?). In the film's conflict between its narrative strategies of containment and its marks of excess in performance style and mise-en-scène, between, in other words, its antifeminist representations and the lesbian encoding of those representations, women, lesbian and straight, may have been able to create an alternative and oppositional reading. Just as the film can be seen as two-sided, adhering to the ideology of the mystique on one side and exploding the terms of that mystique on the other, I believe that the response of female viewers could be two-sided—that female viewers could simultaneously identify with the film's antifeminist message and laugh at it. Perhaps in the film's incoherence, female viewers could recognize the mystique as a form of masquerade, as a role that they could choose to adopt or not.

Rather than attempting to rescue Crawford or *Johnny Guitar* from camp, I have attempted to locate the possibility for both a feminist reading of camp and a reading of what I call feminist camp. By analyzing Crawford's placement in the historical phenomenon of gay camp, I have shown how camp dissolves a contradiction in her star text between notions of success and expectations about women's roles into a negative image of artificiality and hard professionalism. But reading *Johnny Guitar* as feminist camp suggests that the film's "failure" as a Western and its strategies of containment might represent a successful critique of the dominant 1950s ideology concerning women's roles. While the first camp reading operates to contain Vienna, and Crawford, as masculinized and therefore undesirable, the second feminist camp reading undermines these patriarchal terms. If taken as playing to the phallic economy, Vienna's masculinization personifies the negative stereotype of the castrating female. But, if we read her butch-femme alternations as androgynous and flexible, as playing on the phallic economy to ironize it, we see that sometimes a guitar is just a guitar and ultimately it doesn't matter who wears the pants in the family. As Emma says, "that's big talk for a little gun."

F O U R

Does Feminist Camp

Make a Difference? or, What

We Talk about When

We Talk about Madonna

Madonna's *Veronica Lake* pose in the *"Vogue"* music video.
Video frame enlargement (author's collection).

B eginning with the appearance of her first singles and music videos over a decade ago, Madonna has been a more consistent subject of public debate than virtually any other entertainer in history. She has graced countless magazine covers, ranging from *Vanity Fair* and *Rolling Stone* to *Fortune* and the *National Review*, and has become a fixture in national newspaper editorials and gossip columns. She has appeared on many talk shows, including a memorable 1990 appearance on ABC's *Nightline* with Forrest Sawyer and two notorious appearances on David Letterman's late night show. She has been the subject of a TV movie-of-the-week and a feature length documentary, *Truth or Dare* (which was in turn the object of one-hour-long cable TV parody by Julie Brown and another half-hour parody on the TV show *Blossom*). In addition to numerous biographies and picture books of Madonna, and her own book *Sex*, there is a Madonna comic book, a book of women's dreams about Madonna, even an "I Hate Madonna" handbook.[1] Madonna is as ubiquitous in academic discourse as she is in the popular media. Already the subject of numerous academic essays in the mid-1980s, three collections of essays published in 1993—one devoted exclusively to Madonna's book *Sex*—cemented the institutionalization of a major subdivision of American media studies into Madonna studies.[2]

As Steven Anderson already noted in 1989, the glut of debates revolving around Madonna run the gamut of concerns about the nature of contemporary society itself:

> The tidal wave of Madonna's renown has swept over adulaters and detractors. Once a flesh-and-blood superstar, she's now a metaphysic unto herself. Not that she doesn't have feelings, desires, or stomach gas, but she's achieved such ineffable "being-ness" that old controversies—is she Pop incarnate? Glamorized Fuckdoll?—are largely irrelevant. The only aspect left to consider is Madonna's resonance in the minds of the public, for whom—like it or not—she's become a repository for all our ideas about fame, money, sex, feminism, pop culture, even death.[3]

Anderson suggests that "old controversies" about Madonna are dead; but her "resonance" in the public sphere, while serving as a "repository" for ideas about other matters, still manifests itself in replays of these very controversies. For instance, making a joke about the prevalence of opinions about Madonna in all strata of society, jewelry thieves in Quentin Tarantino's *Reservoir Dogs* argue if "Like A Virgin" is about "big dick" or female desire. Hal Hartley's *Simple Men*, similarly, features generally laconic characters engaged in an extended discussion of whether Madonna's self-exploitation is exploitative. And, in academia, feminists query whether Madonna represents parody or pastiche, a healthy break from essentialism or a rejection of traditional feminist concerns. A hall-of-mirrors effect occurs in the construction of Madonna's star text: media attention fuels academic discourse, which in turn fuels media discourse, and ultimately all becomes a part of "Madonna." Rather than ask "Can pop culture be critical of society?" or "What is the meaning of feminism today?" cultural critics ask "Is Madonna a glamorized fuckdoll or the queen of parodic critique? Pop incarnate or an artist/provocateur?"

If Madonna serves as the repository for our ideas about "fame, money, sex, feminism, pop culture, even death," those ideas are filtered primarily through academic and media discussions about the political effectiveness of gender parody and the manipulation of negative stereotypes. The "controversies" Madonna generates echo, in short, controversies about the value and appeal of camp. Thus, a February 1993 item in the *New Yorker* announces, "Camp is dead, thanks to Madonna."[4] The article, a brief review of a drag show, proclaims that "gender tripping can't be subversive anymore" because Madonna "has opened all the closets, turning deviance into a theme park." On the one hand, the article signals the prominence and accessibility of the discourse of camp in the eighties and early nineties—related to the mainstreaming of the spectacle of drag culture symbolized by, among other things, the much hyped "secret" of *The Crying Game*, the popularity of video "queen" RuPaul, *Paris Is Burning*, and *The Adventures of Priscilla, Queen of the Desert*, as well as Madonna's use of drag and vogueing in her videos and tours. On the other hand, by hanging such a quick assessment of the condition of camp on the signifier "Madonna," the article also underscores that Madonna's status in the public mind has come to be that of unique author of gender bending, parody, and female masquerade.

Madonna, clearly, did not invent feminist camp nor has she effected any major changes in the production of feminist camp. The open secret of the Madonna phenomenon is that, in large part, it and she are astonishingly uninteresting and unoriginal. As Russell Baker cogently assesses, "Madonna isn't the cultural elite. . . . She's just Mae West for yuppies."[5] She engages in forms of female masquerade and gender parody similar to those of West in the 1930s, who was herself imitating nineteenth-century burlesque and female impersonation. Like West, she foregrounds her identifications with both African American and gay male culture. Her play with drag and gender bending can be traced to lesbian idols Dietrich and Garbo. Her "Boy Toy" and "Material Girl" personae revitalize the knowing masquerade of countless gold diggers from the 1920s, 1930s, and 1950s. Yet no analysis of feminist camp would be complete without an acknowledgment of Madonna's role in bringing camp to the forefront in a transnational consumer society. While aiming to inscribe Madonna in an ongoing tradition of feminist camp, I suggest that Madonna's *difference* from previous instances of feminist camp, including West, has to do with the changing meaning of camp from the 1960s to the present. As Baker suggests, Madonna is not just Mae West but Mae West for *yuppies*. If the stuff of camp has not changed significantly since West, what has changed is the context in which camp is produced, how it is consumed, and who consumes it.

Camp has undergone two important changes since the 1960s to become a more overt, more public sensibility, and a mainstream fashion. The first is the "outing" and "heterosexualization" of camp, its virtual equation with first pop and then postmodernism, coincident with the publication of Sontag's essay. The second is a more recent shift to overtly politicized camp and radical drag, dating back to gay camp's changed status following Stonewall and the 1970s gay liberation movement, and its revitalization in the 1980s with the onset of AIDS and "queer" politics.

The first predominantly heterosexual pop and/or postmodern style of camp applies to Madonna's career as a whole — in her extraordinary self-marketing, her changing images, and her retro-cinephilia. The second, more explicitly homosexual and political style of camp inheres primarily in Madonna's explicit references to gay subcultures, especially drag and vogueing, in conjunction with her stated identification with gay men, her flirtation with lesbianism, and her AIDS charity work. In this chapter, I examine these two trajectories of camp through Madonna's star text. My aim is less to provide a history of Madonna's career than to use her as a lens through which to view post-1960s camp. In particular, I explore the debate about Madonna as a debate about camp, so as to determine what this debate tells us about the status of camp today.

Cashing in on Camp: Camp, Pop, and Postmodernism

The publication of Susan Sontag's "Notes on 'Camp'" in 1964 disseminated camp to the general populace, attracting attention in such mainstream publications as *Time*. Despite Sontag's identification of camp as a primarily gay male practice, the publicity surrounding "Notes on 'Camp'" gave the camp sensibility currency for heterosexuals, initiating what Paul Rudnick and Kurt Anderson call the "world of heterosexual camp, Camp Lite." According to Rudnick and Anderson, "The most serious woman in America gave her imprimatur to a jolly, perverse sensibility that was, back then and in the main, homosexual and male": "Sontag's essay was like a thrilling, open-ended mother's excuse note to a whole generation of gifted children: *To Whom It May Concern: Johnny has my permission to enjoy TV and Jacqueline Susann books.*"[6] In defining, if only loosely, the camp sensibility, Sontag must certainly be credited with publicizing the term among heterosexuals. In addition, by legitimating camp as a serious object of study, Sontag opened the way for 1970s gay intellectuals—including Richard Dyer, Andrew Britton, and Jack Babuscio—to engage the topic of camp, often in contention with her characterization.[7]

Sontag's influence, however, cannot be separated from the context in which her essay appeared: namely, pop art. As Andrew Ross points out, pop differs markedly from camp, because camp is the "in" taste of a minority elite, while pop "was supposed to declare that everyday cultural currency had value, and that this value could be communicated in a simple language."[8] Nevertheless, pop problematized the question of taste itself, rejecting an elitist past based on cultural acts of judgment and the notion that objects had intrinsic aesthetic value. Pop, in this sense, created a context for the mainstreaming of camp taste—justifying the democratic spirit of camp, its collapsing of high-low boundaries, while opening the sensibility up to a majority audience. In a curious twist, camp taste became the dominant code. Rather than a covert, cult sensibility, camp became a commercialized taste—and a taste for commercialism—a determinedly unguilty pleasure.

Pop, in its broadest sense, was also the context in which notions of the postmodern took shape. Outside its architectural context, the term "postmodern" is by and large a slippery and unstable signifier, defined, as Anne Friedberg notes, largely through its overusage.[9] The term serves, on the one hand, as a kind of historical marker, isolating contemporary society's explosion of technologies, mass-media fragmentation and globalization, and accelerated information access. On the other hand, the sweeping connotations of the term include discourses of style in various media, as well as theories about the period and its cultural objects. While it is tempting to abandon the term "postmodern" altogether, given its semiotic instability, the various values attached to notions of postmodernity need to be acknowledged and accounted for as part of the cultural current that shapes the discourse around contemporary notions of camp, parody, kitsch — and Madonna.

Andreas Huyssen notes the link between Robert Venturi's influential *Learning from Las Vegas* ("one of the most telling documents of the break of postmodernism with the modernist dogma") and the 1960s pop sensibility: "Time and again the authors use pop art's break with the austere canon of high modernist painting and pop's uncritical espousal of the commercial vernacular of consumer culture as an inspiration for their work. What Madison Avenue was for Andy Warhol, what the comics and the Western were for Leslie Fiedler, the landscape of Las Vegas was for Venturi and his group." [10] Venturi's celebration of Las Vegas style furthered the new camp sensibility's emphasis on the ironic, "thus pushing architecture off on its own snickery detour." [11] Ironic, but no longer parodic, camp came to be equated with postmodern pastiche, which Fredric Jameson has famously labeled "blank parody." [12]

If the mainstreaming of camp taste represents a revolution of sorts, that revolution has, in large part, been televised and televisual. Much of the public discourse on drag, vogueing, and transvestites, as well as other "gay" topics, has since the 1970s taken place on the daytime talk shows hosted by Phil Donahue, Oprah Winfrey, and others. At the same time, a form of camp cinephilia, dedicated to film trivia, the showcasing of "Bad Movies We Love" and classical Hollywood cinema, formerly the stuff of revival movie houses and midnight movies, became a frequent feature on locally syndicated stations across the United States and then on cable TV stations like TNT. Television exposed new generations of audiences to Berkeley musicals, historical camp figures like West, and cult figures like Maria Montez, thus providing an additional context for the rise of camp coextensive with Sontag's writing.

More than just serving as a medium for the "outing" of pre- and post-1960s camp, however, television has itself seemingly become the definitive reference point for the Camp Lite sensibility. The "irony epidemic," as Rudnick and Anderson describe it, filters its jokey baby-boomer ambivalence through insider references to television shows and characters from the 1950s forward as much as, if not more than, through its recycling of retro objects and fashions. This ironic sensibility, which eulogizes a fantasy of the baby boomers' American innocence through nostalgia, has its own television station in the cable network Nickelodeon. Nickelodeon's *Nick at Nite* programming, similar in spirit to midnight movies and the camp fetishization of "bad" movies, most closely captures the spirit of Camp Lite. Nick at Nite devotes itself exclusively to rebroadcasting syndicated shows from the '50s, '60s, and '70s. Not content to simply broadcast the shows, Nick at Nite underscores its ironic attitude toward them, bracketing them with promos using clips from the shows to delineate the use of triple takes and the history of amnesia plots, or subjecting the shows to mock-serious psycho-academic analysis ("What does Rob Petrie's ottoman signify?"), all in the interest of its quasi-ironic mission of "Preserving our Television Heritage." Despite its ironic jokiness, then, Nick at Nite fetishizes and collects TV trivia, promulgating a kind of nightmare vision of E. D. Hirsch's "cultural literacy" with respect to "classic TV." Beyond Nickelodeon, this nostalgia for "classic TV" has now infiltrated Hollywood, which is in the midst of a trend for "based on TV" films—including the Star Trek cycle, The Addams Family, Dragnet, The Fugitive, Boris and Natasha, Wayne's World, The Coneheads, The Flintstones, The Beverly Hillbillies, The Brady Bunch, and The Little Rascals. It can also be seen in the hip citations of "classic TV" in Dream On, Natural Born Killers, and Pulp Fiction.

Both camp's alliance with pop and its downshifting into the small screen of television could be taken as evidence of its demise. The term Camp Lite, after all, suggests a watering down of camp's critical and political edge. As Christin Mamiya argues, pop art not only drew upon the mechanisms, imagery, and ideology of consumer culture but also helped to legitimize that system: "Pop art not only depicted and reflected this rampant consumption but also appropriated the mechanisms and strategies of corporate society, ensuring the effective marketing of this movement and its absorption into the matrix of consumer institutions." [13] Due to pop's complicity with corporate society, many critics view camp's sublimation into pop as a betrayal of "true" "authentic" camp, an appropriation of a subculture by the culture industry. In a similar vein, for many critics, the mainstreaming of camp in its appropriation by the widely accessible medium of television, and in its related glorification of a television past shared by most Americans, signifies a loss of perspicuity in camp: televisual camp is no longer the province of an elite few, and the range of objects considered camp have similarly lost their specificity as marginal. Camp's relation to dominant culture, however, was always already parasitic. Rather than an avant-garde oppositional stance, camp represents a subculture's negotiated means of access to the dominant culture; it operates as much by taking alternative pleasures in mass-cultural objects as it does by creating its own objects. In this sense, it registers a subculture's recognition of failed access to and not simply a refusal of the culture industry. In legitimating both camp and consumer society, post-1960s pop camp simply makes public the consumerism already implicit in camp.

Madonna, especially in her Boy Toy and Material Girl incarnations, seemed the epitome of the newly defined camp style, embracing crass consumer culture, like pop, and updating it through new media forms. "The ultimate postmodern video star,"[14] Madonna appeared on the cultural scene simultaneously with, and depended on, the introduction of MTV, the cable television station that paradigmatically represents the postmodern explosion of technologies, acceleration of images and information, and mass-media access. Her shifting media images, borrowed largely from stereotypes and cinematic images from the past, seemingly embody the postmodern discourse of style. Madonna is most often compared to Monroe, but her sexy images borrow from other film stars, film genres, and photographic styles. For example, the video for "Open Your Heart" (dir. Mondino, 1986) has echoes of Giulietta Masina in Fellini's *Nights of Cabiria* (1957). *Who's That Girl?* (dir. Foley, 1987) updates *Bringing Up Baby* (dir. Hawks, 1938). And the video for "Vogue" (dir. Fincher, 1990) appropriates images from black-and-white 1930s glamour photography of Hollywood stars. A paradigmatic figure from the Reagan-Bush era, Madonna, moreover, typifies 1980s tropes of mobility and consumption. Resolutely commercial, and flaunting it ("we are living in a material world, and I am a material girl"), Madonna represents herself as a self-commodifying commodity for whom pastiche becomes a marketing strategy.

Joyce Millman aptly describes Madonna as "the video generation's Barbie."[15] Like Barbie, Madonna sells because, like Mattel, she continuously updates the model, making her former selves obsolete. It is not enough to own a Barbie doll, one must own the latest Barbie—Bridal Barbie, Aviation Barbie, Barbie for President, et cetera. Madonna constantly offers new models, all Madonna but each differentiated through her costume and accessories—Boy Toy Madonna, Material Girl Madonna, Thin Madonna, Madonna in Drag, S&M Madonna, and so on. Millman characterizes Barbie as "the madonna/whore complex molded into shapely plastic," reflecting, in part, "the fallout of sixties social change and the trickle down of seventies permissiveness." Madonna, similarly, portrays herself as a series of teasingly sexual female stereotypes, the Madonna/whore complex made flesh and blood. She does not just embody a pop or postmodern sensibility but takes that sensibility into the terrain of gender and sexual difference, aligning herself with some of the traditional concerns of camp.

As Ross suggests, the "outing" of camp takes hold in the culture not simply due to its affinity with pop and postmodernism but also because Sontag's essay appears in the context of sexual liberation "for which camp played a crucial role in the redefinition of masculinity and femininity."[16] Ross sees the effect of camp on mainstream popular taste in the eroticized spectacle of performance rock. Madonna has sometimes been compared to performance rock stars, especially David Bowie, because of her shifting images and play with gender roles. Gender bending in performance rock was, however, primarily a masculine privilege.[17] The "redefinition" of sex and gender roles in performance and glam rock was the province of a host of male aesthetes—David Bowie, the New York Dolls, Lou Reed, Iggy Pop, and others. In addition, the gender bending in performance rock, linked in many of the performers' star texts to suggestions of bi- and homosexuality, related more closely to drag and female impersonation than to pop or postmodernism.

While exposing camp style to a heterosexual audience, performance rock differed in spirit from the new camp, disdaining the vulgar consumerism and antielitist judgments of pop. Lisa Lewis notes an ideological division between rock and pop music similar to that between high culture and popular culture: "Rock discourse forged a hierarchy within popular music by creating a structure of value against which 'pop' music could be devalued. Rock was made to stand as a higher form . . . as the representative of art and artfulness."[18] While pop music and pop art are not identical, both embrace consumerism and are positioned as the low other to a "high" culture discourse. Performance rock defined itself in opposition to pop-music discourse and stood instead as the representative of artfulness in popular music. Madonna, in contrast, clearly embodies pop-music discourse: "Image and representation . . . are Madonna's playground. She revels in self-promotion, in the creation of an image or images, in being a personality, a celebrity. She accepts artifice as an integral feature of music production and promotion and is comfortable with textual production."[19] Although Andy Warhol influenced Bowie and Reed, his true heir is Madonna. She captures the full force of Warhol's ironic redefinition of fame and celebrity and his creation of the "superstar" (who becomes one once named).

Male performance-rock artists inhabit a quasi-romantic persona (Ziggy Stardust, Aladdin Sane), their changing images reflecting different voices. Madonna, in contrast, creates different images, the meaning of which exists at the level of style. She does not inhabit personae so much as represent them ironically: "I'm just being ironic. . . . That's the joke of it all. It's a luring device, like the whole boy-toy thing. It's playing into people's idea of what's humiliating to women."[20] In embracing pop discourse, rather than rock, and a postmodern malleability, rather than a romantic star persona, Madonna's eroticized images expose image as artifice and play on the negative connotations attached to images of women.

Some of the controversy Madonna generates has to do with her pop re-production of the lowest forms of aesthetic culture, her commercialism, and the presumably formulaic and trivial pop music she produces.[21] It is, however, largely because she plays on "people's idea of what's humiliating to women" that Madonna has become a controversial figure in academic and popular discourse. Madonna enters the cultural scene following both the 1970s Women's Liberation movement and the 1980s institutionalization of academic feminism and provokes debates about not just postmodernism but "postfeminism" as well.

The status of and need for feminism in the early 1980s especially was extremely foggy. The label "postfeminist" suggested a belief, in the media and especially among younger women, that there was no longer any need for feminist politics, and, subsequently, suggested a feeling among 1970s feminists that activist feminism was losing ground. The debate about post-feminism encompassed many areas—the viability of women's music, for in-stance, as well as a questioning of certain "feminist orthodoxies around the body and self-presentation: the injunction against feminine adornment and its oppressive signifiers—makeup, high heels, skirts, long hair and so on," which, for postfeminists, seemed "oppressive and trapping in itself."[22] As a female superstar, Madonna challenged a lot of the established positions of academic and activist feminism and functioned on both sides of the "post-feminist" debate as a touchstone for the rearticulation of a host of feminist issues including pornography, fashion, makeup, and sex.

In discussing the negative female stereotypes contained in Madonna's image, feminist critics echo the post-Stonewall debate about the politics of camp for gay men: they ask whether Madonna fuels or dismantles those stereotypes, whether she represents a retrograde and antifeminist image of oppression, or embodies a new vision of powerful and independent femi-ninity. Most of the negative criticism of Madonna relates to her sexuality and gender—her image as a kind of female grotesque and as the antithesis of feminism and feminist identity politics. In a survey of "Madonna-haters," Madonna is called antifeminist and a backward step for women; further, she is likened to a social disease, a narcissist, a succubus, a vampire, and—linking her sexuality and her commercialism—a prostitute.[23] *The I Hate Madonna Hand-book* also compares her to a prostitute and features a quiz: "Feminist or Slut?"

Some feminists consider Madonna's postmodernism a liability for femi-nism insofar as her changing images challenge the unified concept of "woman."[24] However, contrary to Camille Paglia's assertion that she alone recognizes Madonna's permutations as the "future of feminism," many feminists dismiss the charge that postmodern style is apolitical and empty of content and have considered Madonna's use of borrowed styles to be parodic and critical.[25] For example, discussing Madonna's changing images, and particularly her retro-cinephilia, Ramona Curry argues that Madonna "functions not as mere imitation or pastiche, but as a *parody* of female star images, indeed of the concept of stardom altogether." Curry notes that the repetition of this parody may seem ultimately to be pastiche, but "what adheres to Madonna's cumulative image from her varied and multiple performances is her status as a kind of meta-masquerade."[26]

The turning point in feminist attitudes toward Madonna and the beginning of her acceptance by an adult female audience, along with her established popularity among teenage "wanna-be" fans, seems to have been the video for "Material Girl" (dir. Lambert, 1985). Here, Madonna imitates Marilyn Monroe's "Diamonds Are a Girl's Best Friend" number from *Gentlemen Prefer Blondes* (dir. Hawks, 1953). In a video-within-the-video, Madonna performs "Material Girl" dressed in a pink sleeveless gown that is an exact replica of Monroe's dress. The song simultaneously celebrates and parodies the gold digger's self-commodification as a form of 1980s crass materialism: "The boy with the cold, hard cash is always Mr. Right / Cause we are living in a material world, and I am a material girl."

Because this video invokes a famous text, and especially a famous sex symbol, "Material Girl" could be taken as simple nostalgia or pastiche. The video, however, reproduces elements of the Monroe image (blondness, sexuality, gold digging) and simultaneously recasts that image in a potentially critical manner. First, the framing narrative suggests that "Madonna" is not really the material girl of the song, differentiating her from the Monroe character. Greg Seigworth cites the video's "self-conscious disjunction of the singer and the song as ironic commentary on the then-predominant image of Madonna as Boy Toy" and asserts that "Madonna was trying to intervene in and influence the shape her own emerging mythology would take."[27] Second, both Madonna's witty performance and the song's pointed lyrics attribute to the Monroe character a knowingness and degree of control absent from most nostalgic treatments of Monroe, which generally remember her as a witless sex object and/or tragic victim. Thus, the video creates a dialectical constellation of Monroe-Madonna, revealing a stronger and more savvy Monroe in the image of Madonna.

Many feminists embrace Madonna not only because her multiple masquerades challenge essentialist notions of identity, but also because, throughout her various incarnations, Madonna asserts her own power and independence, in the economic sphere and in terms of authorship. In claiming Madonna as a parodic text, critics generally cite her presumed control over her own image. Sonya Andermahr claims, "Madonna calls her own shots. . . . [S]he exercises more power and control over the production, marketing and financial value of that image than any female icon before her. She has never been content to be the face that launched a thousand record covers; she has to be the helmswoman too." [28] Similarly, John Fiske observes, "She parodies not just the stereotypes, but the way in which they are made. She represents herself as the one who is in control of her own image and of the process of making it." [29] As one woman who dreamt of Madonna put it, "I had a dream that Madonna's real name was Boswana. . . . It's because she's the boss." [30]

The issue of economic and authorial control relates directly to Madonna's "success in articulating and parading the desire to be desired in an unabashed, aggressive, gutsy manner." [31] In other words, the perception of Madonna's control relates to precisely the same characteristics that lead some to call her a prostitute—her outspokenness in both her songs and press about her own sexual desires and her sexual attractiveness. Many of her videos, including "Open Your Heart," "Borderline," "Express Yourself," and "Material Girl," offer "reflexive commentaries on male 'looking' countered by a feminine 'look'." [32] Revolving around a drama of vision, Madonna's videos subvert and complicate the primacy of classical Hollywood's structured male gaze. Gazed at by a bevy of men, Madonna returns the gaze, asserting her own desires and desirability, her status as sexual subject and not merely a sex object. Extratextually, contesting her frequent comparison to Marilyn Monroe, Madonna says, "I take the preconceived notion of what a sex goddess is and throw it back in your face and say I can be a sex symbol, but I don't have to be a victim." [33]

Madonna's initial popularity among teenage girls has been attributed to fans' identification with her power and independence. According to both Fiske and Lewis, for instance, "Madonna as a site of meaning" offered teenage girls a means of resisting the powerlessness and subordination in their own lives. Teenage "wanna-bes" imitated Madonna's style in the mid-1980s in order to appear sexy and because they admired and identified with her independence, self-reliance, and presumed resistance to patriarchy.

In the same year that "Material Girl" was released, Susan Seidelman's *Desperately Seeking Susan* further broadened Madonna's appeal among adults, especially women. Addressed to young adult women, the film suggests that Madonna's adult female fans, like her teenage fans, identify with her as a figure of power and desire (a suggestion supported by the dreams collected in I *Dream of Madonna*). In the film, Rosanna Arquette's bored suburban house-wife functions as an obsessive "wanna-be" in relation to Madonna's thinly veiled self-portrait, Susan. Arquette's Roberta voyeuristically tracks Susan's romantic life via newspaper classifieds, spies on and follows her through the city, wears her clothes, and carries a photo of her—even into the bathtub. Roberta's identification with Susan is literalized in the portion of the film when her amnesia causes her to "become" Susan. Ultimately, through her identification with Susan, Roberta gets the courage to become her own person, leaving behind her unsatisfactory marriage, bland suburban life, and unhip clothing. The only narrative film that has succeeded because of, and not despite, Madonna, *Desperately Seeking Susan* not only targeted a more mature audience for Madonna but determined, in large part, the way in which that audience would respond to her.

Critics argue that many gay men and lesbians, similarly, identify with Madonna's power and independence. Michael Musto observes, "Her pride, flamboyance, and glamour reach out to gay guys as much as her refusal to be victimized strikes a chord in lesbians." If gay male identification with female stars had been, as Ross claims, "first and foremost, an identification with women as *emotional* subjects in a world in which men 'acted' and women 'felt,' "[34] Madonna, for Musto, offers a more equitable model. He continues: "It's not the divisive old Judy story, with guys weeping along with the diva as she longs to go over the rainbow and track down the man that got away, while women cringe."[35] A diva of a different sort, gay men, lesbians, and straight women can take equal pleasure in Madonna and identify with her as a figure of desire and power. In this sense, she offers camp pleasure without the guilt of affirming negative stereotypes.

The perception of Madonna's power and independence relates not only to her outspoken sexuality but also to her use of politically controversial imagery in her textual productions. Lisa Henderson ties Madonna's popularity among gays and lesbians to her status as a political figure: "The heart of Madonna's appeal to lesbian and gay audiences . . . include(s) her willingness to act as a political figure as well as a popular one and to recognize that such fraught domains as sex, religion, and family are indeed, political constructions, especially for lesbian and gay people."[36] Madonna both parodies sexual stereotypes and blasts the patriarchal institutions that construct those stereotypes. In videos, songs, commercials, and public-service announcements she has taken on such embattled territories as the Catholic church, the family, abortion, condoms, big business (Pepsi), and the American flag. She has, moreover, made public statements about the censorship battles in the

United States and abroad and become a symbol of that struggle due to her banned Pepsi commercial, banned video for "Justify My Love," and threatened boycotts and closings of her live concert tour in Rome and Toronto.[37]

Queer as You Wanna-be: Camp and Identity Politics

Madonna's self-presentation and reception among gays and lesbians as a political figure links her to the second tendency of post-1960s camp I mentioned earlier—its shift to overtly politicized camp and "queer" politics. This trajectory springs directly from and closely resembles pre-1960s gay camp. It differs, however, from earlier "traditional" gay camp in crucial ways because the historical meaning of camp changes for gays after Stonewall. As I noted in the introduction, for many gay intellectuals after Stonewall, camp was initially viewed largely as an embarrassment affirming the dominant culture's negative perception of the gay community. Even theorists like Richard Dyer who valorized camp did so largely from a historical perspective, arguing that camp had functioned as a kind of dress rehearsal for liberation politics and "coming out," but not claiming that it should substitute for politics after Stonewall.

At the same time, though, flamboyant drag and cross-dressing began to be used in the 1970s in Gay Pride parades to signify being "out" in a visible public ritual. By taking on the dominant culture's negative perception of gay men as "queens," the use of camp style in public—much like the use of the slogan "We're Here, We're Queer, Get Used to It"—could assert gay pride, identity, community, and history. If pop camp exposes one side of camp—recognizing the camp subculture's consumerism and desire for access to the dominant culture—queer camp emphasizes the other side—camp's ability to signal difference and alienation from the dominant. Here, rather than make public camp's parasitic relation to the dominant culture, queer camp recodes the subculture's own history to reconceive itself as adversarial.

In the 1980s, camp became a key strategy in gay activist politics aimed at asserting gay rights, and not simply gay pride. Gay activists, in the wake of the AIDS crisis, work to improve AIDS awareness among homosexual and heterosexual communities; to demand more government funding for research and treatment centers, faster FDA approval for drugs, better access to experimental drugs, and nonprejudicial insurance coverage policies; and to combat the increasing problem of gay bashing and hate crimes spawned by AIDS paranoia. With particular attention to the latter, the gay activist group Queer Nation has adopted what Lauren Berlant and Elizabeth Freeman describe as a "camp counterpolitics" in which Queer Nation engages in a "kind of guerrilla warfare." Queer Nation embodies a mobile sense of queerness. According to Berlant and Freeman, it shifts "between a utopian politics of identity, difference, dispersion, and specificity and a pluralist agenda, in the liberal sense, that imagines a 'gorgeous mosaic' of difference without a model of conflict." Staging public events, like Queer Nights Out in bars and parades in shopping malls, Queer Nation claims safe spaces and adopts camp strategies to create visible public spectacles: "Its tactics are to cross borders, to occupy spaces, and to mime the privileges of nationality—in short, to simulate 'the national' with a camp inflection." [38] Queer Nation's use of camp strategies, as well as the prominence of drag in Gay Pride parades, and other overt manifestations linked to gay identity politics, have redefined and revitalized camp within the gay community. The new queer camp style takes on the signs and practices of camp without the pathos, adopting camp not as a mark of oppression but as an index of pride, signaling a refusal to accept oppression anymore.

Andrew Ross rightly claims that for most academics and sex radicals Madonna functions "like what environmentalists call a charismatic megafauna: a highly visible, and lovable, species, like the whale or the spotted owl, in whose sympathetic name entire ecosystems can be protected and safeguarded through public patronage." [39] In large part, Madonna's status as a political figure depends upon her willing identification as a "queer" supporter. She has consistently aligned herself in public with gay culture and politics. Madonna had a gay following early on partly because she made African American–style dance music after the demise of disco. [40] In numerous interviews, she states her identification with gay men, self-identifying as a "fag hag" and describing gay men as "just a f——k of a lot more sensitive than most of the straight men I know. They're more fun to be around. They're freer. I also feel that they're persecuted and I can relate to that." [41] Interviews and biographies refer constantly to Madonna's relationship with her gay dance teacher, Christopher Flynn, who was both mentor and close friend and who introduced Madonna to the world of gay discos in Michigan. Madonna is also one of the earliest well-known celebrities who performed in AIDS benefits; and she included safer-sex instructions and a condom in the packaging for her album Like a Prayer.

Moreover, in Madonna's gender bending, she identifies herself with a wide range of sex and gender roles, expanding the range of erotic representation and identification. In masculine suit, grabbing her crotch for "Express Yourself" (dir. Fincher, 1989), she imitates Michael Jackson's already androgynous (and parodic?) interpretation of phallic masculinity. In "Justify My Love" (dir. Mondino, 1990), she occupies multiple sexual subject positions, leaving open whether we are to read them as lesbian, straight, and/or bisexual. Beyond videos, Madonna invites us to be confused about her "real-life" sexual identity, in joking about and refusing to clarify the nature of her "friendship" with Sandra Bernhard on *Late Night with David Letterman*, or in offering us *Sex*, her book of fantasies, presumably her own, which features pictures of Madonna with lesbian skinheads, posing in gay and lesbian clubs.

Madonna takes advantage of the pop or postmodern mainstreaming of camp to introduce elements of queer politics into popular culture. John Leland argues that "in exchange for her genuine affection, [Madonna has] raided gay subculture's closet for the best of her ideas."[42] Although each of Madonna's videos contain some element of gender parody, and her career as a whole can be read as meta-masquerade, the video for "Vogue" (dir. Fincher, 1990), in particular, articulates a relationship between gay subcultures, Hollywood stars, and feminist camp. The video mainstreams the subcultural gay practice of vogueing in which African American and Latino gays combine quasi-breakdance movements with impersonations of specific female stars, as well as generic male and female types (e.g., the executive, the schoolgirl). The song and video obscure vogueing's racial and homosexual specificity while opening the practice out to a larger audience. The video shows the men in suits, not drag, and the lyrics exclaim, "It doesn't matter if you're black or white, if you're a boy or a girl." While mainstreaming this practice, however, the video makes sex and gender roles ambiguous enough that its affiliation, and Madonna's, with a gay subculture cannot be ignored or erased.

"Vogue" uses gay subcultural references in conjunction with postmodern pastiche and retro-cinephilia to create a queer camp effect. Although the men do not cross-dress, Madonna does. Each time she appears with the male dancers, she wears a dark masculine suit. Her use of drag mixes gender signs — she wears an enormous cone-bra with a man's suit, for instance — and underscores her status as a female female impersonator when she appears singly in various glamorous female guises in other sections of the video. She reappropriates female images from the male dancers, who vogue but do not dress in drag, and yet maintains vogueing's sense of parody and fun. Because no single image-identity seems to be her own, and because she exaggerates and heightens the pose — wearing a ridiculous Veronica Lake wig and reflecting that image in a mirror, for example — she flaunts the masquerade as masquerade.

Madonna's poses in "Vogue" could be taken as simply nostalgic, since the black-and-white glamour photography refers directly and indirectly to well-known Hollywood stars and famous photographs of them. But the song ironizes these star images, even while paying homage to them. After repetitions of the phrase "beauty's where you find it," Madonna raps a catalogue of select Hollywood stars ("ladies with an attitude, fellows that were in the mood") who have overlapping gay camp, straight camp, and nostalgic associations: "Greta Garbo and Monroe. / Dietrich and DiMaggio. / Marlon Brando. Jimmy Dean. / On the cover of a magazine. / Grace Kelly. Harlow, Jean. / Picture of a beauty queen. / Gene Kelly. Fred Astaire. / Ginger Rogers. Dance on air. / They had style, they had grace. / Rita Hayworth gave good face. / Lauren, Katharine, Lana, too. / Bette Davis, we love you." The monotone rap flattens out the differences between these stars and their different camp and nostalgic attributes and empties them of content (in a manner similar to Warhol's portraits of celebrities). Rather than emphasize Monroe's tragic connotations, Hepburn's androgyny, or Astaire's talent, Madonna confines them all and the pleasure we take in them ("we love you") to the reduced categories of beauty, style, grace, and "attitude." Instead of the mournful aura of nostalgia, or the complexities of a star matrix, they, like Warhol's "superstars," are invested with the status of brand-names for a way of being, giving good face, which is easily accessible to all of us: "Strike a pose, there's nothing to it." The lyrics let us imagine that we too can strike the pose, while they emphasize that these star images represent nothing but a pose. "Vogue" suggests that women and gay men alike can gain access to their desires by recognizing and manipulating the illusion, seeing through the mask and giving good face.

Of course, for many critics, Madonna's politics are empty of content. The I Hate Madonna Handbook claims that Madonna's politics are "as phony as her hair color."[43] Similarly, in parodying Truth or Dare, both Julie Brown and Blossom suggest that Madonna's sexual politics are just fuel for more publicity. Making fun of Madonna's politics, Julie Brown's Medusa: Dare to Be Truthful parodies "Vogue" in a song called "Vague." After deliberately exposing her "muffin" to delighted cops who have threatened to arrest her, Medusa sings, "I'm not thinking nothing. / C'mon get vague, / Let your body move without thinking. / C'mon get vague, / Let your IQ drop while you bop." Instead of Madonna's catalogue of cult stars, Medusa raps a list of has-beens and mediocre talents ("Brooke Shields / Dawber, Pam / Personality of Spam"). Brown sums up their appeal, and, by implication, Madonna's: "Ladies with no point-of-view. / Fellas who don't have a clue. / If they're stars, then you can do it. / Just be vague, there's nothing to it." For Brown, and others,

Madonna is not so much a political spokesperson as a narcissist who mouths a "vague" politics to mask a mediocre talent—a claim Madonna obliquely supports in *Truth or Dare* when she tells her backup singers that she knows she is not the most talented singer or dancer, but rather is interested in "pushing people's buttons."

Many critics recognize that Madonna does indeed "push people's buttons" but still find her politics "vague." In particular, many see Madonna's appropriation of gay, racial, and ethnic subcultural practices as an appropriation of style rather than a substantive politics. Marcos Becquer and Jose Gatti argue, for example, that Madonna's "escape to the polymorphous perversity of an idealized universally available dance floor" in "Vogue" subsumes the gay/Other under the myth of equality.[44] Like those feminists who criticize Madonna's postmodernism for challenging feminism's unified concept of "woman," for Becquer and Gatti, Madonna's pluralist queerness, as opposed to gay or feminist identity politics, translates multiculturalism's "gorgeous mosaic" into an unattainable fantasy. In ignoring real difference ("it doesn't matter"), Madonna's "Vogue" denies real antagonisms and real struggles.

More than just a cranky assessment of one video, the opinion put forth by Becquer and Gatti provides a useful point of entry into a whole series of questions about the politics of, not just Madonna, but of contemporary queer camp. These questions, perhaps unanswerable, have to do with the relationship between camp, popular culture, postmodernism, commodification, and politics. How, for example, does camp today negotiate difference? If camp is rooted in a culture of oppression and struggle, is it possible to articulate anything but a power hierarchy through camp? And, once mainstreamed, does camp, even explicitly gay camp, simply become a means for heterosexual performers and spectators to go slumming? To begin to address these questions, or at least to understand what is at stake in them, requires a reconsideration of Madonna's star text, especially of the issue of power as it relates to camp.

As I have suggested, the issue of power is key to Madonna's star text and fan identification with her. Madonna's cultural clout and the controversies she generates are deeply rooted in perceptions of her as powerful. As Lynne Layton notes, "Madonna's art and its reception by critics and fans reflect and shape some of our culture's anxieties about identity and power inequalities. Madonna disturbs the status quo not only because she is an outspoken, sexy woman, but because she has a lot of social and economic power."[45] Layton suggests that the critics' focus on gender relations in Madonna's textual productions functions to obscure a focus on power relations. For Layton,

"Madonna presents the perplexing case of someone who accepts the concept of a natural hierarchy of power but attacks the version of the concept that excludes women, gays, and minorities."[46] By this account, Madonna's gender bending simply reverses the structure of patriarchal power relations. The female takes the gaze from the male, the weepy diva becomes dominatrix. Gender relations are still predicated on a master-slave model, but now the slaves subjugate the master. Madonna's power may well enable her to function as an important symbol of interventionist politics, but if we understand that power is privilege and that Madonna speaks from a privileged position—related to her economic power, whiteness, and influence—we need to consider what, if any, access we and others have to the kind of mobile and flexible subjectivity inherent to Madonna's project.

Madonna masks the actual powerlessness of subcultural groups through her performance of agency and power. To adapt Kaja Silverman's reading of what Foucault calls "discursive fellowships," Madonna compensates for a lack of agency by pretending to occupy the positions of both speaking and spoken subject: "Discourse always requires a speaking position (a position from which power-knowledge is exercised) and a spoken subject (a position brought into existence through the exercise of power-knowledge)." According to Silverman, the male subject is capable of occupying both positions. The female subject, by contrast, is "automatically excluded from all current discursive fellowships except those like feminism, which have grown up in opposition to the dominant symbolic order."[47] When Madonna argues, in her interview with Forrest Sawyer, that the video for "Express Yourself" (dir. Fincher, 1989) does not exploit women because she chained herself to the bed, she asserts her ability to control current stereotypical, pornographic, and hierarchical discourses, thus obscuring the fact that she is spoken by those discourses and incapable of speaking them. Silverman allows for the possibility of the "unusual" woman who gains admittance to a discursive fellowship. However, even if we take Madonna to be an "unusual" woman, the exception to the rule, her "unique" deviation from the female norm merely confirms the larger rule of exclusion.

David Tetzlaff astutely captures the ideological effect of Madonna's privileged position as an "unusual" woman: "The discourses engaged by Chameleon Madonna have no claim on her. How could she be free for her ultimate self-actualization if she were bound to the historically rooted struggles of the subaltern groups who populate her videos? . . . She has won for herself an unlimited ticket for subcultural tourism—she can visit any locale she likes, but she doesn't have to live there."[48] Here, Tetzlaff suggests that Madonna does not reverse power relations so much as ignore and, therefore, mask them. Madonna's masquerade lacks the pathos of oppression—taking camp pleasure in dismantling stereotypes without camp's guilty self-recognition in stereotypes. It is not, however, the case that these stereotypes have been rendered defunct. Rather, Madonna's individual economic and social power removes her from the conditions and struggles of subaltern groups so that her appropriation of these subcultures and stereotypes, no matter how well intentioned, can never be more than a form of subcultural tourism at the level of style. As Douglas Crimp and Michael Warner assert, "She can be as queer as she wants to, but only because we know she's not."[49]

At worst, Madonna's own focus on power and independence leads her to adopt a patronizing attitude toward all those less powerful than herself, causing bell hooks to compare her to a modern-day plantation mistress. Hooks notes how, after choosing a cast of characters from marginalized groups (white gays, straight and gay non-whites) for her "Blonde Ambition" tour, Madonna, in *Truth or Dare*, publicly describes them as "emotional cripples."[50] John Champagne, similarly, observes that *Sex* reinstantiates middle-class privilege because it expresses the same revulsion toward sexuality that it claims to contest—presenting portraits of sexual freaks, instead of highlighting the sensuality of the images.[51] Champagne notes how the photographs emphasize Madonna's separation from the sexual activity taking place around her. The book features, for instance, images that create a sharp contrast between Madonna's blond glamour and the dark-haired, pierced, and tattooed lesbian skinheads or between her whiteness and African Americans Naomi Campbell and Big Daddy Kane. Further, Madonna is pictured as the lone female and lone sexual subject at the Gaiety Theater; Madonna is at the center of virtually every image, foregrounded, and mugging for the camera.

This condescension becomes, at times, positively sinister when Madonna simply fails to recognize her privileged position with respect to different groups and different individuals. It becomes increasingly difficult to attribute to Madonna a genuinely progressive or coalitional politics for instance, when, she ignores the hairdresser who has been drugged and raped in *Truth or Dare*, seeing in the young woman's ordeal only a reflection of her own greatness (assuming by some strange logic that the woman was attacked because she was with the tour), or when she claims in *Sex* that abused women "must be digging it" and that women are not degraded in pornography because the models choose to pose (as if her decision to make *Sex* mirrors the average porn model's options). These moments, in Kate Tentler's words, "are the glitches that make a feminist cringe, the ruptures in my faith. Can her life, her songs, her videos really stand in as the visuals for my feminist politics?"[52]

The point here is not to rake Madonna over the coals for failing to live up to my political ideals or to ask of her that she be a role model. Instead, I take Madonna to be as representative of the limitations of camp as she is of its potential. While we can see a difference between pre-1960s and post-1960s camp, between Mae West and Madonna, it would be a mistake to view the history of camp as a lapsarian narrative. Rather than assume a linear history of camp's fall from authenticity, we need to examine pre- and post-1960s camp in a constellation, to read Mae West through Madonna and vice versa. In this way, we can see the dormant affinity between West and Madonna, and, in their similarity, locate the utopian promise in Madonna and the dystopian aspects of West. Madonna and West are both "unusual" women struggling to situate themselves in a discursive fellowship to which they have no access, while at the same time, they offer a view of how a female subject might be imagined as speaking and not merely as spoken.

If Madonna represents the death of camp, it is not because camp itself has changed but because camp's context and mode of consumption have changed. Camp's always already parasitic relation to the dominant culture surfaces in post-1960s camp. At issue is a conflict in camp between a subculture's desire for access to the mainstream and that subculture's desire for a unique identity. In Madonna, these two sides of camp engage in a kind of internal warfare. The desire on the part of Madonna's advocates for her to articulate an identity politics through camp, to assert difference, conflicts with the desire for the mainstream, for equality and admittance to the dominant culture.

The difficulty posed by Madonna's status as an "unusual" woman overlaps with the difficulty posed by the mainstreaming of camp: namely, the issue of appropriation. Discussing the fact that *Sex* does not seem queer enough because Madonna's queerness feels like appropriation, Crimp and Warner address the "inevitable ambivalence" of the term: "Appropriation is a weird term, though, because in a way you always win these battles by being appropriated. If you're going to conquer cultural turf and gain a certain amount of legitimacy, how else is it going to happen except through the appropriation of certain rhetorics by people who haven't hitherto been part of the minority culture?"[53] The issue of appropriation lurks in virtually every analysis of, not just Madonna, but camp in general, usually obscuring the fact that camp itself operates largely through appropriating objects from dominant culture. Camp's advocates and opponents alike, myself included, are continuously beleaguered by the question, "Who does camp belong to?" Is camp strictly a gay male sensibility? Can lesbians camp? Is "straight" camp still camp? The question remains, however, whether the appropriation of camp connotes the erasure of identity or the acceptance of difference. To gain acceptance without loss of identity, we cling to the notion of a subculture while still yearning to be part of mainstream culture.

What is finally at stake here is the value of difference in identity politics. As Alexander Doty observes, "[W]e queers have become locked into ways of seeing ourselves in relation to mass culture that perpetuate our status as subcultural, parasitic, self-oppressive hangers-on: alienated, yet grabbing for crumbs or crusts and wishfully making this into a whole meal."[54] Camp and queer alike can only be defined in opposition to the non-camp and non-queer. Queers cannot be overly interested in multiplying themselves or their camp sensibility because they require the other for their self-definition and for their self-conception as resistant or alternative. In searching for a "whole meal," self-defined queers face a quandary: How to demand simultaneously the right to maintain a unique identity and gain equal rights, justice, and access to power?

Doty's tentative solution to this problem would be to emphasize the porousness of culture, to redefine the dominant, and recognize the queerness in and of mass culture so that the notion that what is mass or popular is "straight" would become "a highly questionable given" in culture. This solution suggests that dominant culture cannot appropriate or subsume our difference because that difference already permeates the dominant—both through the dominant culture's appropriation of what is queer and through the queer and camp appropriation of objects from the dominant culture for queer or camp readings. Perhaps Doty is right, and the ultimate blandness of the Madonna phenomenon testifies to just this. However, to assert that queerness is everywhere still assumes necessarily that such a thing as non-queer exists: it merely reverses the power relation to assert that what is non-queer is less rather than more prevalent than what is queer.

We can just as easily reverse the direction of Doty's argument to emphasize the porousness of identity. We could argue, in other words, that the ultimate blandness of the Madonna phenomenon inheres in the ultimate blandness of queer difference instead of the ultimate complexity or queerness of dominant culture. If queerness has been posited as unique and other because dominant culture wants it that way, then perhaps the ultimate move of de-essentializing would be to say not that queers are just like "straights" or that "straight" culture is really queer, but that sex and gender identities are porous and that queer difference is largely a matter of self-conception. This solution, however, begs the question of the value of difference in queer self-conceptions: If difference has been reified by queer and non-queer culture alike that is because we still cling to some belief that there are real differences and that some of these matter deeply.

In this perhaps unresolvable problematic, we are caught once again in the either/or "dominant versus resistant" model of cultural politics, replayed now on the field of identity politics. Just as before we faced a theoretical duality between ascribing an unqualified power to either texts or readers, with the subsequent reification of pleasure as wholly good or wholly bad, here we face a similar duality between mainstream culture and its subcultures, with the potential reification of difference. What is needed then is a means of reconceiving sex and gender identities in such a way as to maintain the difference we value in both our self-definition and our social roles without sliding into either vulgar essentialism or vulgar constructionism.

What makes the Madonna phenomenon interesting is, perhaps, its restaging of this controversy in cultural criticism as a controversy in the area of identity politics. Madonna and her reception provide a caution about too easily conflating camp with progressive politics. Madonna's reception, both positive and negative, suggests that camp can still be a political and critical force—perhaps even more so since becoming a more public sensibility—yet suggests that the pool of persons with access to those forces is still severely restricted. The mainstreaming of camp taste in contemporary culture may help articulate a queer subjectivity and coalitional politics, but it may also serve to obscure real difference and to reduce gay politics to a discourse of style. Perhaps, in the future, camp will be dead—if the conditions of oppression are gone and there is no longer any need for camp as a survival strategy. But, in the meantime, we need to scrutinize our camp icons, and our own camp readings and practices, to ensure that we do not naively substitute camp for politics.

CONCLUSION

The Queens Are Dead,

Long Live the Queens

Designing Women's Mary Jo (*Annie Potts*) and
Julia (*Dixie Carter*) masquerade as Bette Davis and Joan Crawford in
Whatever Happened to Baby Jane? *Video frame enlargement*
(*author's collection*).

It would have interested me to know how, by being insisted upon, the best discoveries spoil, and what is the process that ankyloses and discolors a character so rich, so hardy, so un-American: the woman without scruples, the female rival of the male debauch, the brave enemy of the male, valorous enough to use the same weapons as he. —Colette, on Mae West's apparent decline in 1938

People make their own history, but they do not make it just as they please; they do not make it under circumstances chosen by themselves, but under circumstances directly encountered, given and transmitted from the past. —Karl Marx, "The Eighteenth Brumaire of Louis Bonaparte"

What is reassuring is that camp will re-emerge. . . . Camp is always in the future; that is why the present needs it so badly. —Philip Core, *Camp: The Lie That Tells the Truth*

The end of what we call "Madonna" is happening now. Madonna is on the verge of becoming a camp grotesque. A victim of the stereotypes she—and we—thought she could dismantle. Already there is a backlash from academia: we still talk about her but feel compelled now to apologize for doing so, embarrassed at our own very public enthusiasm. She appears on David Letterman's talk show in 1994 and refuses to leave, swearing the whole time, in a battle of wills, if not wits— and, by most accounts, loses to Letterman, America's new sweetheart. A Fox network made-for-TV movie later that same year, *Madonna: Innocence Lost*, portrays the beginning of Madonna's career up to her live performance of "Like A Virgin" on the 1984 MTV awards, emphasizing familiar camp tropes: sexual promiscuity, narcissism, the betrayal of friends and lovers in a ruthless climb to the top, and the loneliness at the top—all "explained" by Madonna's loss of her mother at an early age.

Perhaps as with Mae West, we will forget we ever found Madonna beautiful and will find her belief in her own attractiveness laughable (already we are laughing at her sexual desires and appetites). Maybe like Joan Crawford, it will be the bitchiness, the hard professionalism and artificiality, we cling to. Or she will be another poor little rich girl, lonely and lost, like Marilyn

Monroe. Will she end up like Judy Garland? Or will she get domesticated in more banal ways?—gain weight and start a perfume line, make a workout tape, end up in Vegas on a comeback tour?

When Colette asks how "the best discoveries spoil," we could answer: camp. If camp is the weapon of "the woman without scruples," it is also often, sadly, almost inevitably, the weapon we use against her. Camp may appropriate and expose stereotypes, but it also, in some measure, keeps them alive. Camp is both a mode of excess and a method of containment. Camp depends on our simultaneously recognizing stereotypes as stereotypes to distance ourselves from them and at the same time recognizing, and loving, the hold and power those stereotypes have over us. It is always a guilty pleasure. Thus, the stereotypes at play in camp are recoupable. And, therefore, the positive camp effect one generation attributes to Madonna, or Mae West, or Joan Crawford, becomes, in the next, available to be used against her, to turn her into a camp object.

This is not to say that the work done by feminist and gay camp spectators and producers to express what is "basically serious" about gender and sexuality "in terms of fun and artifice and elegance" has been in vain. At the same time that camp recoups stereotypes, it also displaces them by historicizing them and recoding them according to contemporary tastes and needs. Camp needs, then, to be considered as a mode of productive anachronism, a form of recycling.

The trope of recycling suggests, in part, a logic of diminishing returns and diminishing resources. As the recycling bins remind us: reduce, reuse. But recycling also signifies transformation, change. It depends on our recognizing in a seemingly outmoded object, a throwaway, the potential for new use. The recycled object still carries traces of the original but is reconfigured, remade for a new purpose.

In the preceding chapters, I have emphasized how feminist camp operates at moments of antifeminist backlash to regroup and revitalize seemingly outmoded feminist issues. In the case of Mae West, for instance, I argued that West played on the gap between 1930s and 1890s entertainment forms both to depict and render outmoded the gender-segregated world of nineteenth-century entertainment and to parody contemporary screen stars and sex stereotypes. My chapter on Berkeley emphasized the way in which *Gold Diggers of 1933* links Progressive Era antiprostitution discourses to the economic concerns of women trying to survive in the Depression. In describing how Joan Crawford became recoded as a camp grotesque, I suggested that female spectators might use her star text's residual affiliation with the desires and dissatisfactions of working women as a means to counter the 1950s ideology of domestic satisfaction. And in my chapter on Madonna, I described the ways in which feminist and queer interpretations of her star text seek to align her postmodern "postfeminism" with feminist and queer politics.

I have also attempted to sketch a history of feminist camp. Rather than either a progressive or lapsarian narrative, the history of camp needs to be understood as cyclical, as a response to particular historical circumstances that is partly progressive and partly retrograde. Camp is a sensibility rooted in the status quo, yet it is a critical sensibility that somewhat modifies our understanding of and attitude toward the status quo. The work done by feminist and gay camp spectators and producers to entice alternate meanings into existence in the past has not been momentary in its effects but continues to affect our understanding of a wide range of stars and texts.

The history of camp thus affects our understanding of the past and present. Camp can, moreover, be utilized in the present to alter the way we perceive sex and gender stereotypes in the future. If camp is a weapon that we often turn against ourselves, then it is also a weapon we can use to re-code and historicize camp itself in order to render some of its stereotypes outmoded. In enabling viewers to express their felt alienation from dominant culture, camp spectatorship has changed forever the way large parts of the population have seen and experienced sexual and gender stereotypes and identities constructed in and through mass culture. By recycling feminist camp—in television, video, film, and through feminist criticism and feminist histories of camp—camp spectators, producers, and critics can potentially insure that we never see these stereotypes the same way again.

The ghosts of camp past, present, and future are with us today. To be sure, the present tense of camp consists in large part of what Rudnick and Anderson call Camp Lite and Jameson refers to as postmodern pastiche. Contemporary camp also, however, bears residual traces of "traditional" camp. As I discussed in the preceding chapter, queer camp practices have been revitalized and aligned with queer identity politics. The renewed interest in "traditional" forms of camp can be seen in the popularity of such films as *Paris Is Burning*, *Orlando*, and *The Adventures of Priscilla, Queen of the Desert*. In addition, the contemporary moment has witnessed a burgeoning academic and media interest in drag, cross-dressing, and transsexualism, as well as renewed interest in historical camp figures like Oscar Wilde, Dusty Springfield, and Liberace.[1]

There are also emergent forms of camp alive today that create their camp effect by recycling camp itself, thus rendering forms of "classic" camp outmoded. Some camp is undeniably better (smarter, funnier, more critical) than others, and much post-1960s camp does seem to slip into an easy nostalgia without much of a critical edge. *Nick at Nite* and other instances of Camp Lite fail to redefine cultural objects critically, because they are steeped in nostalgia rather than a historical sense of camp. However, others have productively used television, video, and film to recontextualize, recycle, and redefine camp objects critically, thereby creating new camp effects. In the following pages, I discuss a variety of texts that seem to me to be exemplary in the way they appropriate camp objects and use them to articulate alternative and resistant positions, bringing critical pressure to bear on camp readings and practices.

The Strange Case of Designing Women

In fall 1991, an episode of the sitcom *Designing Women* ("The Strange Case of Clarence and Anita") explored women's anger over the outcome of the Clarence Thomas Supreme Court confirmation hearings by recycling 1960s gay camp for feminist purposes. *Designing Women* targets a female audience and negotiates such female topics as popular culture, female friendship, femininity, and feminism.[2] *Designing Women* was created by — and reflects the liberal politics of — the husband-and-wife production team of Harry Thomason and Linda Bloodworth-Thomason, who are close friends of Bill and Hillary Clinton (for whom Bloodworth-Thomason created the short film about Clinton's youth in Hope, Arkansas, shown at the 1992 Democratic convention). The TV show, which focuses on a female-owned and -run design firm in Atlanta, features a group of white middle-to-upper-class Southern women and a black ex-con/law student, Anthony (Meshach Taylor).[3] During its run, the show's fast-talking and inventive women characters, its willingness to deal with feminist and gay topics, and, most importantly, its exploration of femininity and female relationships, appealed simultaneously to a loyal female audience and a large gay camp following.

In the Anita Hill episode, Julia Sugarbaker (Dixie Carter) and Mary Jo Shively (Annie Potts) express their anger over the confirmation of Clarence Thomas as a U.S. Supreme Court justice, despite Anita Hill's accusing Thomas of sexual harassment. The show uses actual footage of the hearings and, for the first half of the show, the characters watch and respond to the hearings until Thomas is confirmed. As they debate the merits of Thomas's and Hill's respective positions, discussing their own work histories and Anthony's claim that they harass him at work, the characters raise a number of related feminist issues. When Carlene (Jan Hooks) mentions, for example, that polls show that most American women believe Thomas, Mary Jo, who wears a T-shirt with the words "He Lied" printed on it, dismantles the patriarchal bias of polls. She argues that most polls also say most women are not feminists, "but if you ask most women about individual feminist issues, the majority of them are for them," and she adds, "If believing in equal pay and mandated child-care makes me a feminist, then I am proud to be one." Even Carlene, who sides with Thomas, criticizes the bias of the Senate's Supreme Court confirmation committee, especially Ted Kennedy: "Putting him in charge of sexual harassment is like asking that Dom DeLuise to guard the dessert bar at Shoney's."

During the hearings, Julia and Mary Jo are in rehearsal for a community theater production of *Whatever Happened to Baby Jane?* in which they impersonate Joan Crawford and Bette Davis, who portrayed Blanche and Jane Hudson in the 1962 camp classic of the same title. (*Baby Jane* coincidentally creates its camp effect in part by showing the aged stars watching their own old films on TV.) In the second half of the episode, Mary Jo, dressed as Bette Davis/Baby Jane, suggests that they stay in costume to attend the birthday party of coworker Allison (Julia Duffy), who supports Thomas and wears a "She Lied" T-shirt. Puffing on a cigarette and speaking in a clipped Davis-like manner, Mary Jo explains why she wants to stay in character: "I dunno . . . kinda makes me feel . . . I dunno . . . like when I had those big ole fake breasts. . . . Makes me feel *macho*." Julia, as Crawford/Blanche, agrees: "It's only fitting that on this day of infamy we should stay dressed up as two of the toughest talking, big-shouldered broads ever to live in this country."

In impersonating these two camp figures, Julia and Mary Jo recode them as figures of feminist identification. Rather than misogynist grotesques, they interpret Crawford and Davis as tough-talking women who articulate feminist dissatisfaction with the status quo. Mary Jo and Julia parodically re-appropriate the already camp image of Crawford and Davis to create a new, determinedly feminist camp effect. Mary Jo links this theatrical masquerade to the female masquerade of an earlier episode in which she considered breast implants and tried on fake breasts. Their masquerade as these two "broads" renders the earlier camp stereotypes of *Whatever Happened to Baby Jane?* incredible in the same way that Mary Jo's mimicry of full-breasted femininity distanced her from stereotypical images of femininity. Exaggerating a female aesthetic makes Mary Jo feel ironically empowered, "macho," and this feeling helps her express her views on true womanhood.

Emboldened by her impersonation of Davis, Mary Jo delivers a feminist diatribe to a local television news reporter, criticizing not only the Thomas decision, but also a host of other feminist issues:

I'm mad because we're 51 percent of the population and only 2 percent of the United States Senate. I'm mad because 406 men in the
House of Representatives have a pool, a sauna, and a gym, and we have
six hairdryers and a ping-pong table. I'm mad because in a Seminole,
Oklahoma, police station, there's a poster of a naked woman that says,
"Women make bad cops." I'm mad because . . . still we only make
fifty-eight cents on the dollar. And I don't know about the rest of you
women out there but I don't give a damn anymore if people think I'm
a feminist or a fruitcake! What I'm gonna do is get in my car and drive
to the centermost point of the United States of America and climb the
tallest tower and yell, "Hey, don't get me wrong, we love ya, but who
the hell do you men think you are?"

Here, Mary Jo, remaining in character as Davis/Baby Jane throughout, presents herself as simultaneously a grotesque spectacle and as a feminist, thus
occupying the positions of both spoken and speaking subject. She takes on
Davis's persona as an "unusual" woman in order to empower herself as a
speaking subject using the discourse of feminism. In aligning herself with
feminist concerns and with American women (using the pronoun "we" not
"I" in her final statement), Mary Jo does not, however, relegate to herself the
privileged status of being an "unusual" woman. Reaffirming the bonds of
feminism and playing on lesbian rumors about Crawford and Davis, rather
than the preferred gay male reading of a major feud between the two stars,
the episode ends with Mary Jo and Julia dancing together, both leading.
Thus, in relying on a viewer's understanding of Davis and Crawford as camp
figures, the show recodes their camp effect from that of feuding female grotesques into powerful figures of feminist identification.

   This episode of Designing Women is extraordinary in many ways—in its topi-
cality, its use of footage from the Senate hearings, its bald statements of
feminist positions, its lingering on a still image of Hill at the show's end,
and not least among these extraordinary features, its use of the discourse of
camp to articulate its political position.

Theory in the Box

In Joan Does Dynasty (1986), Joan Braderman uses interactive video technology
to criticize the ideology at play in mainstream television and to counter the
passivity of television viewing.[4] Referring to herself as "an American, like TV
itself . . . [a] local beatnik professor doing stand-up theory as TV infiltrator,

media counterspy, and image cop," Braderman inserts herself as a speaking spectator and spectacle into the narrative of the TV show Dynasty. Braderman, peering through chroma-key constructions cut like a mask or superimposed over chroma-keyed backdrops, wearing accessories like a sequined hat to "match" the show's style, performs what Martha Gever aptly calls an "electronically choreographed monologue,"[5] inserted into and hovering above the goings-on of Dynasty's "campy creatures [who] have been interceding in my personal relationships."

In addition to describing the show's plot complications to viewers unfamiliar with Dynasty, Braderman presents an ongoing critique of the show's ideology and its pleasures. Even as she notes the show's "seductive narrative thrust pulling on you," Braderman frustrates the viewer's narrative desire, obscuring the plot by talking over and through it, inserting her own flashback into the narrative, and complicating our understanding of the show with a counterdiscourse of academic feminist film theory. While deconstructing the "pseudo-progressive trajectories" of Dynasty, she admits to her own guilty pleasure in the show's bitchy narratives and in the spectacle of Alexis Carrington, "a female impersonator of the first order" (played by the video's other Joan, Joan Collins): "Centuries of women's oppression, a huge passionate movement against it, and where are we in 1986? Engaged by twisted pleasure, while this monstrous victim of fashion delivers verbal karate chops while issuing bursts of smoke through her shiny blood-red key-light [sic] lips." She confesses her "unreconstructed Dynasty delectation, though I've got the intellectual tools to deconstruct its odious subtext," and asks, "Is deconstructing it merely the invention of a new way to love it?"

At the end of the video, Braderman replays an earlier scene when Alexis went to jail in an off-the-shoulder red evening gown (Braderman notes the "high-camp irony"). Her voice-over narration moves from an analysis of the scene to an exploration of the limitations of female spectatorship: "They're incarcerating her in the panopticon in the narrative of this show, but where she really is is installed in our lives, in your life, in my life. . . . We're the spectators. We're outside the box. She's inside. And indeed, the question for our times, ladies and gentlemen, is, 'Who's in the box?' because that's where power lives." As Braderman notes elsewhere in the video, "Power, while it's everywhere, as Foucault says, is more someplaces than others." Although Braderman suggests that viewers do not typically have access to power, her account of her own critical camp spectatorship opens up the possibility that television viewers can and do produce counternarratives and oppositional discourses. By placing herself "in the box," conflating the roles of spectator and producer, spectacle and speaker, Braderman is able to critique the power relations of *Dynasty* and, by extension, dominant television. If deconstruction is just "a new way to love" *Dynasty*, we should not discount the pleasure that deconstructing *Dynasty* offers—a pleasure that in acknowledging its own complicity with the dominant stereotypes, narratives, and desires of TV may enable us to distance ourselves from those oppressive paradigms.[6]

Stolen Meetings

Cecilia Barriga's video *Meeting Two Queens* (1991) edits together muted images of Marlene Dietrich and Greta Garbo, using parallel scenes from their movies to construct a series of vignettes in a lesbian narrative, silent except for a nondiegetic musical score. Each sequence is bracketed with an intertitle identifying the structuring paradigm of the clips that follow. For instance, in the first segment, "the lake," shots of Garbo fishing at the side of a lake are interspersed with shots of Dietrich arriving at the lakeshore in a boat with a man. Eyeline matches create the illusion that Dietrich is arriving at the same lakeshore where Garbo sits and that Garbo's reaction shots, at first happy and excited and later worried and upset, are reactions first to Dietrich's arrival and then to her kissing the man. The sequence that gives the video its title, "the meeting," intercuts scenes from Dietrich's *The Scarlet Empress* (1934) and Garbo's *Queen Christina* (1933). Decorative intertitles within this segment identify the respective queens, "Catalina de Rusia" (Dietrich's Catherine the Great) and "Cristina de Suecia," (Garbo's Queen Christina). They each walk in procession through a line of soldiers, among trumpets and bayonets, as if meeting in the middle. Other sequences include "the library," which shows Garbo looking up and talking while Dietrich looks down and talks, and "the persecution," in which Garbo and Dietrich are seen to be racing in, respectively, a horse-drawn buggy and a motorcar.

In some sequences, "the dialogue," for instance, Dietrich and Garbo are spliced into the same frame so that they appear to both be talking not just side by side but to each other. In others, "the gesture" and "the end," Barriga uses dissolves to superimpose images of Dietrich and Garbo onto each other. A chroma-key construction at the end of the video creates the effect of Garbo falling from a teardrop in Dietrich's eye, then a dissolve turns the teardrop into Dietrich and the image fades.

Barriga plays on multiple meanings of "queens," suggesting that Dietrich and Garbo not only play queens in their films but are queens—possibly drag "queens," given the androgyny and cross-dressing identified with both stars, but also queens of Hollywood and of lesbian subculture. The video works potentially as an "outing" of Dietrich and Garbo but functions more importantly, as Mary Desjardins has argued, as a lesbian fantasy, recycling these two stars' images to construct a fictional narrative that asserts the relationship between the public sphere of filmgoing and the private knowledge and pleasures of gays and lesbians, who have long speculated about the sexual identities of these two women.[7]

Fine and Dandy Masquerades

No exploration of contemporary feminist camp would be complete without a discussion of the German filmmaker, Ulrike Ottinger. Initially reviled by feminist critics in the 1970s in *Frauen und Film* for her fondness for fetishism and her presumed decadence, Ottinger's narrative films have gained a sort of cult status among feminist film theorists who now view her films as productive of new forms of visual pleasure for women and of a new feminist aesthetic, linked to postmodern pastiche, which radically undermines normative definitions of gender and difference.[8]

Ottinger's films recycle a whole panoply of female stereotypes in wickedly humorous visual and verbal jokes. As Sabine Hake observes, Ottinger uses "the textual strategies of irony, exaggeration, and simulation," appropriating old images for "subversive purposes" that promise "a new femininity." Ottinger's films typically feature outlandish, fetishistic costumes — such as the backless tin-foil dress and skintight leather ensembles worn and designed by Tabea Blumenschein in *Ticket of No Return* and *Madame X*, respectively. Miriam Hansen views Ottinger's foregrounding of fetishism as a form of masquerade that parades the costumes as "representations, signs, masks of femininity." Ottinger's characters represent overdetermined social female types who serve, as Patricia White notes, "as so many figures in a mise-en-scène of female bodies" — such as Betty Brillo, the 1950s housewife; Noa-Noa, the primitive exotic; Blow Up, the model from *Madame X*; or the trio, Exact Statistics, Social Question, and Common Sense in *Ticket of No Return*.

Linking these social types to camp traditions, Ottinger appropriates gay male aestheticism for feminist purposes. References to Oscar Wilde abound in her films. There are explicit borrowings, such as the films *The Image of Dorian Gray in the Yellow Press*, which substitutes the model Veruschka for Wilde's character, and *Johanna d'Arc*, which features Delphine Seyrig's character, Lady Windermere, the private scholar and anthropologist. In addition, an underlying visual aestheticism can be seen in the films' visual style and use of color, which reflect Ottinger's background as a painter, and in the outrageous costumes, which are, like Mae West's, "trimmed with excitement." Aestheticism also serves as a trope in the films' narratives, as when the Drinker in Ticket of No Return peels an orange and throws away the fruit to cherish the peel.

In claiming aestheticism for women, Ottinger revises and feminizes Wildean aestheticism to create, as Hansen argues in reference to Ticket of No Return, a female dandy. Ottinger aligns this female dandy with a lesbian aesthetic, rewriting the history of camp to include Sapphic modernism as well as Wildean aestheticism. In particular, her films refer to Woolf's Orlando: the pirate ship in Madame X is named for Orlando, Madame X's former lover (played by Ottinger herself); and Freak Orlando represents a sustained rewriting of Virginia Woolf's novel, situating its parodic play within the genre of historical fiction in an historical representation of the world of freaks.

However, rather than privilege Wildean aestheticism and Sapphic modernism, Ottinger links them to a range of entertainment traditions, thus reinscribing high modernism within popular traditions and playing literary camp tropes against cinematic and popular clichés. Freak Orlando incorporates circuses as well as Todd Browning's film Freaks. Madame X effectively remakes Hollywood's many versions of Madame X, the melodrama of the unknown mother.[9] Fritz Lang's maniacal underworld leader Dr. Mabuse becomes Frau Dr. Mabuse, the ruthless manipulator of the yellow press and ruler of a video-dominated "metropolis," in The Image of Dorian Gray in the Yellow Press. In Johanna d'Arc of Mongolia, Ottinger incorporates a variety of figures from musical entertainment traditions: Mickey Katz, "eloquent tenor of the Yiddish-American musical"; the Kalinke sisters, a Georgian ladies combo, reminiscent of the Andrews or McGuire Sisters and of backup singers; and Fanny Ziegfeld, an American musical comedy star, who bears traces not just of her namesakes, Ziegfeld and Fanny Brice, but of Streisand's Brice as well.

Most importantly, Ottinger produces not only a new feminist aesthetic, appropriating fetishism and visual pleasure for women but also inscribes that female aestheticism in the public sphere. Ottinger's female characters are wanderers—nomads, in part, but also female versions of Benjamin and Baudelaire's flaneur.[10] The Drinker in Ticket of No Return wanders the streets of Berlin, voyaging on an urban odyssey in search of booze. Orlando in Freak Orlando wanders through the mall, the public space originally and stereotypically allowed for the flaneuse; but s/he also moves through history, circulating in a landscape of freaks and circuses, subject to neither time nor mortality. Madame X, which Ottinger describes as a comedy about the women's movement, brings its female pirates/representatives together on the high seas with the promise of "Gold, Love, Adventure"—the same promises offered women by the cinema but here made concrete and requiring mobility instead of the immobile spectatorship of the cinema. And the female passengers on the Trans-Siberian railway in *Johanna d'Arc of Mongolia* travel from the European train to the Mongolian steppes (as the film shifts from a Hollywood-style highly artificial studio setting into a style influenced by feminist ethnography), moving literally across different cultures and seemingly across time. In Ottinger's films, these public spaces are not merely traversed by women but dominated by them, in woman-centered narratives that are frequently about creating space for women—whether the all-female pirate ship in *Madame X*, the woman warriors' camp in *Johanna d'Arc*, or the oddly feminized streets of Berlin in *Ticket of No Return*. The movements of these characters are by no means without effort or conflict but instead serve to display, in exaggerated form, the contradictions of a feminized public sphere. Difference (gender difference, cultural difference, historical difference, stylistic difference) is contextualized in these unconventional settings and, at the same time, displaced—made strange all over again. It is also made beautiful and pleasurable and fun.[11]

Taken as a whole, Ottinger's narrative films can be seen as moving beyond debates around *postmodernism* or *postfeminism* to produce a mobilized and recycled camp sensibility that offers simultaneously a new feminist aesthetic and a new view of women's relation to modernity and the relationship between women and the public sphere.

I could cite additional examples—for instance, Akerman's recycling of the Hollywood musical in her film, *Window Shopping*, Sally Potter's *Orlando*, the use of ABBA in *Muriel's Wedding*'s lip-synching female bonding scene, or the female aestheticism of *Absolutely Fabulous*. But, rather than offer a complete catalogue of contemporary feminist camp, in concluding with these texts, I want in part simply to underscore that post-1960s camp does not necessarily signal a loss of perspicuity in camp but can still be a critical force. *Designing Women* demonstrates television's potential to not simply reproduce the dominant but to bring feminist messages to a mainstream audience. In other words, by using camp to articulate its political position, it relates camp spectatorship to women's everyday lives. *Joan Does Dynasty* and *Meeting Two Queens* suggest ways in which spectators might use the interactive technologies of video to appropriate images from the dominant—whether TV or cinema—to create alternative images. Braderman and Barriga take techniques from the avant-garde—collage, photomontage, found footage—to produce a feminist aesthetic, expressive of academic feminism and lesbian fantasy, respectively. Ottinger's films suggest that postmodern style can mobilize a historical understanding of gay and feminist camp both to critique and revitalize feminist politics.

In addition, these texts provide another perspective on the issue of appropriation discussed in the preceding chapter. Each text appropriates camp images—through parodic imitation in the case of *Designing Women*, through quotation in Ottinger's films, and quite literally (raising the issue of copyright infringement) in *Joan Does Dynasty* and *Meeting Two Queens*—and by recontextualizing them recodes them to produce new meanings. Although much post-1960s camp seems to be reinventing the wheel, imitating or borrowing camp style without making camp that differs significantly from earlier camp, these texts recycle camp itself and, in doing so, produce feminist camp effects with respect to the original camp objects.

In appropriating Wilde, Woolf, *Dynasty*, and the images of Crawford, Davis, Dietrich, and Garbo, the examples above appropriate texts and images from the dominant and thus assert female spectators' pleasure in dominant culture. But these texts are already inflected with queer and camp readings, and their appropriation by Braderman, Barriga, Ottinger, and *Designing Women* furthers these readings. Thus, these texts redefine the dominant even as they appropriate from it. In Doty's terms, they make the notion that mass culture is "straight" a "highly questionable given." They underscore both the important role that literary, cinematic, and televisual public spheres have played in queer self-conception and -definition and the importance of queer and camp reading practices in shaping even the dominant culture's understanding of literature, film, and TV histories and ideologies.

The notion of recycling might suggest, on the one hand, that feminist interpretations of camp occur only after the fact, through a historical recontextualization of gay male camp. But, on the other hand, these recyclings represent a recognition that feminist interpretations of camp objects were always already available to female spectators.

We still need, however, to consider the institutional conditions under which camp gets recycled. The examples I describe in this chapter represent consciously oppositional production practices, yet each in its way remains marginal. Video art clearly occupies a marginal place not only in the culture at large but even in art and academic institutions. Ottinger remains a relatively marginal figure in film culture, outside both German commercial cinema and the relatively established male avant-garde; and she still struggles to get her films funded. Showings of her films are limited primarily to gay and lesbian or women's films festivals and academic conferences or are dependent upon noncommercial outlets like the German embassy or Goethe institutes.[12] Women Make Movies currently distributes a 35mm subtitled version of *Johanna d'Arc of Mongolia*, but subtitled videotapes of Ottinger's films are still largely unavailable. *Designing Women*, in contrast, is a popular TV sitcom that fits neatly into the dominant; as a show willing to voice oppositional feminist discourses and one created by very powerful friends of the Clintons—let alone in its redeployment of camp for political purposes—it is, however, an extremely unusual instance within mainstream television. It suggests the potential of television to offer counterpractices but also serves to remind us how rarely television uses that potential.

As earlier chapters have argued, West and Madonna consciously produce a camp aesthetic but stand out as "unusual" insofar as they are positioned as speaking subjects and manage to create a counterpractice within dominant institutions. While West is allowed relative freedom to deploy camp as a conscious aesthetic practice, her physique and her displacement into an 1890s setting emphasizes her difference from the norm and thereby reduces somewhat her threat. Madonna, in contrast, gains access to discursive fellowships not generally available to women because of her economic power. Everything Madonna does is qualified, ironically, by her success—the scale of her business and celebrity. Madonna makes clear that camp can be redeployed as a conscious artistic practice, but at the same time, Madonna's success in cornering the market on camp cannot be easily duplicated and underscores how little room there normally is for a feminist camp practice within dominant institutions.

We need, therefore, to consider whether or how camp can be consciously redeployed as an aesthetic counterpractice from within dominant institutions and not simply from the margins. Recognizing the history of camp as a countertradition is a first step, but, for feminist camp to move significantly beyond the margins, we will still need to redeploy feminist camp as an artistic practice—and not as an exception to the rule.

NOTES

Introduction: *What Makes the Feminist Camp?*

1 See William White, " 'Camp' as Adjective: 1909–1966," *American Speech* 41 (1966): 70–72.

2 Christopher Isherwood, *The World in the Evening* (New York: Noonday Press, 1954), 110.

3 Susan Sontag, "Notes on 'Camp' " (1964), reprinted in Sontag *Against Interpretation* (New York: Farrar, Straus & Giroux, 1966), 275–92.

4 Sontag, "Notes on 'Camp,' " 277. Later, Sontag somewhat modified her claim that camp was essentially apolitical. She credited the diffusion of camp taste with "a considerable if inadvertent role in the upsurge of feminist consciousness in the late 1960s" insofar as camp helped undermine "certain stereotyped femininities." See Susan Sontag, "The 'Salmagundi' Interview," with Robert Boyars and Maxine Bernstein, in *A Susan Sontag Reader* (New York: Farrar, Straus & Giroux, 1982), 338–39.

5 See, for example, Robert F. Kiernan, *Frivolity Unbound: Six Masters of the Camp Novel* (New York: Continuum, 1990).

6 On Friday, 28 June 1969, the day Judy Garland died, New York City vice squad raided the Stonewall Inn on Christopher Street and were attacked by an angry homosexual mob. The police locked themselves in the bar while the mob threw broken bottles and cobblestones, uprooted a parking meter, battered down the door, and tried to set the bar on fire. On Saturday night, another riot occurred. The Stonewall riots "established a homosexual militancy and identity in the public imagination" and are commonly taken to be the originary moment for the modern gay liberation movement. On the importance of Stonewall, see Michael Bronski, *Culture Clash: The Making of Gay Sensibility* (Boston: South End Press, 1984), 2–13 and Martin Duberman, *Stonewall* (1993; reprint, New York: Plume Books, 1994).

7   See Andrew Britton, "For Interpretation—Notes Against Camp," *Gay Left* (winter 1978/79). George Melly refers to post-Stonewall attitudes toward camp, "the Stepin Fetchit of the leather bars," in his preface to Philip Core, *Camp: The Lie that Tells the Truth* (New York: Delilah, 1984), 5. See also Andrew Ross, "Uses of Camp," in *No Respect: Intellectuals and Popular Culture* (New York: Routledge, 1989), 143–44.

8   Richard Dyer, "Judy Garland and Gay Men," in *Heavenly Bodies: Film Stars and Society* (New York: St. Martin's Press, 1986), 115.

9   Richard Dyer, "It's Being So Camp as Keeps Us Going" (1976), reprinted in Dyer, *Only Entertainment* (New York: Routledge, 1992), 145.

10   Fredric Jameson, "Postmodernism, Or, The Cultural Logic of Late Capitalism," *New Left Review*, no. 146 (July–August 1984): 65.

11   Linda Hutcheon, *The Politics of Postmodernism* (New York: Routledge, 1989), 93, 8, 101.

12   Ross 139.

13   This quotation comes from a footnote to the 1977 reprint of Dyer, "It's Being So Camp as Keeps Us Going," *Body Politic Review Supplement* 10 (September 1977): 11. This note no longer appears in the 1992 reprint, nor does any discussion of women's access to camp.

14   On gay men's appropriation of these aspects of women's culture, see George Chauncey, *Gay New York: Gender, Urban Culture, and the Making of the Gay Male World, 1890–1940* (New York: Basic Books, 1994), esp. 289.

15   Mark Booth, *Camp* (New York: Quartet Books, 1983), 18.

16   Wayne Koestenbaum, "Callas and Her Fans," *Yale Review* 79, no. 1 (May 1990): 13–14. See also Catherine Clement, *Opera, or the Undoing of Women*, trans. Betsy Wing (Minneapolis: University of Minnesota Press, 1988), 28.

17   Ross 161.

18   Shari Roberts offers an analysis of the female audience for musicals in *Seeing Stars: Spectacles of Difference in World War II Hollywood Musicals* (Durham, N.C.: Duke University Press, forthcoming).

19   Perhaps not surprisingly, when I looked online for books on gay male friendships with women, the only title that came up with "women" and "gay men" in it was a book about marriages between gay men and straight women. Catherine Whitney, *Uncommon Lives: Gay Men and Straight Women* (New York: New American Library, 1990).

20   Dawne Moon analyzes the use of the term "fag hag" among gay men and finds that the term is used sometimes to mark certain women's exclusion from gay male culture and, contradictorily, to mark others' acceptance by gay men. Dawne Moon, "Insult and Inclusion: The Term 'Fag Hag' and Gay Male 'Community,'" *Social Forces* 74, no. 2 (December 1995). I am also grateful to Eve Kosofsky Sedgwick for helping me sort through the meanings of this term.

21   Some critics seek to bridge the gap between feminist and gay theory. Eve Kosofsky Sedgwick, in particular, has consistently and elegantly negotiated feminist

and gay theory and has demonstrated the joint articulations of antifeminist and homophobic discourses in a variety of contexts. Richard Dyer, as well, seems exemplary in his attention to the intersections of sex and gender oppression. And the shift toward "queer" theory, as I discuss below, may encourage more alliances.

22 Alexander Doty, *Making Things Perfectly Queer: Interpreting Mass Culture* (Minneapolis: University of Minnesota Press, 1993), 3.

23 Moe Meyer, "Reclaiming the Discourse of Camp," in *The Politics and Poetics of Camp*, ed. Moe Meyer (New York: Routledge, 1994), 1–22. Meyer dismisses not only pop camp as camp trace but also, explicitly, criticizes Dyer's analysis of Judy Garland for not "addressing the problem of her nongay sexual identity, and without a political analysis of the relationship between gay discourse and nongay producers of camp."

24 Mary Ann Doane, *The Desire to Desire: The Woman's Film of the 1940s* (Bloomington: Indiana University Press, 1987), 180.

25 Ibid., 182.

26 Judith Butler, *Gender Trouble: Feminism and the Subversion of Identity* (New York: Routledge, 1990), 32, 141.

27 Ibid., 137.

28 Esther Newton, *Mother Camp: Female Impersonators in America* (Chicago: University of Chicago Press, 1979), 103.

29 Judith Butler, *Bodies That Matter: On the Discursive Limits of "Sex"* (New York: Routledge, 1993), 125.

30 See Joan Riviere, "Womanliness as a Masquerade" (1929), reprinted in *Formations of Fantasy*, ed. Victor Burgin, James Donald, Cora Kaplan (London: Methuen, 1986), 35–44. For the introduction of the concept into film studies, see Mary Ann Doane, "Film and the Masquerade: Theorizing the Female Spectator" (1982) and "Masquerade Reconsidered: Further Thoughts on the Female Spectator" (1988–89), reprinted in Doane, *Femmes Fatales: Feminism, Film Theory, Psychoanalysis* (New York: Routledge, 1991), 17–32 and 33–43, respectively; and Claire Johnston, "Femininity and the Masquerade: *Anne of the Indies*" (1975), reprinted in *Psychoanalysis and Cinema*, ed. E. Ann Kaplan (New York: Routledge, 1990), 64–72. See also Stephen Heath, "Joan Riviere and the Masquerade," in *Formations of Fantasy*, 45–61; and Butler, *Gender Trouble*, 43–57.

31 Riviere 35.

32 Riviere 38.

33 Heath 49.

34 Doane, "Film and the Masquerade," 25, 26.

35 Butler, *Gender Trouble*, 138.

36 Doane, for example, would resist camp and discounts her own model of masquerade due to its overlapping passivity and activity. She says that there is a "pronounced difficulty in aligning the notion of masquerade with that of female

spectatorship" due to "the curious blend of activity and passivity in the masquerade" and "the corresponding blurring of the opposition between production and reception." Doane, "Masquerade Reconsidered," 39.

37 See Janet Bergstrom and Mary Ann Doane, "The Female Spectator: Contexts and Directions," *Camera Obscura* 20–21 (May–September 1989): 16–17. See also E. Deidre Pribram, ed., *Female Spectators: Looking at Film and Television* (New York: Verso, 1988); Lorraine Gamman and Margaret Marshment, eds., *The Female Gaze: Women as Viewers of Popular Culture* (Seattle: Real Comet Press, 1989); and Jackie Stacey, *Star Gazing: Hollywood Cinema and Female Spectatorship* (New York: Routledge, 1994). For an overview of theories of spectatorship in film studies generally, see Judith Mayne, *Cinema and Spectatorship* (New York: Routledge, 1993).

38 Miriam Hansen, Individual response to questionnaire, *Camera Obscura* 20–21 (May–Sept. 1989): 173.

39 Doane, "Film and the Masquerade," 26. For a critique of Doane's emphasis on the text, see Tania Modleski, "Rape versus Mans/laughter: Hitchcock's *Blackmail* and Feminist Interpretation," *PMLA* 102, no. 3 (May 1987): 310.

40 Christine Gledhill, "Pleasurable Negotiations," in *Female Spectators: Looking at Film and Television*, ed. E. Deidre Pribram (New York: Verso, 1988), 73. See also Stuart Hall, "Encoding/Decoding," in *Culture Media, Language*, ed. Stuart Hall, et al. (London: Hutchinson, 1980), 128–39.

41 Laura Mulvey, "Afterthoughts on 'Visual Pleasure and Narrative Cinema' inspired by King Vidor's *Duel in the Sun*," in *Visual and Other Pleasures* (Bloomington: Indiana University Press, 1989), 29–38.

42 Mayne 93.

43 Elspeth Probyn, *Sexing the Self: Gendered Positions in Cultural Studies* (New York: Routledge, 1993), 52. Both Mayne and Probyn cite John Fiske, in particular, as exemplary of this tendency in cultural studies. I would argue, and I think they would agree, that the redemptive model is much more widespread. I explore this problem more fully in chapter 4.

44 Meaghan Morris, "Banality in Cultural Studies," in *Logics of Television: Essays in Cultural Criticism*, ed. Patricia Mellencamp (Bloomington: Indiana University Press, 1990), 30.

45 Susan Rubin Suleiman, *Subversive Intent: Gender, Politics and the Avant-Garde* (Cambridge: Harvard University Press, 1990), 179. On comedic forms of female transgression and women's laughter, see Kathleen Rowe, *The Unruly Woman: Gender and the Genres of Laughter* (Austin: University of Texas Press, 1995).

46 Mayne 93.

47 Thomas Hess, "J'Accuse Marcel Duchamp," *Art News* 53, 10 (1965): 53.

48 Sontag, "Notes on 'Camp,'" 277.

49 Richard Dyer, for example, describes a letter he received while researching his piece on Garland and gay men in which the author tells a story about himself and another young boy defending Garland in a high school class, each unaware

that the other was gay and unaware of Garland's association with gay subcultures. Dyer, "Judy Garland and Gay Men," 193.

50 Doty xiii.

51 My description of these class sensibilities are not meant to describe economic or power relations. Rather, I take it to be true that, through camp, gay men of different classes identify with a perceived or imaginary upper-class sensibility and that women of different classes identify with a perceived or imaginary working-class position.

52 Shari Roberts, for example, sees an affinity between Carmen Miranda's "spectacle of ethnicity" and her camp appeal. See Shari Roberts, " 'The Lady in the Tutti-Frutti Hat': Carmen Miranda, a Spectacle of Ethnicity," *Cinema Journal* 32, no. 3 (spring 1993): 3–23.

53 Meyer 5–7.

54 A notable exception is bell hooks, "Is Paris Burning?" in *Black Looks: Race and Representation* (Boston: South End Press, 1992), 145–56.

55 Quoted in Dyer, "It's Being So Camp," 146.

56 Melly, in Core 5; Ross 143.

57 David Bergman, "Introduction," in *Camp Grounds: Style and Homosexuality*, ed. David Bergman (Amherst: University of Massachusetts Press, 1993), 10.

58 Richard Dyer, "White," *Screen* 29, no. 4 (autumn 1988): 44.

59 Patricia Juliana Smith, " 'You Don't Have to Say You Love Me': The Camp Masquerades of Dusty Springfield," and William Lane Clark, "Degenerate Personality: Deviant Sexuality and Race in Ronald Firbank's Novels," in Bergman 185–205 and 134–55, respectively.

1 *"The Kinda Comedy Where They Imitate Me":*
   Mae West's Identification with the Feminist Camp

1 Robert C. Jennings, "Mae West: A Candid Conversation with the Indestructible Queen of Vamp and Camp," *Playboy*, January 1971, 78.

2 Jennings 74.

3 Other honorees, James Stewart and Mervyn LeRoy, simply sat on plain stools and took audience questions.

4 For this description of West's "comeback," I have relied on George Eells and Stanley Musgrove, *Mae West: The Lies, the Legends, the Truth* (London: Robson Books Ltd, 1984), 266–70; and Carol M. Ward, *Mae West: A Bio-Bibliography* (New York: Greenwood Press, 1989).

5 Eells and Musgrove 268.

6 On this point, see Joan Mellen, "The Mae West Nobody Knows," in *Women and Their Sexuality in the New Film* (New York: Horizon Press, 1973), 243.

7 William Troy, "Mae West and the Classic Tradition," *Nation*, 8 November 1933, 547–48.

8   For an account of the history of burlesque, see Robert C. Allen, *Horrible Pretti-ness: Burlesque and American Culture* (Chapel Hill: University of North Carolina Press, 1991).

9   Allen 148.

10   Quoted in Robert C. Toll, *On with the Show: The First Century of Show Business in America* (New York: Oxford University Press, 1976), 226; and Ward 9.

11   According to Maurice Leonard, West's mother, Tillie, idolized Tanguay and made Mae copy her mannerisms and speech. Maurice Leonard, *Mae West: Empress of Sex* (Glasgow: Harper Collins, 1991), 12. See also Eells and Musgrove 35.

12   Most accounts describe Tanguay as a sort of frantic madwoman. See, for instance, Allen 273.

13   Parker Tyler, *The Hollywood Hallucination*, cited by Tyler in his introduction to Jon Tuska, *The Films of Mae West* (Secaucus, N.J.: The Citadel Press, 1973), 10–11.

14   See, for instance, Miriam Hansen, "Pleasure, Ambivalence, Identification: Valen-tino and Female Spectatorship," in *Stardom: Industry of Desire*, ed. by Christine Gled-hill (New York: Routledge, 1991), 277; and Ramona Curry, "Power and Allure: The Mediation of Sexual Difference in the Star Image of Mae West" (Ph.D. diss., Northwestern University, 1990), 257–320 and passim. Although she refers to early appreciations of West as a female impersonator, Curry focuses primarily on gay camp readings of West as an impersonator from the 1960s onward.

15   Eells and Musgrove 36.

16   George Davis, "The Decline of the West," *Vanity Fair*, May 1934, 82.

17   Library of Congress manuscript 11. Hereafter, all play-script citations will be in text. I have cited act, scene, and page when available, but the manuscripts gen-erally mark act and page only.

18   West recruited about fifty chorus boys from a Greenwich Village hangout for homosexuals. During rehearsals, she let the performers "cavort and carry on" as much as they wanted and during the play's run much of the dialogue was ad-libbed. (See Eells and Musgrove 65–66.)

19   Ethan Mordden, "No One's Woman: Mae West," in *Movie Star: A Look at the Women Who Made Hollywood* (New York: St. Martin's Press, 1983), 123.

20   Curry, "Power and Allure," 389.

21   Lawrence F. LaMae, "Writers Fear Hazel Scott Has Become 'Hollywood,' One Writes," *Chicago Defender*, 31 July 1943.

22   John Kobal, "Mae West," in *People Will Talk* (New York: Knopf, 1986), 154.

23   Ramona Curry, "*Goin' to Town* and Beyond: Mae West, Film Censorship and the Comedy of UnMarriage," in *Classical Hollywood Comedy*, ed. Kristine Brunovska Kar-nick and Henry Jenkins (New York: Routledge, 1995), 220.

24   Hazel Carby, "It Jus Be's Dat Way Sometime: The Sexual Politics of Women's Blues," in *Gender and Discourse: The Power of Talk*, ed. Alexandra D. Todd and Sue Fisher (New York: Ablex, 1988), 231.

25   John F. Szwed, "Race and the Embodiment of Culture," *Ethnicity* 2 (1975): 27.

26   Donald Bogle, *Toms, Coons, Mulattoes, Mammies, and Bucks: An Interpretive History of Blacks in American Films* (1973; reprint, New York: Bantam Books, 1974), 60.

27   *Mae West and the Men Who Knew Her* (dir. Gene Feldman, 1993).

28   John Corbett, "Siren Song to Banshee Wail: On the Status of the Background Vocalist," in *Extended Play: Sounding Off from John Cage to Dr. Funkenstein* (Durham, N.C.: Duke University Press, 1994), 56–67.

29   Kaja Silverman, *The Acoustic Mirror: The Female Voice in Psychoanalysis and Cinema* (Bloomington: Indiana University Press, 1988), 61.

30   SDiane Bogus, "The Queen 'B' Figure in Black Literature," in *Lesbian Texts and Contexts: Radical Revisions*, ed. Karla Jay and Joanne Glasgow (New York: New York University Press, 1990), 275–90.

31   Linda Nochlin, "The Imaginary Orient," in *The Politics of Vision: Essays in Nineteenth-Century Art and Society* (New York: Harper Row Publishers, 1989), 49.

32   Review of *Klondike Annie*, *Time*, 9 March 1936, 44.

33   Jay Brian Chapman, "Is Mae West Garbo's Greatest Rival?" *Motion Picture*, July 1933, 28–29, 76–77; Constance Champion, "Katharine Hepburn, Mae West—And Sex Appeal!" *Motion Picture*, March 1934, 28–29, 87–88; Kenneth Baker, "War Clouds in the West?" *Photoplay*, December 1933, 47, 109.

34   Andre Sennewald, "Lines for a Mae West Scrapbook," *New York Times*, 30 September 1934, Sec. 9, p. 4.

35   Leo McCarey, "Mae West Can Play Anything," *Photoplay*, June 1935, 126.

36   Elza Schallert, "Go West—If You're an Adult," *Motion Picture*, May 1933, 32.

37   Anne Cannon Palumbo and Ann Uhry Abrams, "Proliferation of the Image," in *Liberty: The French-American Statue in Art and History*, ed. June Hargrove and Pierre Provoyeur (New York: Harper & Row, 1986), 230–64.

38   June Hargrove, "Unveiling the Colossus," in Hargrove and Provoyeur 201.

39   Stark Young, "Diamond Lil," *New Republic*, 27 June 1928, 146.

40   Kathy Peiss, *Cheap Amusements: Working Women and Leisure in Turn-of-the-Century New York* (Philadelphia: Temple University Press, 1986), 142–45.

41   Allen 76.

42   Miriam Hansen, "Adventures of Goldilocks: Spectatorship, Consumerism and Public Life," *Camera Obscura* 22 (January 1991): 51–54. See also Peiss 148.

43   Colette, "Mae West," in *Colette at the Movies: Criticism and Screenplays*, trans. Sarah W. R. Smith, ed. Alain and Odette Virmaux (New York: Frederick Ungar Publishing Co., 1980), 63.

44   Kirtley Baskette, "Mae West Talks about Her 'Marriage,' " *Photoplay*, August 1935, 40.

45   "New York's 'Dirt' Shows," *Variety*, 2 February 1927, 41.

46   Eells and Musgrove 68.

47   According to Marybeth Hamilton, the play, *Pleasure Man*, was banned because West explicitly linked female impersonation with homosexuality, in opposition to contemporary heterosexualized images of impersonators. This may be part

of the reason, but I would emphasize other facts: namely, that the play ends with a castration scene and treats homosexuality as morally superior to straight male promiscuity. Curiously, when West wrote a novelization of the play in the 1970s, she eliminated all references to female impersonation and homosexuality. See Hamilton, " 'I'm the Queen of the Bitches': Female Impersonation and Mae West's *Pleasure Man*," in *Crossing the Stage: Controversies on Cross-Dressing*, ed. Lesley Ferris (New York: Routledge, 1993), 107–19; and Mae West, *Pleasure Man: The Novel* (New York: Dell Press, 1975).

48   Leonard J. Leff and Jerold L. Simmons, *The Dame in the Kimono: Hollywood, Censorship and the Production Code from the 1920s to the 1960s* (New York: Grove Weidenfeld, 1990), 20–21.

49   Ramona Curry, "Mae West as Censored Commodity: The Case of *Klondike Annie*," *Cinema Journal* 31, no. 1 (fall 1991): 67. See also Marybeth Hamilton, " 'A Little Bit Spicy, but Not Too Raw': Mae West, Pornography and Popular Culture," in *Sex Exposed: Sexuality and the Pornography Debate*, ed. Lynne Segal and Mary McIntosh (New Brunswick, N.J.: Rutgers University Press, 1993), 295–311.

50   Quoted in Eells and Musgrove 280.

51   Leff and Simmons 40.

52   Lea Jacobs, *The Wages of Sin: Censorship and the Fallen Woman Film, 1928–1942* (Madison: University of Wisconsin Press, 1991), 66 and passim.

53   William F. French, "What Price Glamour?" *Motion Picture*, November 1934, 29.

54   See, for instance, Edward Churchill, "So You Think You Know Mae West," *Motion Picture*, July 1935: 49, 70–71; and William French, " 'It's All in Fun,' Says Mae West," *Movie Classic*, December 1934, 27, 70.

55   Gladys Hall, "The Crime of the Day in Hollywood," *Motion Picture*, January 1934, 28.

56   Beulah Leake, "Defending Mae West" (First Prize Letter), *Movie Classic*, March 1935, 10. Although fan letters may not be wholly reliable, as a published document, this forms part of West's star discourse.

57   Jackie Stacey, "Feminine Fascinations: Forms of Identification in Star-Audience Relations," in *Stardom: Industry of Desire*, ed. Christine Gledhill (New York: Routledge, 1991), 141–63; and *Star Gazing: Hollywood Cinema and Female Spectatorship* (New York: Routledge, 1994). Christian Metz adopted the psychoanalytic terminology of three registers of identification (primary, secondary, and partial) for cinematic identification. The cultural and social forms Stacey highlights relate most closely to the psychoanalytic concept of secondary identification—identification with an actor, character, or star. See Christian Metz, *The Imaginary Signifier: Psychoanalysis and the Cinema*, trans. Celia Britton, Annwyl Williams, Ben Brewster, and Alfred Guzzetti (Bloomington: Indiana University Press, 1977), 1–88. For a thorough analysis and summary of the psychoanalytic concept of identification in film studies, see Anne Friedberg, "A Denial of Difference: Theories of Cinematic Identification," in *Psychoanalysis and Cinema*, ed. E. Ann Kaplan (New York: Routledge, 1990), 36–45. The most cogent critique of film studies' use of

psychoanalytic models of identification is in D. N. Rodowick, *The Difficulty of Difference: Psychoanalysis, Sexual Difference & Film Theory* (New York: Routledge, 1991).

58 Alexander Walker, *The Celluloid Sacrifice: Aspects of Sex in the Movies* (London: Michael Joseph, 1966), 74.

59 McCarey 127.

60 Schallert 32.

61 Madame Sylvia, "Is Mae West Skidding on the Curves?" *Photoplay* Nov. 1936: 86.

62 Ruth Tildesley, "Curves! Hollywood Wants Them — And So Will You!" *Motion Picture*, July 1933, 34–35.

63 Cecelia Ager, "Mae West Reveals the Foundation of the 1900 Mode," *Vogue*, 1 September 1933, 67, 86.

64 Colette 62.

65 Review of *I'm No Angel*, *Time*, 16 October 1933: 34.

66 Mae West, *Goodness Had Nothing to Do with It* (Englewood Cliffs, N.J.: Prentice-Hall, 1959), 106–7.

67 Ward 57.

68 Chapman 76.

69 Mae West, interview by Richard Meryman, *Life*, 18 April 1969, 62C.

70 Hall 70.

71 Kirtley Baskette, "Has Mae West Gone High Hat?" *Photoplay*, July 1934, 39, 110–12.

2 *What Trixie and God Know: Feminist Camp*
   in Gold Diggers of 1933

1   Susan Sontag, "Notes on 'Camp'" (1964), reprinted in *Against Interpretation* (New York: Farrar, Straus & Giroux, 1966), 275–92.

2   Jane Feuer, *The Hollywood Musical*, 2d ed. (Bloomington: University of Indiana Press, 1993), ix.

3   Gerald Mast, *Can't Help Singin': The American Musical on Stage and Screen* (New York: Overlook Press, 1987), 2.

4   Ibid. 37.

5   Ibid.

6   Feuer 143 and 141.

7   Ibid. 140.

8   Ibid. 143.

9   See Janet Staiger, "The Logic of Alternative Readings: A Star is Born," in *Interpreting Films: Studies in the Historical Reception of American Cinema* (Princeton: Princeton University Press, 1992), 154–77.

10 *American Thesaurus of Slang* (New York: Thomas Crowell) 580, subheading 594.b.

11 See Feuer 26ff.

12 Bob Pike and Dave Martin, *The Genius of Busby Berkeley* (Reseda, Calif.: Creative Film Society Books, 1973), 33.

13 Mast 123.

14   Feuer 69. See also Rick Altman, *The American Film Musical* (Bloomington: Indiana University Press, 1989), 200–271. Rather than a narrative/number split, Altman emphasizes four "sites" in the backstage musical: city and theater, stage and backstage.

15   Arthur Hove, "Introduction: In Search of Happiness," in *Gold Diggers of 1933*, ed. Arthur Hove (Madison: University of Wisconsin Press, 1980), 19.

16   Ibid. 27–30.

17   Mast 120.

18   See Mark Roth, "Some Warners Musicals and the Spirit of the New Deal," in *Genre: The Musical — A Reader*, ed. Rick Altman (New York: Routledge & Kegan Paul, 1986), 41–56.

19   Richard Dyer, "Entertainment and Utopia," in Altman 186.

20   Lucy Fischer, "The Image of Woman as Image: The Optical Politics of *Dames*," in Altman 70–84; Paula Rabinowitz, "Commodity Fetishism: Women in *Gold Diggers of 1933*," *Film Reader* 5 (1982): 141–49.

21   Patricia Mellencamp, "The Sexual Economics of *Gold Diggers of 1933*," in *Close Viewings: An Anthology of New Film Criticism*, ed. Peter Lehman (Tallahassee: Florida State University Press, 1990), 181.

22   Ibid.

23   Mellencamp clearly distinguishes her use of masochism from recent feminist rewritings that claim masochism for feminism as a female spectatorial mechanism. Gaylyn Studlar, for instance defines masochism as a mother-centered, pre-Oedipal phenomenon and argues for the importance of a "masochistic aesthetic" in film. See Gaylyn Studlar, *In the Realm of Pleasure: Von Sternberg, Dietrich, and the Masochistic Aesthetic* (Chicago: University of Illinois Press, 1988). A principal text on the theory of masochism is that of Gilles Deleuze, *Sacher-Masoch: An Interpretation*, trans. Jean McNeil (London: Faber and Faber, 1971).

24   On this point, see Alexander Doty, *Making Things Perfectly Queer: Interpreting Mass Culture* (Minneapolis: University of Minnesota Press, 1993), 13–14.

25   Although the success of this film motivated Warners to produce variations on the theme in *Gold Diggers of 1935*, *Gold Diggers of 1937*, and *Gold Diggers in Paris* (1938), none of these films were as successful as the 1929 and 1933 versions, and they do not feature true gold diggers so much as attach the term generally to chorus girls, much as Dean Martin did in his TV variety show.

26   For histories of antiprostitution reform movements in the Progressive Era, see Mark Thomas Connelly, *The Response to Prostitution in the Progressive Era* (Chapel Hill: University of North Carolina Press, 1980); Ruth Rosen, *The Lost Sisterhood: Prostitution in America, 1900–1918* (Baltimore: The Johns Hopkins University Press, 1982); and Barbara Meil Hobson, *Uneasy Virtue: The Politics of Prostitution and the American Reform Tradition* (New York: Basic Books, 1987; Chicago: University of Chicago Press, 1990).

27   Hobson 183ff.

28 Numerous films capitalized on the white slavery panic, notably *The White Slave* (dir. Miles Brothers, 1907), *Traffic in Souls* (dir. Tucker, 1913), *The Inside of the White Slave Traffic* (dir. Beal, 1913), *The House of Bondage* (dir. Kingsley, 1914), and *Intolerance* (dir. Griffith, 1916). See Kay Sloan, *The Loud Silents: Origins of the Social Problem Film* (Chicago: University of Illinois Press, 1988), 80–86; Kevin Brownlow, *Behind the Mask of Innocence—Sex, Violence, Prejudice, Crime: Films of Social Conscience in the Silent Era* (Berkeley: University of California Press, 1990), 70–85; and Miriam Hansen, *Babel and Babylon: Spectatorship in American Silent Film* (Cambridge: Harvard University Press, 1991), 221–25.

29 Rosen 47–48.

30 Definitions from *Oxford English Dictionary, Thesaurus of Slang, Dictionary of Slang.* See also Kathy Peiss's discussion of "treating" in " 'Charity Girls' and City Pleasures: Historical Notes on Working-Class Sexuality, 1880–1920," in *Powers of Desire: The Politics of Sexuality,* ed. Ann Snitow, Christine Stansell, and Sharon Thompson (New York: Monthly Review Press, 1983), 74–87.

31 According to Lea Jacobs, 1930s comic gold-digger films were considered "sex pictures" like melodramas of the fallen woman. The tendency in these pictures to glamorize the heroine and to associate the scenario of class rise with female sexuality was considered to be especially repugnant by the industry censors. See Lea Jacobs, *The Wages of Sin: Censorship and the Fallen Woman Film, 1928–1942* (Madison: University of Wisconsin Press, 1991), 66–67. While censors criticized Mae West's "sex pictures," her gold digger is, as I argue in chapter 1, anachronistically inserted into an 1890s setting.

32 Richard Dyer, "It's Being So Camp as Keeps Us Going" (1976), reprinted in Dyer, *Only Entertainment* (New York: Routledge, 1992), 144.

33 Mellencamp 188.

34 John Tiller was a British theater devotee who thought the effect of the chorus would be better if the chorus girls could be drilled to perform numbers in concert, all dancing together and mirroring each other. He formed Tiller Schools, which became extremely influential all over the world. Tiller girls were best known for performing high kicks in unison. The Radio City Rockettes carry on the Tiller tradition today. See Derek and Julia Parker, *The Natural History of the Chorus Girl* (New York: Bobbs Merrill, 1975), 102ff.

35 Siegfried Kracauer, "The Mass Ornament," in *Critical Theory and Society: A Reader,* ed. Stephen Eric Bronner and Douglas MacKay Kellner (New York: Routledge, 1989), 145.

36 Sabine Hake, "Girls and Crisis: The Other Side of Diversion," *New German Critique* 40 (winter 1987): 147–64.

37 Peter Wollen, "Cinema/Americanism/the Robot," in *Modernity and Mass Culture,* ed. James Naremore (Bloomington: Indiana University Press, 1991), 60.

38 Walter Benjamin, "Central Park," trans. Lloyd Spencer, *New German Critique* 34 (winter 1985): 40, 52–53.

39   In aligning Baudelaire with the prostitute, Benjamin also implicitly argues that
the prostitute displaces the myth of individuality and intellectual independence
in both sexes. He writes: "[Baudelaire] proved in his own person what he considered the unavoidable necessity of prostitution for the poet. . . . Baudelaire
stumbled on relations of competition in poetic production. . . . it was a real
discovery of Baudelaire's that he was ranged against individuals. The disorganiza-
tion of the poetic schools, and of 'style' is the complement of the open market
which reveals itself to the poet as the public." Benjamin 53–54.

40   Christine Buci-Glucksman, "Catastrophic Utopia: The Feminine as Allegory of
the Modern," *Representations* 14 (spring 1986): 222.

41   Also see Susan Buck-Morss, "The Flaneur, the Sandwichman and the Whore:
The Politics of Loitering," *New German Critique* 39 (fall 1986): 137.

42   Ibid. 138.

3   *Camping under Western Stars: Joan Crawford*
in Johnny Guitar

1   Evelyn Satz [pseud.], "Camping It Up," *Films and Filming*, no. 342 (March 1983):
22; Crawford quoted in Jane Ellen Wayne, *Crawford's Men* (New York: Prentice-
Hall, 1988), 235.

2   Richard Dyer, *Stars* (London: British Film Institute, 1979), 3, 38.

3   Robert C. Allen and Douglas Gomery, *Film History: Theory and Practice* (New York:
Alfred A. Knopf, 1985), 186.

4   For essays on *Mildred Pierce* in its historical moment, see Peter Biskind, "The Tam-
ing of the Shrew: *Mildred Pierce*," in *Seeing is Believing: How Hollywood Taught Us to Stop
Worrying and Love the Fifties* (New York: Pantheon, 1983), 296–304; Linda Williams,
"Feminist Film Theory: *Mildred Pierce* and the Second World War," in *Female Spectators: Looking at Film and Television*, ed. E. Deidre Pribram (New York: Verso, 1988),
12–30; and Pamela Robertson, "Structural Irony in *Mildred Pierce*, or How Mildred
Lost Her Tongue," *Cinema Journal* 30, no. 1 (fall 1990): 42–54.

5   Joan Crawford with Jane Kerner Ardmore, *A Portrait of Joan* (New York: Paperback
Library, 1964), 123.

6   Allen and Gomery 177.

7   Quoted in Wayne 10.

8   Ben Maddox, "Give Joan Crawford Credit," *Silver Screen*, January 1932, 25.

9   Adela Rogers St. Johns, "Joan Crawford: The Dramatic Rise of a Self-Made Star,"
Photoplay, October 1937, 26.

10   Eric L. Ergenbright, "'Any Clever Woman Can Develop Glamour'—Joan Crawford," *Motion Picture*, November 1934, 27.

11   Jane Marie Gaines and Charlotte Cornelia Herzog, "'Puffed Sleeves Before Tea-
Time': Joan Crawford, Adrian and Women Audiences," in *Stardom: Industry of Desire*,
ed. Christine Gledhill (New York: Routledge, 1991), 85.

12   Ruth Biery, "The Story of a Dancing Girl," *Photoplay*, 28 September 1928, 34.

13   Maddox 71.

14   Crawford was married to Philip Terry from 1942 to 1946 and Alfred Steele from 1955 to 1959.

15   See, for example, "Evolution of Joan Crawford: In which lies pictorial proof that glamour is not always inherent, but can also be acquired — witness these amazing portraits," *Movie Classic*, June 1936, 34–35; Ruth Biery, "From Jazz to Gentility," *Motion Picture*, May 1930, 66, 122–23; and Dorothy Manners, "The Girl without a Past," *Photoplay* Oct. 1935: 32–33, 86.

16   Lea Jacobs, *The Wages of Sin: Censorship and the Fallen Woman Film, 1928–1942* (Madison: University of Wisconsin Press, 1991). See also, Jean-Loup Bourget, "Faces of the American Melodrama," in *Imitations of Life: A Reader on Film and Television Melodrama*, ed. Marcia Landry (Detroit: Wayne State University Press, 1991), 429–40.

17   Allen and Gomery 180–81.

18   Gladys Hall, "Can You Pass Joan Crawford's Love Test?" *Movie Classic*, November 1936, 30–31, 68–69; and Sonia Lee, "How Joan Crawford Keeps Her Men Friends Interested," *Movie Classic*, December 1934, 28–29, 67, 69.

19   Wayne 8.

20   Bob Thomas, *Joan Crawford: A Biography* (New York: Simon & Schuster, 1978), 89.

21   Sonia Lee, "Joan Crawford Answers Her Critics," *Movie Classic*, June 1935, 26.

22   Thomas 123.

23   See Lea Jacobs, "Censorship and the Fallen Woman Cycle," in *Home Is Where the Heart Is: Studies in Melodrama and the Woman's Film*, ed. Christine Gledhill (London: BFI Publishing, 1990), 110–12.

24   Richard Dyer, "Judy Garland and Gay Men," in *Heavenly Bodies: Film Stars and Society* (New York: St. Martin's Press, 1986), 150–56.

25   Stephen Harvey, *Joan Crawford* (New York: Pyramid Publications, 1974), 100.

26   Mary Ann Doane, "The 'Woman's Film': Possession and Address," in Gledhill (1990), 285.

27   Joan Crawford, "I've Been Lonely," *Photoplay*, April 1943, 56, 80.

28   John R. Franchey, "Bachelor Mother," *Silver Screen*, August 1942, 38.

29   For a typical example see Marynia Farnham and Ferdinand Lundberg, *Modern Women: The Lost Sex* (New York: Harper and Brothers, 1947). For an account of the way in which the media ignored Kinsey's more radical findings about clitoral orgasm, see Regina Cornwell Morantz, "The Scientist as Sex Crusader: Alfred C. Kinsey and American Culture," *American Quarterly* 29, no. 5 (1977). Richard Dyer discusses the image of female sexual passivity in relation to Marilyn Monroe's image in *Heavenly Bodies*, 19–66.

30   Susan Faludi, *Backlash: The Undeclared War against American Women* (New York: Crown Publishers, 1992), 53.

31   For accounts of this incident, I have relied on Wayne 196–97 and Thomas 181–83. Thomas was the reporter responsible for the AP article.

32   For accounts of publicity surrounding *Johnny Guitar*, I have relied on Wayne 201–2 and Thomas 188–93. Crawford's own account of the feud between herself and McCambridge does indeed suggest that Crawford was jealous of her younger co-star. In her autobiography, she refers to McCambridge as "an actress who hadn't worked in ten years" despite the fact that McCambridge had won an Academy Award only four years before for her performance in *All the King's Men*. Crawford describes McCambridge as a "rabble rouser" and says she "was perfectly cast in the picture, but she played her part offstage as well." Crawford with Ardmore 118.

33   Nicholas Ray, quote from a public appearance at the Orson Welles Cinema in Cambridge, October 1973, in John Francis Kreide, *Nicholas Ray* (Boston: Twayne Publishers, 1977), 49–50.

34   François Truffaut, "'A Wonderful Certainty': Review of *Johnny Guitar*. April 1955," in *Cahiers du Cinema—The 1950s: Neo-Realism, Hollywood, New Wave*, ed. Jim Hillier (Cambridge: Harvard University Press, 1984), 107.

35   Ibid.

36   Jacques Rivette, "'On Imagination': Review of *The Lusty Men*, October 1953," in Hillier 105.

37   Michael Wilmington, "Nicholas Ray's *Johnny Guitar*," *Velvet Light Trap* 12 (spring 1974): 21.

38   Philip French, *Westerns: Aspects of a Movie Genre* (London: Secker & Warburg in Association with BFI, 1973), 67.

39   Leo Charney, "Historical Excess: *Johnny Guitar's* Containment," *Cinema Journal* 25, no. 4 (summer 1990): 25.

40   Ibid. 27–28.

41   Ibid. 31.

42   Ibid. 29.

43   *Catholic World* June 1954: 27; Virginia Graham, "Cinema," *Spectator*, 4 June 1954, 678.

44   John McCarten, "The Current Cinema: Kill or Be Killed," *New Yorker*, 5 June 1954, 65.

45   Moira Walsh, "Films," *America*, 5 June 1954, 287.

46   Review, *Variety*, 5 May 1954, 6.

47   Ibid.

48   "Cinema: The New Pictures," *Time*, 14 June 1954, 106.

49   Betty Friedan, *The Feminine Mystique* (1963; reprint, New York: Dell, 1983), 103–49.

50   Janet Staiger, "Hollywood, Freud and the Representations of Women: Regulations and Contradiction, 1945–early 60s," in Gledhill (1990), 197.

51   Roy Chanslor, *Johnny Guitar* (New York: Simon and Schuster, 1953), 12. This edition, dedicated to Joan Crawford, claims to be the first printing of the novel. It seems likely, however, that the novel first appeared in a pulp version and was printed by Simon and Schuster after work on the film began.

52 Lillian Faderman, *Odd Girls and Twilight Lovers: A History of Lesbian Life in Twentieth Century America* (New York: Columbia University Press, 1991), 139–58.

53 Ibid. 146–48.

54 Wilmington 24.

55 Ibid.

56 Gaines and Herzog 78.

57 Philip Core, *Camp: The Lie that Tells The Truth* (New York: Delilah, 1984), 58.

58 "New Films," *Newsweek*, 14 June 1954, 104.

59 Rebecca Bell-Metereau, *Hollywood Androgyny* (New York: Columbia University Press, 1985), 92.

60 Charney 30.

61 Esther Newton, "The Mythic Mannish Lesbian: Radclyffe Hall and the New Woman," in *Hidden from History: Reclaiming the Gay and Lesbian Past*, ed. Martin Duberman, Martha Vicinus, and George Chauncey Jr. (New York: Meridian, 1990), 281–93.

62 See Elizabeth Lapovsky Kennedy and Madeline Davis, *Boots of Leather, Slippers of Gold: The History of a Lesbian Community* (New York: Routledge, 1993).

63 Sue-Ellen Case, "Toward a Butch-Femme Aesthetic," *Discourse* 11, no. 1 (fall–winter 1988–89): 64.

4   *Does Feminist Camp Make a Difference? or, What We Talk about When We Talk about Madonna*

1   Madonna, Personality Comics, 1991; Kay Turner, ed., *I Dream of Madonna: Women's Dreams of the Goddess of Pop* (London: Thames and Hudson, 1993); Ilene Rosenzweig, *The I Hate Madonna Handbook* (London: Virgin, 1994).

2   Adam Sexton, ed., *Desperately Seeking Madonna: In Search of the Meaning of the World's Most Famous Woman* (New York: Dell, 1993); Cathy Schwichtenberg, ed., *The Madonna Connection: Representational Politics, Subcultural Identities, and Cultural Theory* (San Francisco: Westview Press, 1993); Lisa Frank and Paul Smith, eds., *Madonnarama: Essays on Sex and Popular Culture* (San Francisco: Cleiss Press, 1993). Sexton's book includes essays from the popular as well as academic press, magazine polls, poems, cartoons, and other instances of Madonna's ubiquitous presence in the popular imagination, serving as a book about both Madonna and Madonna's public. Frank and Smith's book, a collection of essays about *Sex*, published roughly eight months after *Sex*, signals the shockingly quick institutionalization of Madonna studies. The Sexton and Schwichtenberg collections contain a majority of positive responses to Madonna, while Frank and Smith's book is mostly negative, a sign that Madonna's fans and advocates are tiring of her.

3   Steve Anderson, "Forgive Me Father," *Village Voice*, 4 April 1989, 67–68.

4   "Goings on About Town," *New Yorker*, 22 February 1993, 10.

5   Russell Baker, "Those Vile Few," *New York Times*, 24 October 1992, 15.

6   Paul Rudnick and Kurt Anderson, "The Irony Epidemic," *Spy*, March 1989, 94.

7   See, for instance, Richard Dyer, "It's Being So Camp as Keeps Us Going" (1976), reprinted in Dyer, *Only Entertainment* (New York: Routledge, 1992), 135–48; Andrew Britton, "For Interpretation—Notes Against Camp," *Gay Left* (winter 1978/79); and Jack Babuscio, "Camp and the Gay Sensibility," in *Gays and Film*, ed. Richard Dyer (London: British Film Institute, 1980), 40–57.

8   Andrew Ross, "Uses of Camp," in *No Respect: Intellectuals and Popular Culture* (New York: Routledge, 1989), 150.

9   Anne Friedberg, *Window Shopping: Cinema and the Postmodern* (Berkeley: University of California Press, 1993), 9–12. Friedberg makes her point using Dick Hebdige's description of postmodernism as a "buzzword." See Hebdige, "Postmodernism and 'The Other Side,' " *Journal of Communication Inquiry* 10, no. 2 (summer 1986): 78.

10 Andreas Huyssen, *After the Great Divide: Modernism, Mass Culture, Postmodernism* (Bloomington: Indiana University Press, 1986), 187. See also Christin J. Mamiya, "The Legacy of Pop Art: The Roots of Postmodernism," in *Pop Art and Consumer Culture: American Super Market* (Austin: University of Texas Press, 1992), 158–71. For theories of architectural postmodernism, see Robert Venturi, Denise Scott Brown, Stephen Izenour, *Learning from Las Vegas* (Cambridge: MIT Press, 1972) and Venturi, *Complexity and Contradiction in Architecture* (New York: Museum of Modern Art, 1966).

11 Rudnick and Anderson 95.

12 Fredric Jameson, "Postmodernism, Or, The Cultural Logic of Late Capitalism," *New Left Review*, no. 146 (July–August 1984): 65.

13 Mamiya 1.

14 Dan Rubey, "Vogueing at the Carnival: Desire and Pleasure on MTV," *South Atlantic Quarterly* 90, no. 4 (fall 1991): 902.

15 Joyce Millman, "Primadonna," in Sexton 53.

16 Ross, "Uses of Camp," 148.

17 Of course, female stars like Annie Lennox and Grace Jones have played with gender roles in their concerts and videos. These stars, more pop than rock, might be considered transitional figures between performance rock and Madonna.

18 Lisa Lewis, *Gender Politics and MTV: Voicing the Difference* (Philadelphia: Temple University Press, 1990), 29.

19 Ibid. 104.

20 Madonna, quoted in Brian Johnson, "Madonna: The World's Hottest Star Speaks Her Mind," *Macleans*, 13 May 1991, 48.

21 A significant exception is found in Susan McClary, "Living to Tell: Madonna's Resurrection of the Fleshly," *Genders* 7 (spring 1990): 1–21. McClary challenges critics who automatically dismiss Madonna's music as irrelevant and offers a musicological analysis of Madonna's feminist "counternarrative."

22 Sonya Andermahr, "A Queer Love Affair? Madonna and Lesbian and Gay Culture," in *The Good, the Bad, and the Gorgeous: Popular Culture's Romance with Lesbianism*, ed. Diane Hamer and Belinda Budge (London: Pandora, 1994), 35. In the same

anthology, see also Arlene Stein, "Crossover Dreams: Lesbianism and Popular Music since the 1970s," 15–27.

23 See Laurie Schultze, Anne Barton White, and Jane D. Brown, "'A Sacred Monster in Her Prime': Audience Construction of Madonna as Low Other," in Schwichtenberg 15–38. The authors catalogue the opinions of Madonna haters, sorting responses into four categories, one of which emphasizes Madonna's presumably formulaic music and three of which emphasize Madonna's sexuality and gender.

24 See, for instance, Ruth Conniff, "Politics in a Post-Feminist Age," *The Progressive*, July 1991, 17–18.

25 Camille Paglia, "Madonna I: Animality and Artifice," in *Sex, Art, and American Culture: Essays* (New York: Vintage Books, 1992), 3–5. This essay originally appeared in the *New York Times*, 14 December 1990. For discussions of the value of Madonna's postmodernism for feminism, see Cathy Schwichtenberg, "Madonna's Postmodern Feminism: Bringing the Margins to the Center," and Roseann M. Mandziuk, "Feminist Politics and Postmodern Seductions: Madonna and the Struggle for Political Articulation," in Schwichtenberg 129–48 and 167–88, respectively.

26 Ramona Curry, "Madonna from Marilyn to Marlene—Pastiche and/or Parody," *Journal of Film and Video* 42, no. 2 (summer 1990): 25, 28.

27 Greg Seigworth, "The Distance between Me and You: Madonna and Celestial Navigation (or You Can Be My Lucky Star)," in Schwichtenberg 308.

28 Andermahr 29.

29 John Fiske, "British Cultural Studies and Television," in *Channels of Discourse: Television and Contemporary Criticism*, ed. Robert C. Allen (Chapel Hill: University of North Carolina Press, 1987), 277. See also Fiske, "Madonna," in *Reading the Popular* (Boston: Unwin Hyman, 1989).

30 Turner 34.

31 E. Ann Kaplan, "Whose Imaginary? The Televisual Apparatus, the Female Body and Textual Strategies in Select Rock Videos on MTV," in *Female Spectators: Looking at Film and Television*, ed. E. Deidre Pribram (New York: Verso, 1988), 145.

32 Schwichtenberg, "Madonna's Postmodern Feminism," in Schwichtenberg 134.

33 Madonna, quoted in Jay Carr, "Madonna Bares All!" *Boston Globe*, 26 April 1991, 79.

34 Ross, "Uses of Camp," 157.

35 Michael Musto, "Immaculate Connection," *Outweek*, 20 March 1991, 37.

36 Lisa Henderson, "Justify Our Love: Madonna and the Politics of Queer Sex," in Schwichtenberg 117.

37 The British documentary *Banned in the U.S.A.* (1992), about censorship battles in the United States, details the battle over Madonna's Pepsi commercial as well as the controversies surrounding Mapplethorpe, 2 Live Crew, and NEA funding of controversial artists.

38 Lauren Berlant and Elizabeth Freeman, "Queer Nationality," *boundary 2* 19, no. 1 (1992): 154, 152.

39   Andrew Ross, "This Bridge Called My Pussy," in Frank and Smith 52.

40   On disco's relationship to a gay sensibility, see Richard Dyer, "In Defence of Disco," in *Only Entertainment*, 149–58. Since no image of Madonna appeared on her first record cover, most listeners assumed she was an African American woman.

41   See Carrie Fisher, "True Confessions: Part One," *Rolling Stone*, 13 June 1991, 35–36, 39–40, 120; and Johnson, "The World's Hottest Star Speaks Her Mind," 48.

42   John Leland, "The Selling of Sex," *Newsweek*, 2 November 1992, 103.

43   Rosenzweig xii.

44   Marcos Becquer and Jose Gatti, "Elements of Vogue" (paper presented at Society for Cinema Studies Conference, Los Angeles, Calif., May 1991).

45   Lynne Layton, "Like a Virgin: Madonna's Version of the Feminine," in Sexton 171.

46   Ibid. 172.

47   Kaja Silverman, "Histoire d'O: The Construction of a Female Subject," in *Pleasure and Danger: Exploring Female Sexuality*, ed. Carol Vance (1984; reprint, London: Pandora Press, 1989), 326. See also Michel Foucault, *The Archaeology of Knowledge and the Discourse on Language*, trans. A. M. Sheridan (London: Tavistock, 1972), 225–26; and Silverman, *The Subject of Semiotics* (New York: Oxford University Press, 1983).

48   David Tetzlaff, "Metatextual Girl: Patriarchy, Postmodernism, Power, Money, Madonna," in Schwichtenberg 259. See also Rubey's analysis of "Justify My Love" where he argues that Madonna "insists on both her solidarity with minorities and marginal groups, and on her ability to move between worlds, to leave the hotel when she's tired of dressing up." Rubey 901–2.

49   Douglas Crimp and Michael Warner, "No Sex in *Sex*," in Frank and Smith 95.

50   bell hooks, "Madonna: Plantation Mistress or Soul Sister," in *Black Looks: Race and Representation* (Boston: South End Press, 1992), 163.

51   John Champagne, "Stabat Madonna," in Frank and Smith 111–38.

52   Kate Tentler, "Like a Feminist," *Village Voice*, 24 November 1992, 22. Not surprisingly, Madonna's stance on pornography, abuse, and rape are the things Camille Paglia admires in *Sex*. See Paglia, "Camille Paglia, Author of *Sexual Personae*, Talks About *Sex*," *Us Magazine*, December 1992, 18.

53   Crimp and Warner 95. See also Hamer and Budge on "lesbian chic" in popular culture.

54   Alexander Doty, *Making Things Perfectly Queer: Interpreting Mass Culture* (Minneapolis: University of Minnesota Press, 1993), 104.

Conclusion: The Queens Are Dead,
Long Live the Queens

 1   Two anthologies on camp are: David Bergman, ed., *Camp Grounds: Style and Homosexuality* (Amherst: University of Massachusetts Press, 1993) and Moe Meyer, ed., *The Politics and Poetics of Camp* (New York: Routledge, 1994).

 2   My analysis relies on Tara McPherson, "Disregarding Romance and Refashioning

Femininity: Getting Down and Dirty with the *Designing Women*" (paper presented at the Society for Cinema Studies, Pittsburgh, Pa., May 1992). See also Alexander Doty's description of *Designing Women* as a lesbian narrative in *Making Things Perfectly Queer: Interpreting Mass Culture* (Minneapolis: University of Minnesota Press, 1993), 39–62 and passim.

3   Before going off the air, the show underwent numerous changes in personnel, losing some female characters and adding others. Mary Jo and Julia were the only female characters left from the original story line. Initially, Anthony seemed to be coded as gay, but in the last few seasons, the show's narrative strenuously asserted his heterosexuality. See McPherson and Doty for accounts of the changes in personnel and politics over the years.

4   *Joan Does Dynasty* was produced as part of *Paper Tiger Television*, a weekly series on public access cable television. It can be seen in the video compilation *Crack in the Tube*, produced by the Video Data Bank.

5   Martha Gever, "The Feminism Factor: Video and Its Relation to Feminism," in *Illuminating Video: An Essential Guide to Video Art*, ed. Doug Hall and Sally Jo Fifer (New York: Aperture, in association with Bay Area Video Coalition, 1990), 237.

6   I am not suggesting that the formalist device of deconstruction will automatically function critically. A counterexample would be *Mystery Science Theater 3000* in which the "alien"-ation is literalized and the viewers critique the films from a position of superiority (above the earth, mocking the films).

7   Mary Desjardins, "*Meeting Two Queens*: Feminist Filmmaking, Fan Culture, Identity Politics, and the Melodramatic Fantasy," unpublished. Judith Mayne discusses the relationship between "outing" and gay and lesbian spectatorship in *Cinema and Spectatorship* (New York: Routledge, 1993), 160ff.

8   Essays on Ottinger in English include: Ruth Perlmutter, "German Grotesque: Two Films by Sander and Ottinger," Sabine Hake, "'And with Favorable Winds They Sailed Away': *Madame X* and Femininity," Miriam Hansen, "Visual Pleasure, Fetishism, and the Problem of Feminine/Feminist Discourse: Ulrike Ottinger's *Ticket of No Return*," Marc Silberman, "Interview with Ulrike Ottinger: Surreal Images," all reprinted in *Gender and German Cinema: Feminist Interventions*, vol. 1, ed. Sandra Frieden, et al. (Oxford: Berg, 1993); Patricia White, "Madame X of the China Seas," in *Queer Looks: Perspectives on Lesbian and Gay Film and Video*, ed. Martha Gever, Pratibha Parmar, and John Greyson (New York: Routledge, 1993), 275–91; Angela McRobbie, introduction to "Interview with Ulrike Ottinger," interview by Erica Carter, trans. Martin Chalmers, *Screen Education* 41 (1982): 34; Therese Grisham, "Twentieth Century *Theatrum Mundi*: Ulrike Ottinger's *Johanna d'Arc of Mongolia*" and Ulrike Ottinger, "An Interview with Ulrike Ottinger," interview by Therese Grisham, *Wide Angle* 14, no. 2 (April 1992): 23–36; Brenda Longfellow, "Lesbian Phantasy and the Other Woman in Ottinger's *Johanna d'Arc of Mongolia*," *Screen* 34, no. 2 (summer 1993): 124–36; Roswitha Mueller, "The Mirror and the Vamp," *New German Critique*, no. 34 (1985): 176–93; and Ulrike Ottinger, "Minori-

ties and the Majority: An Interview with Ulrike Ottinger," interview by Roy Grundmann and Judith Shulevitz, *Cineaste* 43, no. 3 (1991): 40ff.

9   See Hake and White on "Madame X" in Hollywood.

10 On the gendering of the flaneur and the relation between the flaneur/flaneuse and a postmodern aesthetic, see Anne Friedberg, *Window Shopping: Cinema and the Postmodern* (Berkeley: University of California Press, 1993).

11 See the interview by Grundmann and Shulevitz on Ottinger's view of her films as about difference and the relationship between the minority and majority.

12 On this point, see Hansen, "Visual Pleasure, Fetishism."

BIBLIOGRAPHY

Books, Journals, Manuscripts

Allen, Robert C., and Douglas Gomery. Film History: Theory and Practice. New York: Alfred A. Knopf, 1985.

Allen, Robert C. Horrible Prettiness: Burlesque and American Culture. Chapel Hill: University of North Carolina Press, 1991.

———. Vaudeville and Film 1895–1915: A Study in Media Interaction. New York: Arno Press, 1980.

Altman, Rick. The American Film Musical. Bloomington: Indiana University Press, 1989.

Andermahr, Sonya. "A Queer Love Affair? Madonna and Lesbian and Gay Culture." In The Good, the Bad, and the Gorgeous: Popular Culture's Romance with Lesbianism, edited by Diane Hamer and Belinda Budge. London: Pandora, 1994.

Babuscio, Jack. "Camp and the Gay Sensibility." In Gays and Film, edited by Richard Dyer. London: British Film Institute, 1980.

Becquer, Marcos, and Jose Gatti. "Elements of Vogue." Paper presented at Society for Cinema Studies Conference, Los Angeles, Calif., May 1991.

Bell-Metereau, Rebecca. Hollywood Androgyny. New York: Columbia University Press, 1985.

Benjamin, Walter. "Central Park." Translated by Lloyd Spencer. New German Critique 34 (winter 1985): 32–58.

Bergman, Carol. Mae West. New York: Chelsea House Publishers, 1988.

Bergman, David. Camp Grounds: Style and Homosexuality. Amherst: University of Massachusetts Press, 1993.

Bergstrom, Janet, and Mary Anne Doane. "The Female Spectator: Contexts and Directions." Camera Obscura 20–21 (May–September 1989): 5–27.

Berlant, Lauren, and Elizabeth Freeman. "Queer Nationality." boundary 2 19, no. 1 (1992): 149–80.

Biskind, Peter. Seeing is Believing: How Hollywood Taught Us to Stop Worrying and Love the Fifties. New York: Pantheon, 1983.

Bogle, Donald. *Toms, Coons, Mulattoes, Mammies, and Bucks: An Interpretive History of Blacks in American Films.* 1973. Reprint, New York: Bantam Books, 1974.

Bogus, SDiane. "The Queen 'B' Figure in Black Literature." In *Lesbian Texts and Contexts: Radical Revisions,* edited by Karla Jay and Joanne Glasgow. New York: New York University Press, 1990.

Boone, Joseph A., and Michael Cadden, eds. *Engendering Men: The Question of Male Feminist Criticism.* New York: Routledge, 1990.

Booth, Mark. *Camp.* New York: Quartet Books, 1983.

Bourget, Jean-Loup. "Faces of the American Melodrama." In *Imitations of Life: A Reader on Film and Television Melodrama,* edited by Marcia Landry. Detroit: Wayne State University Press, 1991.

Bronski, Michael. *Culture Clash: The Making of Gay Sensibility.* Boston: South End Press, 1984.

Brownlow, Kevin. *Behind the Mask of Innocence—Sex, Violence, Prejudice, Crime: Films of Social Conscience in the Silent Era.* Berkeley: University of California Press, 1990.

Buci-Glucksman, Christine. "Catastrophic Utopia: The Feminine as Allegory of the Modern." *Representations* 14 (spring 1986): 220–29.

Buck-Morss, Susan. "The Flaneur, the Sandwichman and the Whore: The Politics of Loitering." *New German Critique* 39 (fall 1986): 99–140.

Butler, Judith. *Bodies That Matter: On the Discursive Limits of "Sex."* New York: Routledge, 1993.

———. *Gender Trouble: Feminism and the Subversion of Identity.* New York: Routledge, 1990.

Byars, Jackie. *All That Hollywood Allows: Re-Reading Gender in 1950s Melodrama.* Chapel Hill: The University of North Carolina Press, 1991.

Carby, Hazel. "It Jus Be's Dat Way Sometime: The Sexual Politics of Women's Blues." In *Gender and Discourse: The Power of Talk,* edited by Alexandra D. Todd and Sue Fisher. New York: Ablex, 1988.

Case, Sue-Ellen. "Toward a Butch-Femme Aesthetic." *Discourse* 11, no. 1 (fall–winter 1988–89): 55–73.

Chafe, William Henry. *The American Woman: Her Changing Social, Economic, and Political Roles, 1920–1970.* New York: Oxford University Press, 1972.

Champagne, John. "Stabat Madonna." In *Madonnarama: Essays on Sex and Popular Culture,* edited by Lisa Frank and Paul Smith. San Francisco: Cleiss Press, 1993.

Chanslor, Roy. *Johnny Guitar.* New York: Simon and Schuster, 1953.

Charney, Leo. "Historical Excess: *Johnny Guitar's* Containment." *Cinema Journal* 25, no. 4 (summer 1990): 23–34.

Chauncey, George. *Gay New York: Gender, Urban Culture, and the Making of the Gay Male World, 1890–1940.* New York: Basic Books, 1994.

Clark, William Lane. "Degenerate Personality: Deviant Sexuality and Race in Ronald Firbank's Novels." In *Camp Grounds: Style and Homosexuality,* edited by David Bergman. Amherst: University of Massachusetts Press, 1993.

Clement, Catherine. *Opera, or the Undoing of Women.* Translated by Betsy Wing. Minneapolis: University of Minnesota Press, 1988.

Colette. *Colette at the Movies: Criticism and Screenplays.* Translated by Sarah W. R. Smith. Edited by Alain and Odette Virmaux. New York: Frederick Ungar, 1980.

Connelly, Mark Thomas. *The Response to Prostitution in the Progressive Era.* Chapel Hill: University of North Carolina Press, 1980.

Corbett, John. "Siren Song to Banshee Wail: On the Status of the Background Vocalist." In *Extended Play: Sounding Off from John Cage to Dr. Funkenstein.* Durham, N.C.: Duke University Press, 1994.

Core, Philip. *Camp: The Lie that Tells the Truth.* New York: Delilah, 1984.

Crawford, Joan, with Jane Kerner Ardmore. *A Portrait of Joan.* New York: Paperback Library, 1964.

Crimp, Douglas, and Michael Warner. "No Sex in Sex." In *Madonnarama: Essays on Sex and Popular Culture,* edited by Lisa Frank and Paul Smith. San Francisco: Cleiss Press, 1993.

Curry, Ramona. "*Goin'* to Town and Beyond: Mae West, Film Censorship and the Comedy of UnMarriage." In *Classical Hollywood Comedy,* edited by Kristine Brunovska Karnick and Henry Jenkins. New York: Routledge, 1995.

———. "Mae West as Censored Commodity: The Case of *Klondike Annie.*" *Cinema Journal* 31, no. 1 (fall 1991): 57–84.

———. "Madonna from Marilyn to Marlene—Pastiche and/or Parody." *Journal of Film and Video* 42, no. 2 (summer 1990): 15–30.

———. "Power and Allure: The Mediation of Sexual Difference in the Star Image of Mae West." Ph.D. diss., Northwestern University, 1990.

Da, Lottie, and Jane Alexander. *Bad Girls of the Silver Screen.* New York: Carrol & Graf, 1989.

Desjardins, Mary. "*Meeting Two Queens:* Feminist Filmmaking, Fan Culture, Identity Politics, and Melodramatic Fantasy." Unpublished.

Deleuze, Gilles. *Sacher-Masoch: An Interpretation.* Translated by Jean McNeil. London: Faber and Faber, 1971.

Doan, Laura, ed. *The Lesbian Postmodern.* New York: Columbia University Press, 1994.

Doane, Mary Ann. *Femmes Fatales: Feminism, Film Theory, Psychoanalysis.* New York: Routledge, 1991.

———. *The Desire to Desire: The Woman's Film of the 1940s.* Bloomington: Indiana University Press, 1987.

———. "The 'Woman's Film': Possession and Address." In *Home is Where the Heart Is: Studies in Melodrama and the Woman's Film,* edited by Christine Gledhill. London: BFI Publishing, 1990.

Dolan, Jill. *The Feminist Spectator as Critic.* Ann Arbor: University of Michigan Press, 1991.

Doty, Alexander. *Making Things Perfectly Queer: Interpreting Mass Culture.* Minneapolis: University of Minnesota Press, 1993.

Duberman, Martin. *Stonewall.* 1993. Reprint, New York: Plume Books, 1994.

Dyer, Richard. *The Matter of Images: Essays On Representation.* New York: Routledge, 1993.

———. *Only Entertainment.* New York: Routledge, 1992.

———. *Now You See It: Studies on Lesbian and Gay Film.* New York: Routledge, 1990.

———. "White," *Screen* 29, no. 4 (autumn 1988): 44. Reprinted in *The Matter of Images.*

————. *Heavenly Bodies: Film Stars and Society.* New York: St. Martin's Press, 1986.

————. "Entertainment and Utopia." In *Genre: The Musical—A Reader,* edited by Rick Altman. New York: Routledge & Kegan Paul, 1986.

————. *Stars.* London: British Film Institute, 1979.

Edwards, Tim. *Erotics and Politics: Gay Male Sexuality, Masculinity, and Feminism.* New York: Routledge, 1994.

Eells, George, and Stanley Musgrove. *Mae West: The Lies, the Legend, the Truth.* London: Robson Books, 1984.

Faderman, Lillian. *Odd Girls and Twilight Lovers: A History of Lesbian Life in Twentieth Century America.* New York: Columbia University Press, 1991.

Faludi, Susan. *Backlash: The Undeclared War against American Women.* New York: Crown, 1992.

Farnham, Marynia, and Ferdinand Lundberg. *Modern Woman: The Lost Sex.* New York: Harper and Brothers, 1947.

Feuer, Jane. *The Hollywood Musical.* 2d ed. Bloomington: University of Indiana Press, 1993.

Fischer, Lucy. "The Image of Woman as Image: The Optical Politics of *Dames.*" In *Genre: The Musical—A Reader,* edited by Rick Altman. New York: Routledge & Kegan Paul, 1986.

Fiske, John. *Reading the Popular.* Boston: Unwin Hyman, 1989.

————. "British Cultural Studies and Television." In *Channels of Discourse: Television and Contemporary Criticism,* edited by Robert C. Allen. Chapel Hill: University of North Carolina Press, 1987.

Foucault, Michel. *The Archaeology of Knowledge and the Discourse on Language.* Translated by A. M. Sheridan. London: Tavistock, 1972.

Frank, Lisa, and Paul Smith, eds. *Madonnarama: Essays on Sex and Popular Culture.* San Francisco: Cleiss Press, 1993.

Franklin, S., Celia Lury, and Jackie Stacey, eds. *Off-Centre: Feminism and Cultural Studies.* London: HarperCollins, 1991.

French, Philip. *Westerns: Aspects of a Movie Genre.* London: Secker & Warburg in Association with BFI, 1973.

Friedan, Betty. *The Feminine Mystique.* 1963. Reprint, New York: Dell, 1983.

Friedberg, Anne. *Window Shopping: Cinema and the Postmodern.* Berkeley: University of California Press, 1993.

————. "A Denial of Difference: Theories of Cinematic Identification." In *Psychoanalysis and Cinema,* edited by E. Ann Kaplan. New York: Routledge, 1990.

Gaines, Jane Marie, and Charlotte Cornelia Herzog. " 'Puffed Sleeves Before Tea-Time': Joan Crawford, Adrian and Women Audiences." In *Stardom: Industry of Desire,* edited by Christine Gledhill. New York: Routledge, 1991.

Gamman, Lorraine, and Margaret Marshment, eds. *The Female Gaze: Women as Viewers of Popular Culture.* Seattle: Real Comet Press, 1989.

Garber, Marjorie. *Vested Interests: Cross-Dressing and Cultural Anxiety.* New York: Routledge, 1992.

Gever, Martha. "The Feminism Factor: Video and Its Relation to Feminism." In *Illu-*

minating Video: An Essential Guide to Video Art, edited by Doug Hall and Sally Jo Fifer. New York: Aperture, in association with Bay Area Video Coalition, 1990.

Gledhill, Christine. "Pleasurable Negotiations." In Female Spectators: Looking at Film and Television, edited by E. Deidre Pribram. New York: Verso, 1988.

Grisham, Therese. "Twentieth Century Theatrum Mundi: Ulrike Ottinger's Johanna d'Arc of Mongolia" and "An Interview With Ulrike Ottinger." Wide Angle 14, no. 2 (April 1992): 23–36.

Hake, Sabine. " 'And with Favorable Winds They Sailed Away': Madame X and Femininity." In Gender and German Cinema: Feminist Interventions, vol. 1, edited by Sandra Frieden, et al. Oxford: Berg, 1993.

————. "Girls and Crisis: The Other Side of Diversion." New German Critique 40 (winter 1987): 147–64.

Hall, Stuart. "Encoding/Decoding." In Culture Media, Language edited by Hall et al. London: Hutchinson, 1980.

Hamer, Diane, and Belinda Budge, eds. The Good, the Bad, and the Gorgeous: Popular Culture's Romance with Lesbianism. London: Pandora, 1994.

Hamilton, Marybeth. " 'A Little Bit Spicy, but Not Too Raw': Mae West, Pornography and Popular Culture." In Sex Exposed: Sexuality and the Pornography Debate, edited by Lynne Segal and Mary McIntosh. New Brunswick, N.J.: Rutgers University Press, 1993.

————. " 'I'm the Queen of the Bitches': Female Impersonation and Mae West's Pleasure Man." In Crossing the Stage: Controversies on Cross-Dressing, edited by Lesley Ferris. New York: Routledge, 1993.

Hansen, Miriam. "Visual Pleasure, Fetishism, and the Problem of Feminine/Feminist Discourse: Ulrike Ottinger's Ticket of No Return." In Gender and German Cinema: Feminist Interventions, vol. 1, edited by Sandra Frieden, et al. Oxford: Berg, 1993.

————. Babel and Babylon: Spectatorship in American Silent Film. Cambridge: Harvard University Press, 1991.

————. "Pleasure, Ambivalence, Identification: Valentino and Female Spectatorship." In Stardom: Industry of Desire, edited by Christine Gledhill. New York: Routledge, 1991.

————. "Adventures of Goldilocks: Spectatorship, Consumerism and Public Life." Camera Obscura 22 (January 1991): 51–72.

————. Individual response to questionnaire. Camera Obscura 20–21 (May–September 1989): 169–74.

Hargrove, June, and Pierre Provoyeur. Liberty: The French-American Statue in Art and History. New York: Harper & Row, 1986.

Harvey, Stephen. Joan Crawford. New York: Pyramid Publications, 1974.

Heath, Stephen. "Joan Riviere and the Masquerade." In Formations of Fantasy, edited by Victor Burgin, James Donald, Cora Kaplan. London: Methuen, 1986.

Hebdige, Dick. "Postmodernism and 'The Other Side.' " Journal of Communication Inquiry 10, no. 2 (summer 1986).

————. Subculture: The Meaning of Style. 1979. Reprint. London: Routledge, 1988.

Henderson, Lisa. "Justify Our Love: Madonna and the Politics of Queer Sex." In *The Madonna Connection: Representational Politics, Subcultural Identities, and Cultural Theory*, edited by Cathy Schwichtenberg. San Francisco: Westview Press, 1993.

Hobson, Barbara Meil. *Uneasy Virtue: The Politics of Prostitution and the American Reform Tradition*. 1987. Reprint, Chicago: University of Chicago Press, 1990.

hooks, bell. *Black Looks: Race and Representation*. Boston: South End Press, 1992.

Hove, Arthur, ed. *Gold Diggers of 1933*. Madison: University of Wisconsin Press, 1980.

Hutcheon, Linda. *The Politics of Postmodernism*. New York: Routledge, 1989.

Huyssen, Andreas. *After the Great Divide: Modernism, Mass Culture, Postmodernism*. Bloomington: Indiana University Press, 1986.

Isherwood, Christopher. *The World In the Evening*. New York: Noonday Press, 1954.

Jacobs, Lea. *The Wages of Sin: Censorship and the Fallen Woman Film, 1928–1942*. Madison: University of Wisconsin Press, 1991.

———. "Censorship and the Fallen Woman Cycle." In *Home Is Where the Heart Is: Studies in Melodrama and the Woman's Film*, edited by Christine Gledhill. London: BFI Publishing, 1990.

Jameson, Fredric. "Postmodernism, Or, The Cultural Logic of Late Capitalism." *New Left Review*, no. 146 (July–August 1984): 53–92.

Jardine, Alice, and Paul Smith, eds. *Men in Feminism*. New York: Methuen, 1987.

Johnston, Claire. "Femininity and the Masquerade: *Anne of the Indies*." In *Psychoanalysis and Cinema*, edited by E. Ann Kaplan. New York: Routledge, 1990.

Kaplan, Cora. "Wild Nights: Pleasure/Sexuality/Feminism." In *Formations of Pleasure*, edited by Fredric Jameson, et al. Boston: Routledge & Kegan Paul, 1983.

Kaplan, E. Ann. "Whose Imaginary? The Televisual Appartus, the Female Body and Textual Strategies in Select Rock Videos on MTV." In *Female Spectators: Looking at Film and Television*, edited by E. Deidre Pribram. New York: Verso, 1988.

Kennedy, Elizabeth Lapovsky, and Madeline Davis. *Boots of Leather, Slippers of Gold: The History of a Lesbian Community*. 1991. Reprint, New York: Routledge, 1993.

Kiernan, Robert F. *Frivolity Unbound: Six Masters of the Camp Novel*. New York: Continuum, 1990.

Knight, Julia. *Women and the New German Cinema*. New York: Verso, 1992.

Kobal, John. "Mae West." In *People Will Talk*. New York: Knopf, 1986.

Koestenbaum, Wayne. "Callas and Her Fans." *Yale Review* 79, no. 1 (May 1990): 1–20.

Kracauer, Siegfried. "The Mass Ornament." In *Critical Theory and Society: A Reader*, edited by Stephen Eric Bronner and Douglas MacKay Kellner. New York: Routledge, 1989.

Kreide, John Francis. *Nicholas Ray*. Boston: Twayne Publishers, 1977.

Layton, Lynne. "Like a Virgin: Madonna's Version of the Feminine." In *Desperately Seeking Madonna: In Search of the Meaning of the World's Most Famous Woman*, edited by Adam Sexton. New York: Dell, 1993.

Leff, Leonard J., and Jerold L. Simmons. *The Dame in the Kimono: Hollywood, Censorship, and the Production Code from the 1920s to the 1960s*. New York: Grove Weidenfeld, 1990.

Leonard, Maurice. *Mae West: Empress of Sex*. Glasgow: HarperCollins, 1991.

Lewis, Lisa. *Gender Politics and MTV: Voicing the Difference*. Philadelphia: Temple University Press, 1990.

Longfellow, Brenda. "Lesbian Phantasy and the Other Woman in Ottinger's *Johanna d'Arc of Mongolia*." *Screen* 34, no. 2 (summer 1993): 124–36.

Madonna. *Sex*. Photographs by Steven Meisel. New York: Warner Books, 1992.

Madonna #1. Personality Comics, 1991.

Mamiya, Christin J. *Pop Art and Consumer Culture: American Super Market*. Austin: University of Texas Press, 1992.

Mandziuk, Roseann M. "Feminist Politics and Postmodern Seductions: Madonna and the Struggle for Political Articulation." In *The Madonna Connection: Representational Politics, Subcultural Identities, and Cultural Theory*, edited by Cathy Schwichtenberg. San Francisco: Westview Press, 1993.

Mast, Gerald. *Can't Help Singin': The American Musical on Stage and Screen*. New York: Overlook Press, 1987.

Mayne, Judith. *Cinema and Spectatorship*. New York: Routledge, 1993.

———. *The Woman at the Keyhole: Feminism and Women's Cinema*. Bloomington: Indiana University Press, 1990.

McClary, Susan. "Living to Tell: Madonna's Resurrection of the Fleshly." *Genders* 7 (spring 1990): 1–21.

McCormick, Richard W. *Politics of the Self: Feminism and the Postmodern in West German Literature and Film*. Princeton: Princeton University Press, 1991.

McPherson, Tara. "Disregarding Romance and Refashioning Femininity: Getting Down and Dirty with the *Designing Women*." Paper presented at the Society for Cinema Studies, Pittsburgh, May 1992.

McRobbie, Angela. Introduction to "Interview with Ulrike Ottinger." By Erica Carter. Translated by Martin Chalmers. *Screen Education* 41 (1982): 34.

Mellen, Joan. *Women and Their Sexuality in the New Film*. New York: Horizon Press, 1973.

Mellencamp, Patricia, "The Sexual Economics of *Gold Diggers of 1933*." In *Close Viewings: An Anthology of New Film Criticism*, edited by Peter Lehman. Tallahassee: Florida State University Press, 1990.

Metz, Christian. *The Imaginary Signifier: Psychoanalysis and the Cinema*. Translated by Celia Britton, Annwyl Williams, Ben Brewster, and Alfred Guzzetti. Bloomington: Indiana University Press, 1977.

Meyer, Moe. "Reclaiming the Discourse of Camp." In *The Politics and Poetics of Camp*, edited by Moe Meyer. New York: Routledge, 1994.

Millman, Joyce. "Primadonna." In *Desperately Seeking Madonna: In Search of the Meaning of the World's Most Famous Woman*, edited by Adam Sexton. New York: Dell, 1993.

Modleski, Tania. *Feminism without Women: Culture and Criticism in a "Postfeminist" Age*. New York: Routledge, 1991.

———. "Rape versus Mans/laughter: Hitchcock's *Blackmail* and Feminist Interpretation." *PMLA* 102, no. 3 (May 1987).

Moers, Ellen. *The Dandy: Brummell to Beerbohm.* Lincoln: University of Nebraska Press, 1960.

Moon, Dawne. "Insult and Inclusion: The Term 'Fag Hag' and Gay Male 'Community.'" *Social Forces* 74, no. 2 (December 1995).

Morantz, Regina Cornwell. "The Scientist as Sex Crusader: Alfred C. Kinsey and American Culture." *American Quarterly* 29, no. 5 (1977).

Mordden, Ethan. *Movie Star: A Look at the Women Who Made Hollywood.* New York: St. Martin's Press, 1983.

Morris, Meaghan. "Banality in Cultural Studies." In *Logics of Television: Essays in Cultural Criticism,* edited by Patricia Mellencamp. Bloomington: Indiana University Press, 1990.

Mueller, Roswitha. "The Mirror and the Vamp." *New German Critique* 34 (1985): 176–93.

Mulvey, Laura. *Visual and Other Pleasures.* Bloomington: Indiana University Press, 1989.

Newton, Esther. *Mother Camp: Female Impersonators in America.* Chicago: University of Chicago Press, 1979.

———. "The Mythic Mannish Lesbian: Radclyffe Hall and the New Woman." In *Hidden from History: Reclaiming the Gay and Lesbian Past,* edited by Martin Duberman, Martha Vicinus, and George Chauncey Jr. New York: Meridian, 1990.

Nochlin, Linda. *The Politics of Vision: Essays in Nineteenth-Century Art and Society.* New York: Harper Row Publishers, 1989.

Ottinger, Ulrike. Interview by Therese Grisham. *Wide Angle* 14, no. 2 (April 1992): 23–36.

Paglia, Camille. *Sex, Art, and American Culture: Essays.* New York: Vintage Books, 1992.

Parker, Derek, and Julia Parker. *The Natural History of the Chorus Girl.* New York: Bobbs Merrill, 1975.

Peiss, Kathy. *Cheap Amusements: Working Women and Leisure in Turn-of-the-Century New York.* Philadelphia: Temple University Press, 1986.

———. "'Charity Girls' and City Pleasures: Historical Notes on Working-Class Sexuality, 1880–1920." In *Powers of Desire: The Politics of Sexuality,* edited by Ann Snitow, Christine Stansell, and Sharon Thompson. New York: Monthly Review Press, 1983.

Perlmutter, Ruth. "German Grotesque: Two Films by Sander and Ottinger." In *Gender and German Cinema: Feminist Interventions,* vol. 1, edited by Sandra Frieden et al. Oxford: Berg, 1993.

Pike, Bob, and Dave Martin. *The Genius of Busby Berkeley.* Reseda, Calif.: Creative Film Society Books, 1973.

Pribram, E. Deidre, ed. *Female Spectators: Looking at Film and Television.* New York: Verso, 1988.

Probyn, Elspeth. *Sexing the Self: Gendered Positions in Cultural Studies.* New York: Routledge, 1993.

Rabinowitz, Paula. "Commodity Fetishism: Women in *Gold Diggers of 1933.*" *Film Reader* 5 (1982): 141–49.

Rivette, Jacques. "'On Imagination': Review of *The Lusty Men*, October 1953." In *Cahiers du Cinema — The 1950s: Neo-Realism, Hollywood, New Wave*, edited by Jim Hillier. Cambridge: Harvard University Press, 1984.

Riviere, Joan. "Womanliness as a Masquerade." In *Formations of Fantasy*, edited by Victor Burgin, James Donald, Cora Kaplan. London: Methuen, 1986.

Roberts, Shari. "'The Lady in the Tutti-Frutti Hat': Carmen Miranda, a Spectacle of Ethnicity." *Cinema Journal* 32, no. 3 (spring 1993): 3–23.

———. *Seeing Stars: Spectacles of Difference in World War II Hollywood Musicals*. Durham, N.C.: Duke University Press. Forthcoming.

Robertson, Pamela. "Structural Irony in *Mildred Pierce*, or How Mildred Lost Her Tongue." *Cinema Journal* 30, no. 1 (fall 1990): 42–54.

Rodowick, D. N. *The Difficulty of Difference: Psychoanalysis, Sexual Difference & Film Theory*. New York: Routledge, 1991.

Rosen, Ruth. *The Lost Sisterhood: Prostitution in America, 1900–1918*. Baltimore: The Johns Hopkins University Press, 1982.

Rosenzweig, Ilene. *The I Hate Madonna Handbook*. London: Virgin, 1994.

Ross, Andrew. "Uses of Camp." In *No Respect: Intellectuals and Popular Culture*. New York: Routledge, 1989.

———. "This Bridge Called My Pussy." In *Madonnarama: Essays on Sex and Popular Culture*, edited by Lisa Frank and Paul Smith. San Francisco: Cleiss Press, 1993.

Roth, Mark. "Some Warners Musicals and the Spirit of the New Deal." In *Genre: The Musical — A Reader*, edited by Rick Altman. New York: Routledge & Kegan Paul, 1986.

Rowe, Kathleen. *The Unruly Woman: Gender and the Genres of Laughter*. Austin: University of Texas Press, 1995.

Rubey, Dan. "Vogueing at the Carnival: Desire and Pleasure on MTV." *South Atlantic Quarterly* 90, no. 4 (fall 1991).

Russo, Vito. *The Celluloid Closet: Homosexuality in the Movies*. New York: Harper and Row, 1987.

Sedgwick, Eve Kosofsky. *Tendencies*. Durham, N.C.: Duke University Press, 1993.

———. *Epistemology of the Closet*. Berkeley: University of California Press, 1990.

———. "Tide and Trust." *Critical Inquiry* 15 (summer 1989): 745–57.

Seigworth, Greg. "The Distance Between Me and You: Madonna and Celestial Navigation (or You Can Be My *Lucky Star*)." In *The Madonna Connection: Representational Politics, Subcultural Identities, and Cultural Theory*, edited by Cathy Schwichtenberg. San Francisco: Westview Press, 1993.

Sexton, Adam, ed. *Desperately Seeking Madonna: In Search of the Meaning of the World's Most Famous Woman*. New York: Dell, 1993.

Schultze, Laurie, Ann Barton White, and Jane D. Brown. "'A Sacred Monster in Her Prime': Audience Construction of Madonna as Low Other." In *The Madonna Connection: Representational Politics, Subcultural Identities, and Cultural Theory*, edited by Cathy Schwichtenberg. San Francisco: Westview Press, 1993.

Schwichtenberg, Cathy. "Madonna's Postmodern Feminism: Bringing the Margins to the Center." In *The Madonna Connection: Representational Politics, Subcultural Identities, and Cultural Theory*, edited by Schwichtenberg. San Francisco: Westview Press, 1993.

Silberman, Marc. "Interview with Ulrike Ottinger: Surreal Images." In *Gender and German Cinema: Feminist Interventions*, vol. 1, edited by Sandra Frieden, et al. Oxford: Berg Publishers, 1993.

Silverman, Kaja. *The Acoustic Mirror: The Female Voice in Psychoanalysis and Cinema*. Bloomington: Indiana University Press, 1988.

———. "Histoire d'O: The Construction of a Female Subject." In *Pleasure and Danger: Exploring Female Sexuality*, edited by Carol Vance. 1984. Reprint, London: Pandora Press, 1989.

———. *The Subject of Semiotics*. New York: Oxford University Press, 1983.

Slide, Anthony. *Great Pretenders: A History of Female and Male Impersonation in the Performing Arts*. Lombard, Ill.: Wallace-Homestead Book Company, 1986.

Sloan, Kay. *The Loud Silents: Origins of the Social Problem Film*. Chicago: University of Illinois Press, 1988.

Smith, Patricia Juliana. "'You Don't Have to Say You Love Me': The Camp Masquerades of Dusty Springfield." In *Camp Grounds: Style and Homosexuality*, edited by David Bergman. Amherst: University of Massachusetts Press, 1993.

Snyder, Robert W. *The Voice of the City: Vaudeville and Popular Culture in New York*. New York: Oxford University Press, 1989.

Sontag, Susan. *A Susan Sontag Reader*. New York: Farrar, Straus & Giroux, 1982.

———. "Notes on 'Camp.'" In *Against Interpretation*. New York: Farrar, Straus & Giroux, 1966.

Stacey, Jackie. *Star Gazing: Hollywood Cinema and Female Spectatorship*. New York: Routledge, 1994.

———. "Feminine Fascinations: Forms of Identification in Star-Audience Relations." In *Stardom: Industry of Desire*, edited by Christine Gledhill. New York: Routledge, 1991.

Staiger, Janet. *Interpreting Films: Studies in the Historical Reception of American Cinema*. Princeton: Princeton University Press, 1992.

———. "Hollywood, Freud and the Representations of Women: Regulations and Contradiction, 1945–early 60s." In *Home Is Where the Heart Is: Studies in Melodrama and the Woman's Film*, edited by Christine Gledhill. London: BFI Publishing, 1990.

Steele, Valerie. *Fashion and Eroticism: Ideals of Feminine Beauty from the Victorian Era to the Jazz Age*. New York: Oxford University Press, 1985.

Stein, Arlene. "Crossover Dreams: Lesbianism and Popular Music since the 1970s." In *The Good, the Bad, and the Gorgeous: Popular Culture's Romance with Lesbianism*, edited by Diane Hamer and Belinda Budge. London: Pandora, 1994.

Studlar, Gaylyn. *In the Realm of Pleasure: Von Sternberg, Dietrich, and the Masochistic Aesthetic*. Chicago: University of Illinois Press, 1988.

Suleiman, Susan Rubin. *Subversive Intent: Gender, Politics and the Avant-Garde*. Cambridge: Harvard University Press, 1990.

Szwed, John F. "Race and the Embodiment of Culture." *Ethnicity* 2 (1975): 19–33.

Tetzlaff, David. "Metatextual Girl: Patriarchy, Postmodernism, Power, Money, Madonna." In *The Madonna Connection: Representational Politics, Subcultural Identities, and Cultural Theory*, edited by Cathy Schwichtenberg. San Francisco: Westview Press, 1993.

Thomas, Bob. *Joan Crawford: A Biography*. New York: Simon & Schuster, 1978.

Toll, Robert C. *On with the Show: The First Century of Show Business in America*. New York: Oxford University Press, 1976.

Truffaut, François. "'A Wonderful Certainty': Review of Johnny Guitar. April 1955." In *Cahiers du Cinema — The 1950s: Neo-Realism; Hollywood, New Wave*, edited by Jim Hillier. Cambridge: Harvard University Press, 1984.

Turner, Kay, ed. *I Dream of Madonna: Women's Dreams of the Goddess of Pop*. London: Thames and Hudson, 1993.

Tuska, Jon. *The Films of Mae West*. Secaucus, N.J.: The Citadel Press, 1973.

Tyler, Parker. *Screening the Sexes: Homosexuality in the Movies*. 1972. Reprint, New York: Da Capo Press, 1993.

Van Leer, David. "The Beast of the Closet: Homosociality and the Pathology of Manhood." *Critical Inquiry* 15 (spring 1989): 587–605.

Venturi, Robert. *Complexity and Contradiction in Architecture*. New York: Museum of Modern Art, 1966.

Venturi, Robert, Denise Scott Brown, and Stephen Izenour. *Learning from Las Vegas*. Cambridge: MIT Press, 1972.

Walker, Alexander. *The Celluloid Sacrifice: Aspects of Sex in the Movies*. London: Michael Joseph, 1966.

Ward, Carol M. *Mae West: A Bio-Bibliography*. New York: Greenwood Press, 1989.

Wayne, Jane Ellen. *Crawford's Men*. New York: Prentice-Hall, 1988.

West, Mae. *Pleasure Man: The Novel*. New York: Dell Press, 1975.

———. *Goodness Had Nothing to Do with It*. Englewood Cliffs, N.J.: Prentice-Hall, 1959.

———. Playscripts. Manuscript Reading Room, Library of Congress. Washington, D.C.

White, Patricia. "Madame X of the China Seas." In *Queer Looks: Perspectives on Lesbian and Gay Film and Video*, edited by Martha Gever, Pratibha Parmar, and John Greyson. New York: Routledge, 1993.

White, William. "'Camp' as Adjective: 1909–1966." *American Speech* 41 (1966): 70–72.

Whitney, Catherine. *Uncommon Lives: Gay Men and Straight Women*. New York: New American Library, 1990.

Williams, Linda. "Feminist Film Theory: *Mildred Pierce* and the Second World War." In *Female Spectators: Looking at Film and Television*, edited by E. Deidre Pribram. New York: Verso, 1988.

Wilmington, Michael. "Nicholas Ray's *Johnny Guitar*." *Velvet Light Trap* 12 (spring 1974): 20–25.

Wollen, Peter. "Cinema/Americanism/the Robot." In *Modernity and Mass Culture*, edited by James Naremore. Bloomington: Indiana University Press, 1991.

Newspaper and Magazine Articles Cited

Ager, Cecelia. "Mae West Reveals the Foundation of the 1900 Mode." *Vogue*, 1 September 1933.

Anderson, Steve. "Forgive Me Father." *Village Voice*, 4 April 1989.

Baker, Kenneth. "War Clouds in the West?" *Photoplay*, December 1933.

Baker, Russell. "Those Vile Few." *New York Times*, 24 October 1992.

Baskette, Kirtley. "Mae West Talks about Her 'Marriage.'" *Photoplay*, August 1935.

———. "Has Mae West Gone High Hat?" *Photoplay*, July 1934.

Biery, Ruth. "From Jazz to Gentility." *Motion Picture*, May 1930.

———. "The Story of a Dancing Girl." *Photoplay*, 28 September 1928.

Britton, Andrew. "For Interpretation—Notes Against Camp." *Gay Left*, winter 1978/79.

Carr, Jay. "Madonna Bares All!" *Boston Globe*, 26 April 1991.

Champion, Constance. "Katharine Hepburn, Mae West—And Sex Appeal!" *Motion Picture* March 1934.

Chapman, Jay Brian. "Is Mae West Garbo's Greatest Rival?" *Motion Picture*, July 1933.

Churchill, Edward. "So You Think You Know Mae West." *Motion Picture*, July 1935.

"Cinema: The New Pictures." *Time*, 14 June 1954.

Conniff, Ruth. "Politics in a Post-Feminist Age." *The Progressive*, July 1991.

Crawford, Joan. "I've Been Lonely." *Photoplay*, April 1943.

Davis, George. "The Decline of the West." *Vanity Fair*, May 1934.

Ergenbright, Eric L. "'Any Clever Woman Can Develop Glamour'—Joan Crawford." *Motion Picture*, November 1934.

"Evolution of Joan Crawford: In which lies pictorial proof that glamour is not always inherent, but can also be acquired—witness these amazing portraits." *Movie Classic*, June 1936.

Fisher, Carrie. "True Confessions: Part One." *Rolling Stone*, 13 June 1991.

Franchey, John R. "Bachelor Mother." *Silver Screen*, August 1942.

French, William F. "'It's All in Fun,' Says Mae West." *Movie Classic*, December 1934.

———. "What Price Glamour?" *Motion Picture*, November 1934.

Goings on about Town. *New Yorker*, 22 February 1993.

Graham, Virginia. "Cinema." *Spectator*, 4 June 1954.

Grundmann, Roy, and Judith Shulevitz. "Minorities and the Majority: An Interview With Ulrike Ottinger." *Cineaste* 43, no. 1 (1991): 43ff.

Hall, Gladys. "The Crime of the Day in Hollywood." *Motion Picture*, January 1934.

———. "Can You Pass Joan Crawford's Love Test?" *Movie Classic*, November 1936.

Hess, Thomas. "J'Accuse Marcel Duchamp." *Art News* 63, 10, 1965.

Jennings, Robert C. "Mae West: A Candid Conversation with the Indestructible Queen of Vamp and Camp." *Playboy*, January 1971.

Johnson, Brian. "Madonna: The World's Hottest Star Speaks Her Mind." *Macleans*, 13 May 1991.

LaMae, Lawrence F. "Writers Fear Hazel Scott Has Become 'Hollywood,' One Writes." *Chicago Defender*, 31 July 1943.

Leake, Beulah. "Defending Mae West" (First Prize Letter). *Movie Classic*, March 1935.

Lee, Sonia. "Joan Crawford Answers Her Critics." *Movie Classic*, June 1935.

———. "How Joan Crawford Keeps Her Men Friends Interested." *Movie Classic*, December 1934.

Leland, John. "The Selling of Sex." *Newsweek*, 2 November 1992.

Madame Sylvia. "Is Mae West Skidding on the Curves?" *Photoplay*, November 1936.

Maddox, Ben. "Give Joan Crawford Credit." *Silver Screen*, January 1932.

Manners, Dorothy. "The Girl without a Past." *Photoplay*, October 1935.

McCarey, Leo. "Mae West Can Play Anything." *Photoplay*, June 1935.

McCarten, John. "The Current Cinema: Kill or Be Killed." *New Yorker*, 5 June 1954.

Musto, Michael. "Immaculate Connection." *Outweek*, 20 March 1991.

"New Films." *Newsweek*, 14 June 1954.

"New York's 'Dirt' Shows." *Variety*, 2 February 1927.

Paglia, Camille. "Camille Paglia, Author of *Sexual Personae*, Talks about *Sex*." *Us Magazine*, December 1992.

Review of *Johnny Guitar*. *Variety*, 5 May 1954.

Review of *I'm No Angel*. *Time*, 16 October 1933.

Rogers St. Johns, Adela. "Joan Crawford: The Dramatic Rise of a Self-Made Star." *Photoplay*, October 1937.

Rudnick, Paul and Kurt Anderson. "The Irony Epidemic." *Spy*, March 1989.

Satz, Evelyn [pseud.]. "Camping it Up." *Films and Filming*, no. 342 (March 1983): 20–23.

———. "What a Drag." *Films and Filming*, no. 343 (April 1983): 20–22.

———. "Is There Camp after Cruising?" *Films and Filming*, no. 345 (June 1983): 26–29.

Schallert, Elza. "Go West—If You're an Adult." *Motion Picture*, May 1933.

Sennewald, Andre. "Lines for a Mae West Scrapbook." *New York Times*, 30 September 1934.

Tentler, Kate. "Like a Feminist." *Village Voice*, 24 November 1992.

Tildesley, Ruth. "Curves! Hollywood Wants Them—And So Will You!" *Motion Picture*, July 1933.

Troy, William. "Mae West and the Classic Tradition." *Nation*, 8 November 1933.

Walsh, Moira. "Films." *America*, 5 June 1954.

West, Mae. Interview by Richard Meryman. *Life*, 18 April 1969.

Young, Stark. "Diamond Lil." *New Republic*, 27 June 1928.

INDEX